AF597274

PICTURING TRANSFORMATION

NEXW-ÁYANTSUT

PHOTOGRAPHS BY **NANCY BLECK/SLÁNAY̓ SP'ÁK̲W'US**

WRITTEN BY **KATHERINE DODDS** WITH

CHIEF BILL WILLIAMS/TELÁLSEMK̲IN-SIY̓ÁM̓

AND **NANCY BLECK/SLÁNAY̓ SP'ÁK̲W'US**

From conversations and interviews with

JOHN CLARKE/X̲WUX̲WSÉL'K̲N (from transcripts)

CHIEF IAN CAMPBELL/X̲ÁLEK̲ SEK̲YÚ SIY̓ÁM̓

AARON NELSON-MOODY/TAWX'SIN YEXWULLA/PÚLXTN

EUGENE HARRY/HAYKWILEM

MELANIE RIVERS/7IMLAMELWET

CEASE WYSS/T'UY̓TANAT

DREW LEATHEM/ṬSEWÁTSELTN

LISA BAILE

AMIR ALI ALIBHAI

FOREWORD BY **TANIA WILLARD**

PICTURING

TRANSFORMATION

NEXW-ÁYANTSUT

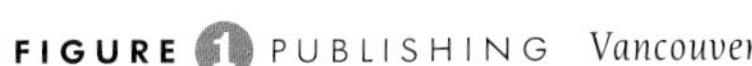

UTSÁM WITNESS SOCIETY | HELLO COOL WORLD

www.utsam-witness.ca *www.HelloCoolWorld.com*

This book is dedicated to the memories of those who have now passed on, but whose impact and influence on this project have been indelible and undeniable.

WITH LOVE
Randy Stoltmann
John Clarke/*X̱wux̱wsél'ḵn*
Rick Hurney
James Nicholas
and the ancestors, especially
David Williams
Laura Williams
Renate Bleck
Margot Bleck

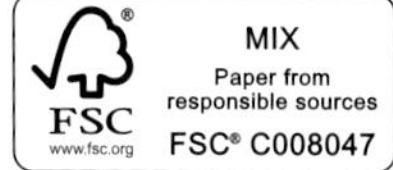

13 14 15 16 17 5 4 3 2 1

Cataloguing data available from Library and Archives Canada
ISBN 978-0-9918588-0-4

Editing by Lucy Kenward
Copyediting by Shirarose Wilensky
Jacket and interior design by Peter Cocking
Jacket photographs by Nancy Bleck
Map by Eric Leinberger
Printed and bound in China on FSC-certified paper
by C&C Offset Printing Co., Ltd.
Distributed in the U.S. by Publishers Group West

Figure 1 Publishing Inc.
Vancouver BC Canada
www.figure1pub.com

Utsám̓ Witness Society and Hello Cool World
www.utsam-witness.ca
www.HelloCoolWorld.com

CONTENTS

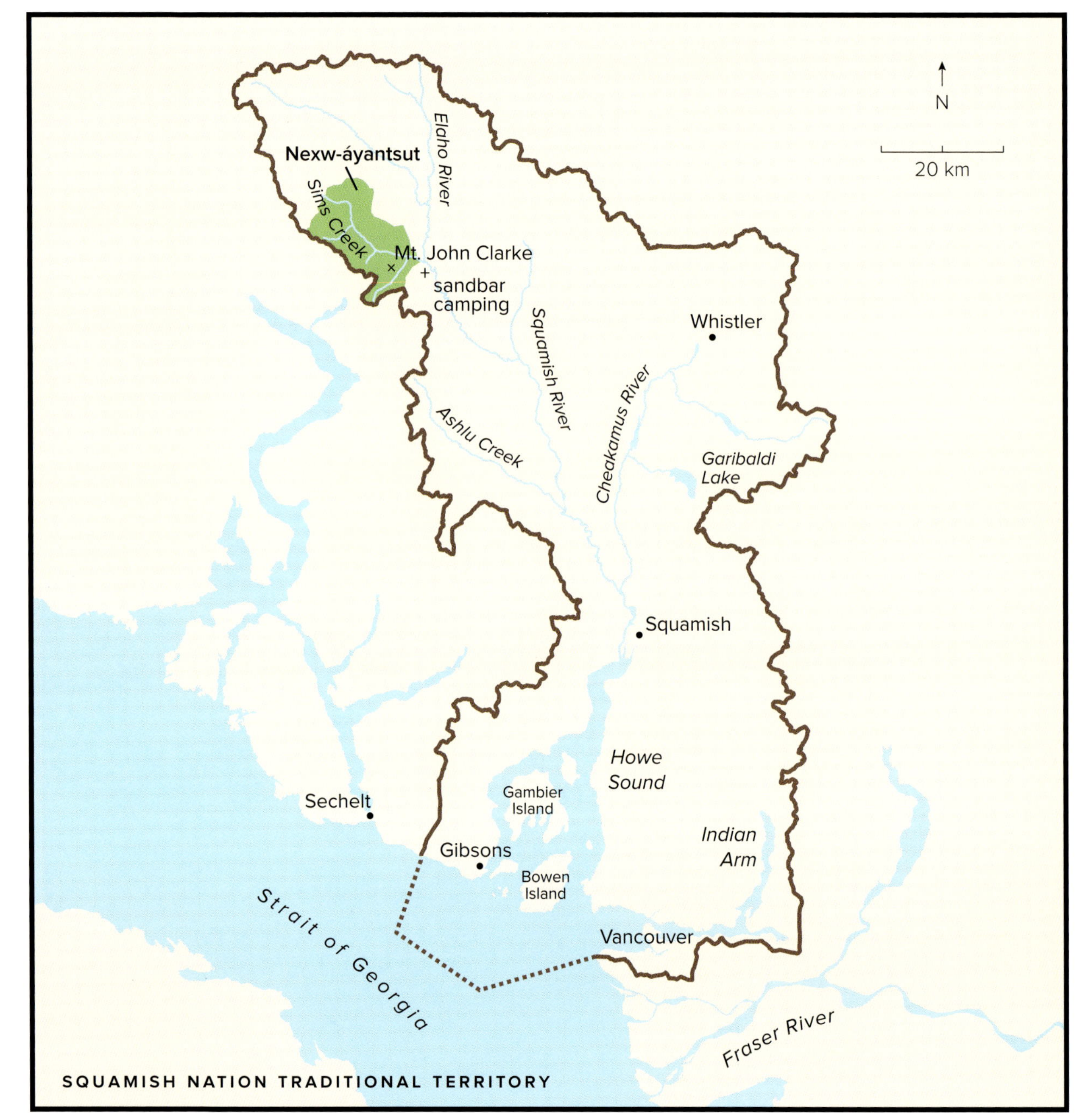
N
20 km
Nexw-áyantsut
Sims Creek
Elaho River
Mt. John Clarke
sandbar camping
Squamish River
Whistler
Cheakamus River
Ashlu Creek
Garibaldi Lake
Squamish
Howe Sound
Gambier Island
Sechelt
Gibsons
Bowen Island
Indian Arm
Vancouver
Strait of Georgia
Fraser River
SQUAMISH NATION TRADITIONAL TERRITORY

FOREWORD
TRANSFORMATION BEGINS AT THE ROOT

THIS IS HOW I learned to dig cedar roots:

say a prayer of thanks
find a good stand of cedar with lots of loose, soft ground
trace your way back from the tree(s) and scrape away the soft earth
find and take hold of one of the interconnected roots
pull up on the root, pulling back and watching the roots heave the soft earth above it
observe the network of roots underneath the top soil, all around the cedar stand
trace and dig out the roots, moving from place to place to disturb as little as possible
loop the supple roots, hanging them on a nearby branch as you work
soak in water to slip the bark/skin off the root
split the roots for use later
say a prayer of thanks.

I am a Witness. In the summer of 2006 I attended one of the weekend camping trips that were a mainstay of Utsám̓ Witness, the community art–based project that introduced many diverse participants to the Nexw-áyantsut (Sims Creek) area, the Squamish Nation's relationship to it and our interwoven paths on this Coast Salish land.

I took part in the camping weekend with a group of young Native women who were participating in the Storyscapes Chinatown project initiated by Kamala Todd, who was a City of Vancouver urban planner at the time. Storyscapes was a way to gather and reassert aboriginal story and experience in Vancouver's cityscape, and part of this process was always to acknowledge the local Indigenous nations: the Squamish, Musqueam and Tsleil-Waututh people. Todd's approach, and her work within Storyscapes, influenced many urban Aboriginal youth at the time, and Utsám̓ Witness fit with this vision of acknowledging Coast Salish land and playing a role in furthering an Indigenous approach to education, activism and organizing for social change. I decided it was a clever way that I could get paid to go camping, join in a forum of activist-generated ideas, participate in local Indigenous culture and have fun. So we went camping, but what really happened was ceremony, a ceremony that I think continues to work inside each and every one of us who visited Nexw-áyantsut.

The Witness Project was a journey of rediscovery for many people. As an urban Aboriginal young woman, getting out onto the land—albeit in Coast Salish territory—was a transformative experience and it left me with many inspirations that continue to fuel my exploration in art and in my own identity as a person of mixed settler and secwepemc culture(s). During that weekend, I participated in a cedar-bracelet weaving workshop led by Squamish women Cease Wyss/*T'uy̓tanat* and Tracy Williams/*Sesemiya*. We stood together dipping small strips of cedar bark in the river to keep it pliable. As we stood riverside, we were not only weaving the cedar; surrounded by the power of mountains and forest and the voices of Squamish elders, leaders and youth, we were weaving memories, knowledge, story, the land and our own sense of self through this gift of cedar.

In the Utsám̓ Witness project, the leadership of the Squamish Nation was central to furthering an understanding of Indigenous rights amidst environmental issues. The project could have stopped at asserting Indigenous rights and title, but it also issued a standing invitation to people to come and be a part of this land, to learn and to witness it and to make a space in their hearts and spirits for it.

Looking through this volume, you can begin to breathe that coastal mountain air, the cedar, soil and moss. You can feel the strength of the Squamish culture and its ancient ties to this land through the empathetic lens of Nancy Bleck/*Slánay̓ Sp'áḵw'us*, whose photographic practice in the context of Utsám̓ Witness symbolically exposes roots. Her work not only represents the landscape but engages with it on a level where interconnectedness is revealed. Accompanied by these macro stills of rocks, moss, riverbanks and thimbleberries, the narrative draws us in, and looking within, seeing up-close, we begin to connect, to remember, to breathe. It carves out the collaborative relationships among John Clarke/*X̱wux̱wsél'ḵn*, Chief Bill Williams/*telálsemḵin siy̓ám̓*, Nancy Bleck, participants of Utsám̓ Witness and the land itself. In so doing, we are confronted with not only the beauty of this place but with the politics of colonialism and resource extraction, with the complete story of what is happening on this land.

A poignant autobiographical image in this collection, *Cedar Elder as Witnessed by Daughter of Immigrants/Daughter of Immigrants as Witnessed by Cedar Elder*, offers a sense of reciprocity and introspection and can be understood as the photographer documenting her complex relationship to place. These works illustrate many of the untold stories that are nonetheless ever-present in the lands we call British Columbia: the story of settlers and their relationship to these lands and to the indigenous peoples of these lands;

the many untold names, languages and stories that remain ignored and erased. These images of the land are fragments, meant to be pieced together to posit new narratives, and they provide an example of how we, settler and Indigenous, may tell stories together in ways that resonate and that help us to see where we are connected, where our roots are.

In another of the photographs in this book, John Clarke holds an image of Magic Grove taken by Shel Neufeld in front of a field of stumps that formerly held the same Magic Grove pictured in the photograph. It shows in sharp contrast the consequence of the logging and resource extraction that the Utsám̓ Witness project and everyone involved with it was trying to stop. This poignant image traces the echoes and shadows of the trees that once stood there; they are powerful reminders of the need to keep on working together, bearing witness and standing up to tell our stories and to invite others to share their stories.

This volume of work attempts to tell just one of those stories, a story of a forest under resource-based economic pressure and a temporary community of caring people from many cultures with a unity of vision to bear witness and protect a place, to come to know that place in its Squamish name, Nexw-áyantsut, and to learn to see this land with new eyes, to help us see where we are connected and uncover our roots.

This book is a witness to the transformative potential of people, of ourselves and of the trio of visionaries who brought their leadership and tenacity to the Utsám̓ Witness project. But this project was not just about individuals; it was about an ecosystem of like-minded participants, artists, revolutionaries and communities who came to know, protect and connect to this sacred area within the ceremonial framework of Squamish culture and knowledge.

Being a Witness changed me. Experiencing the land at Nexw-áyantsut changed me. The land has the power to do that. When we become a witness, we also pledge to protect. You are called here, in this volume of images and story, to witness, to be involved, to be connected and to protect what is precious to all of us because, in the end, we are not just interconnected with the lands and ecosystems around us, we are interdependent.

Now that you have dug the roots
Weave the Basket.

I give thanks, *kukstemc* in my language of Secwepemcstin, *huy chewx a* in the Squamish language, for the brief time I spent in Nexw-áyantsut and what it taught me.

TANIA WILLARD, Secwepemc Nation

PHOTOGRAPHS BY **NANCY BLECK/SLÁNAY̓ SP'ÁK̲W'US**

LAND SPEAK

1995–1996

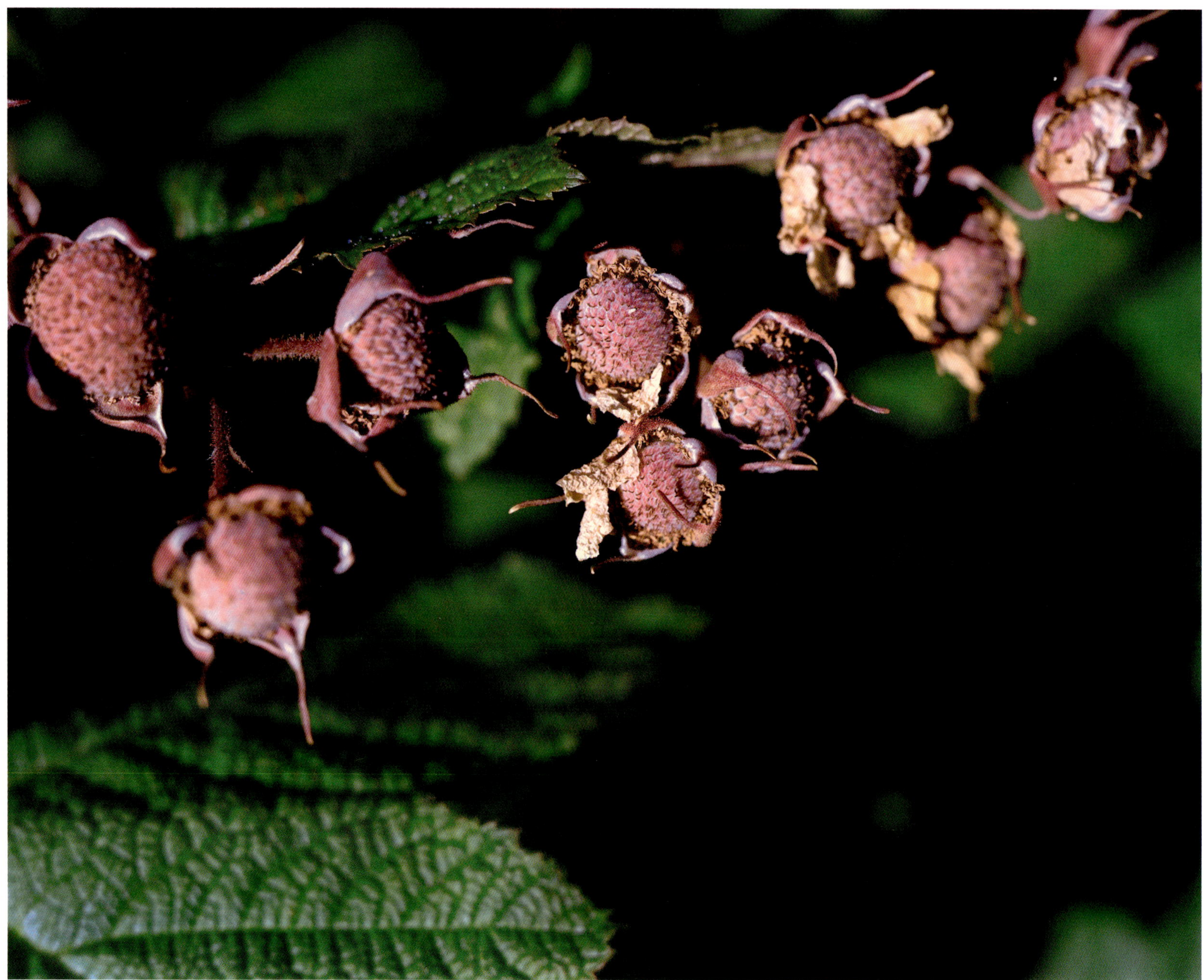

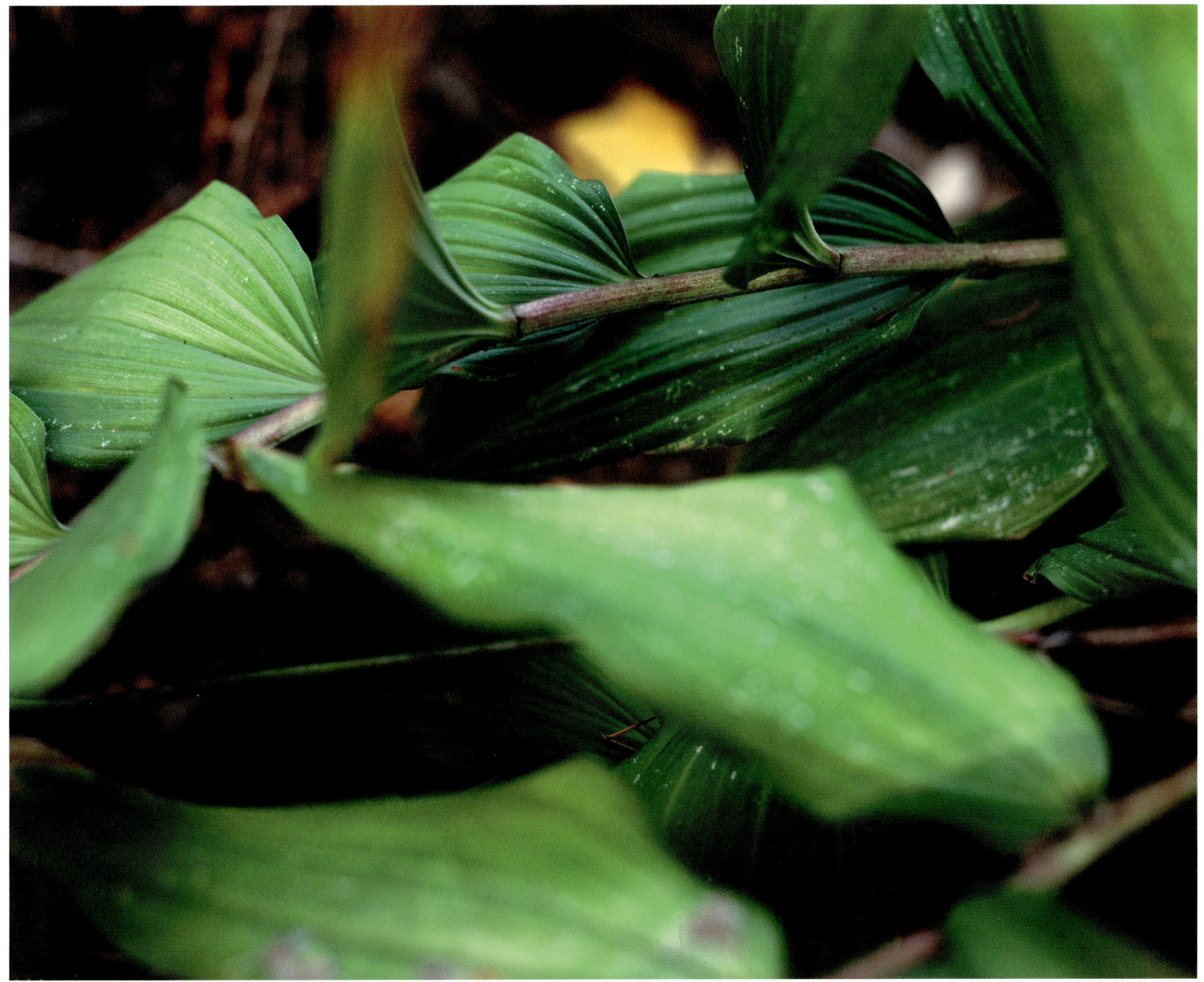

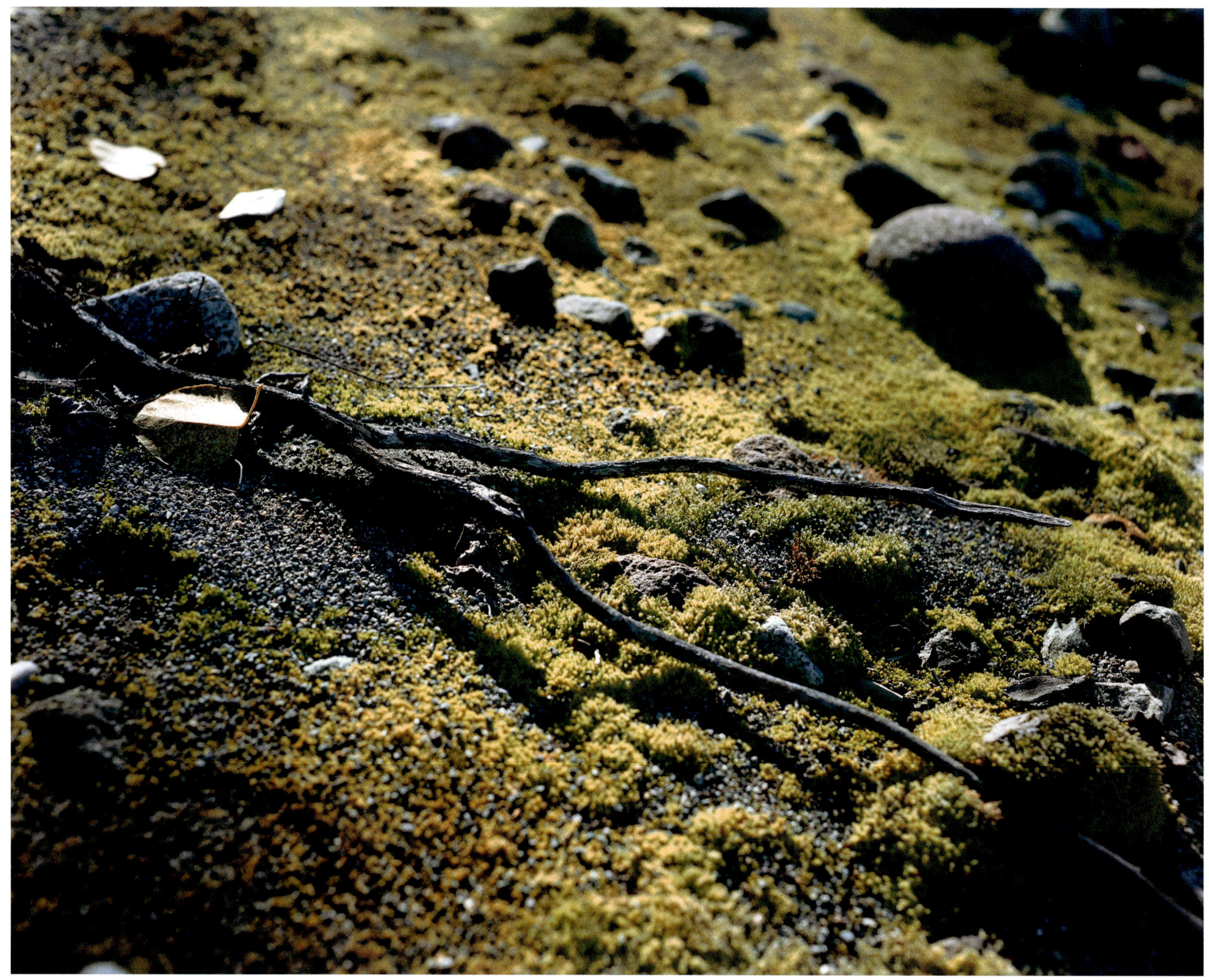

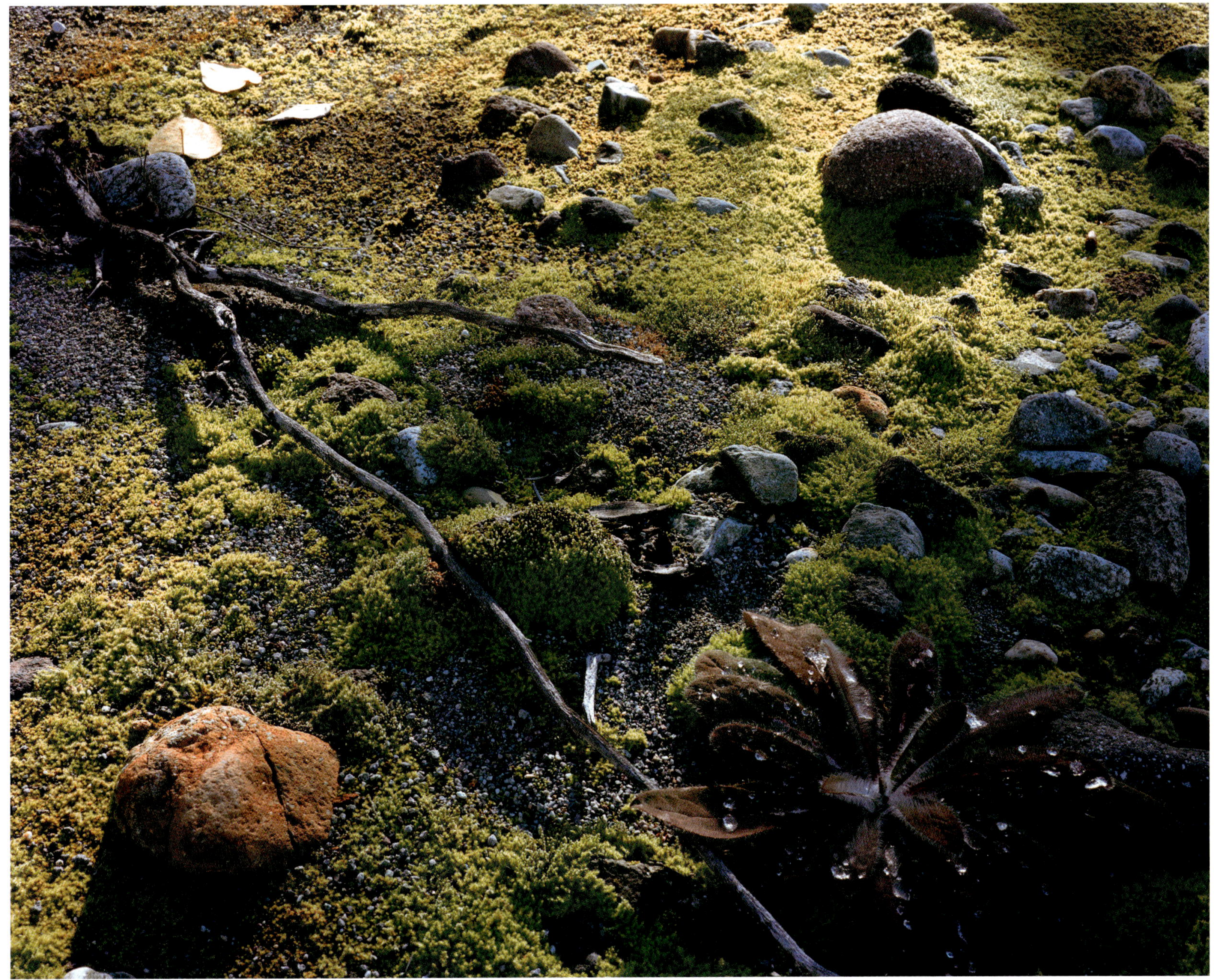

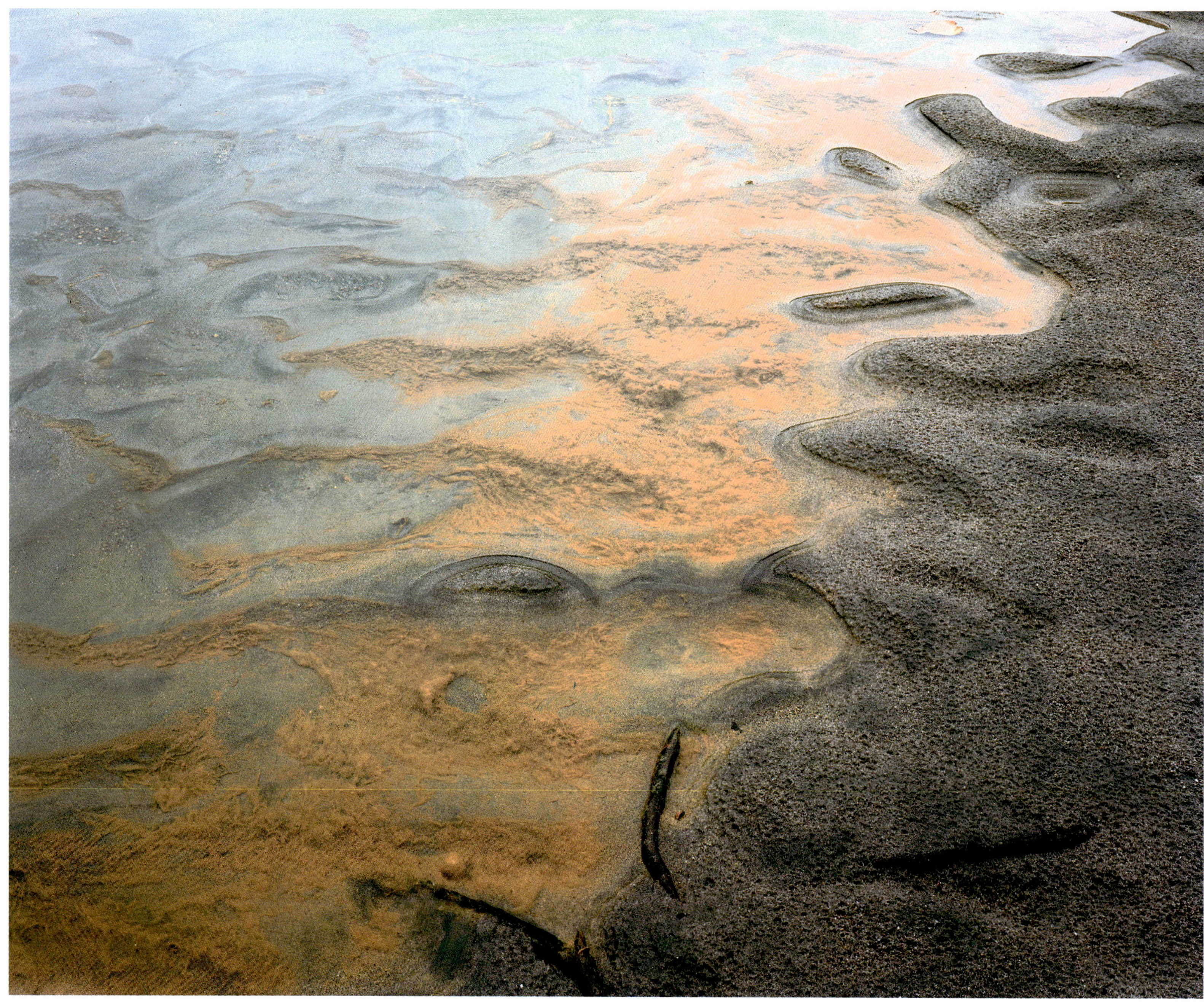

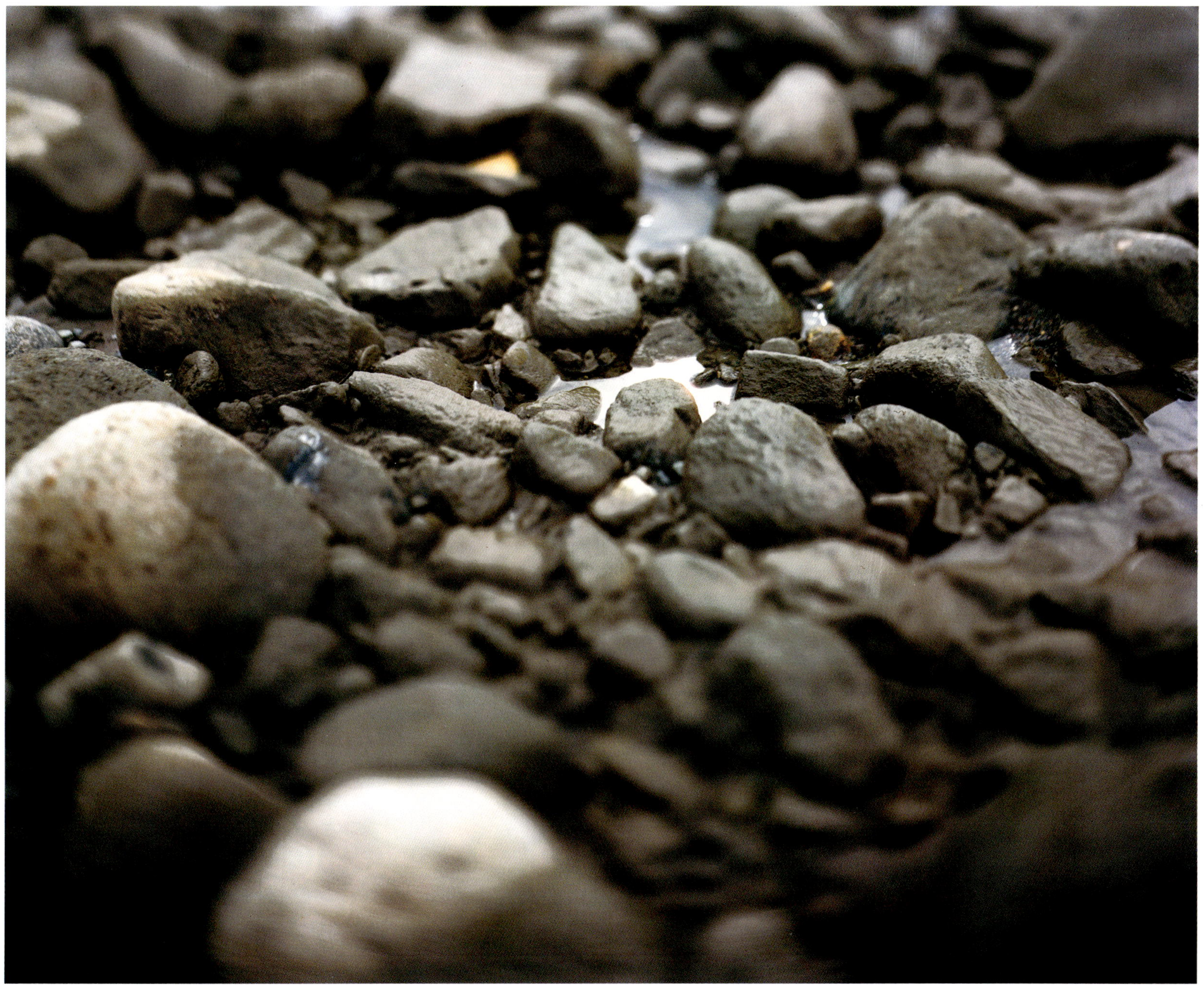

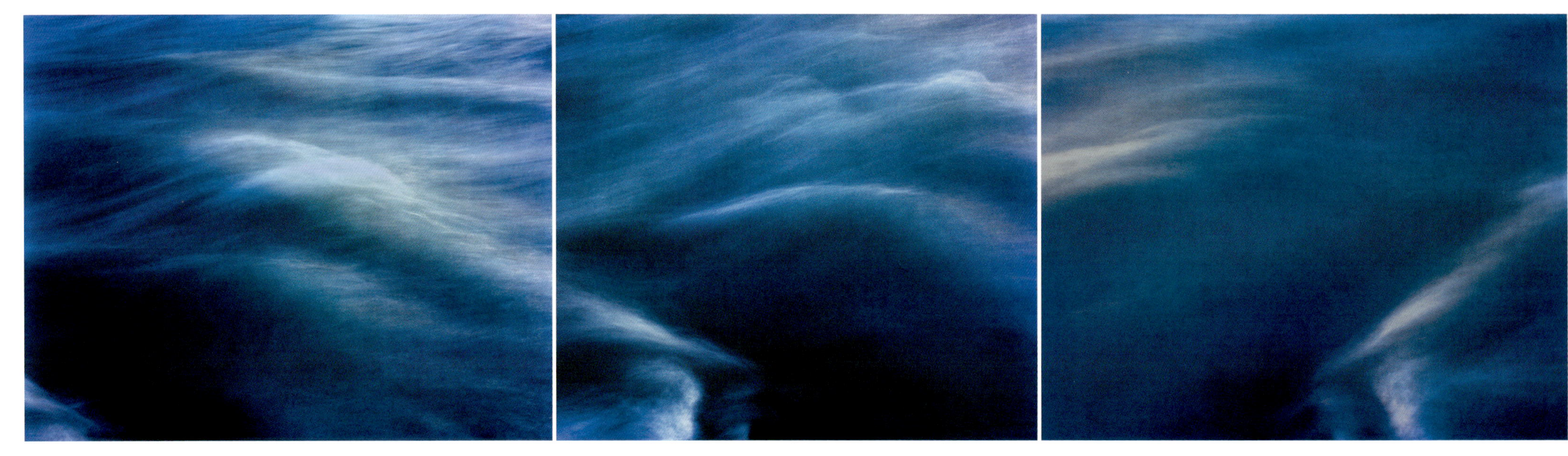

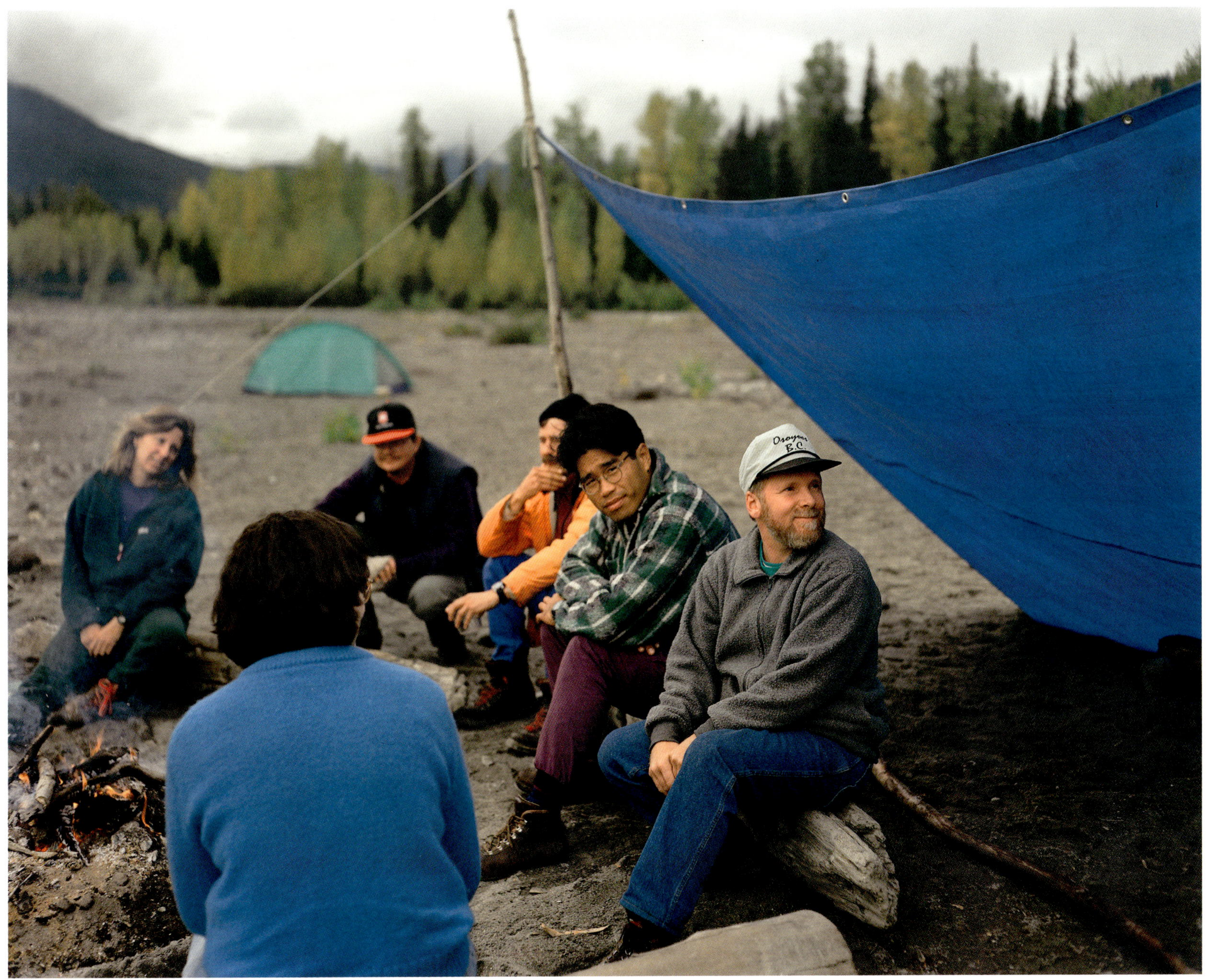

Children of the Earth we are in crisis, our breath is slowly being
usurped as the rainforests of the world disappear.
We are being choked out of our last air by the giant machines we
have ignited, which feed upon the blood of Mother Earth.
There is not one square inch of earth that we have not
contaminated, from Antarctica to the North snow.
Perhaps in the final analysis it will not be the trees that will need
saving; it will be our species—the two-leggeds . . .
It would be a sad world without the two-leggeds.

EXCERPT FROM A POEM BY JAMES NICHOLAS, ROCK CREE WRITER AND ACTOR

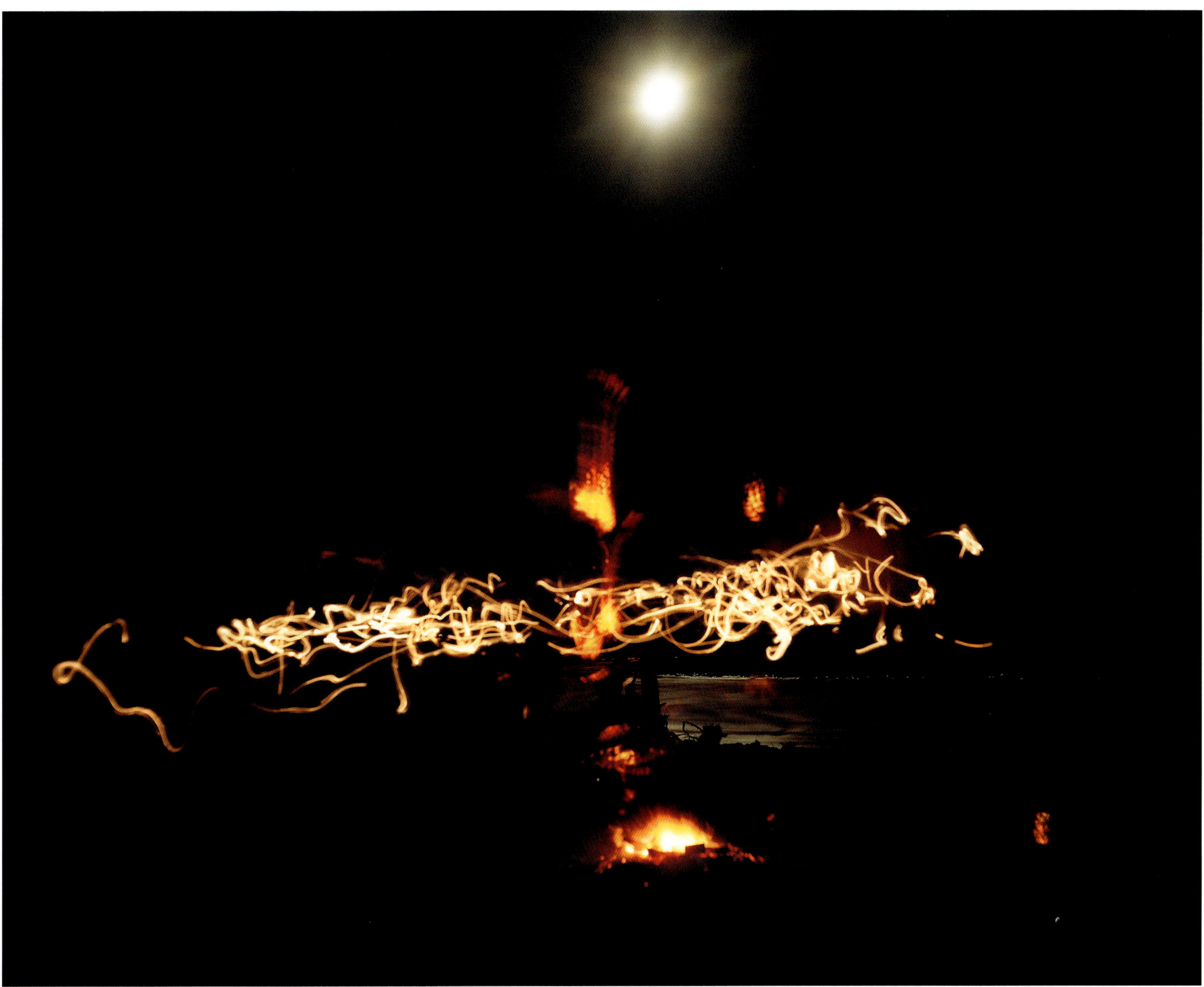

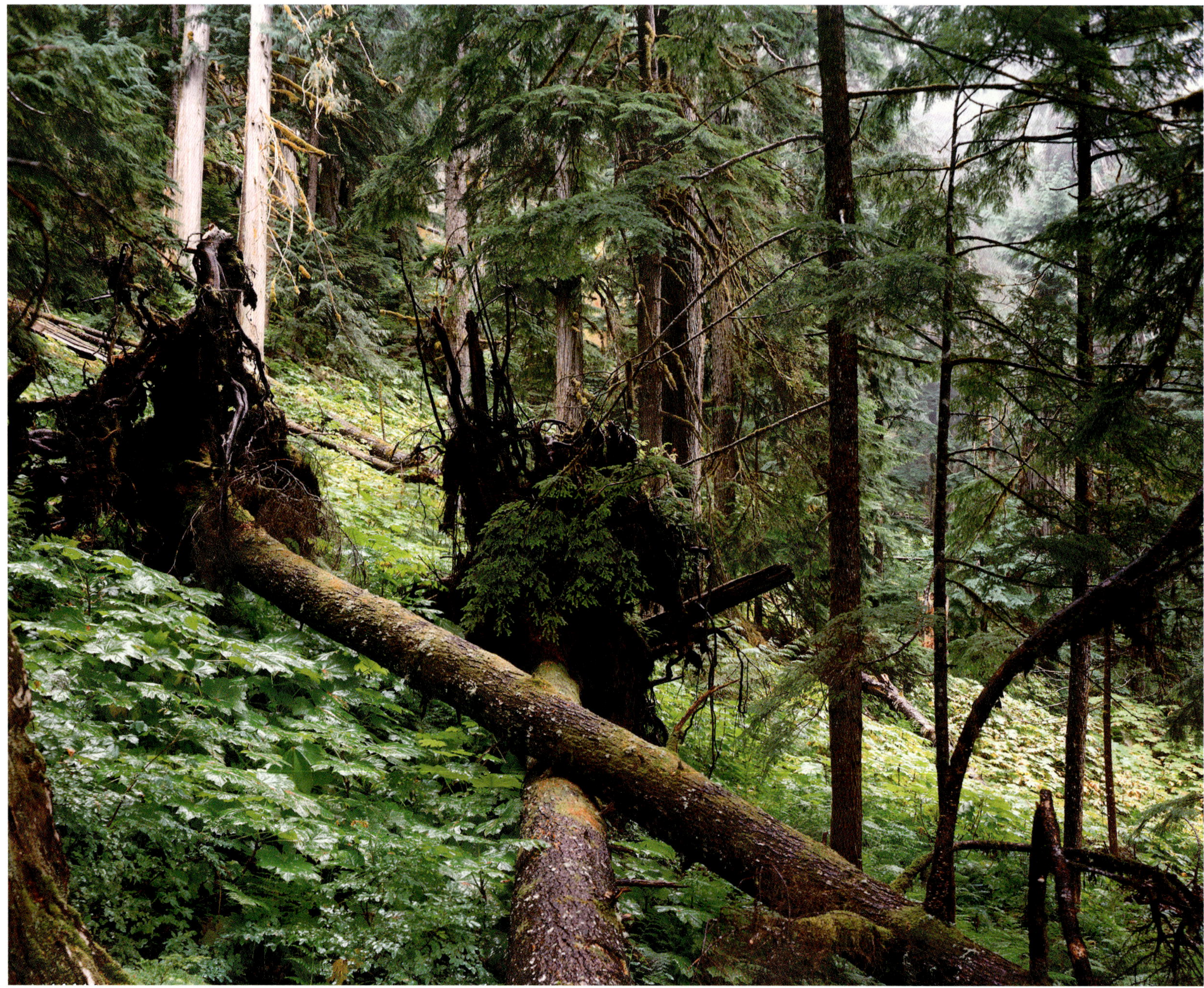

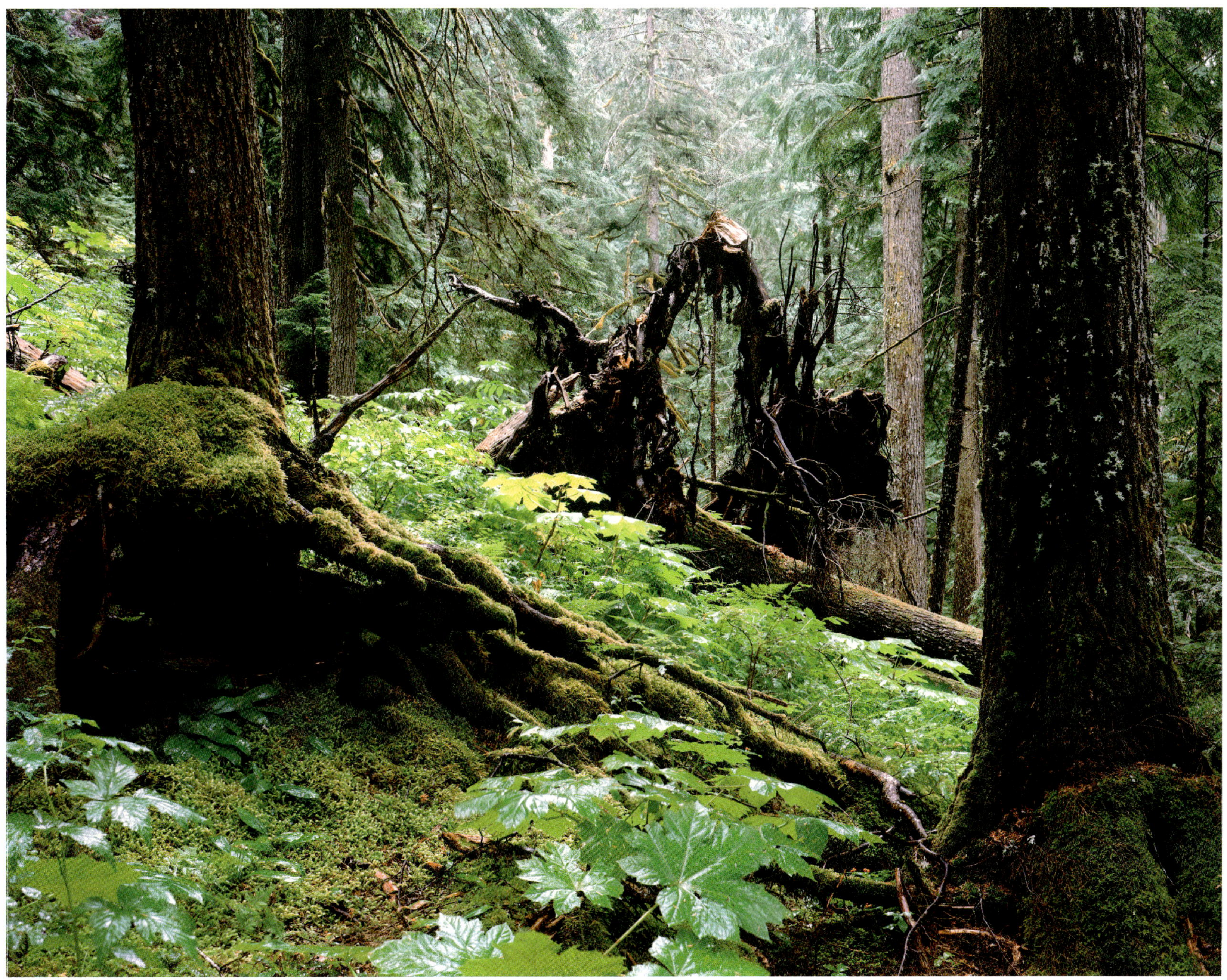

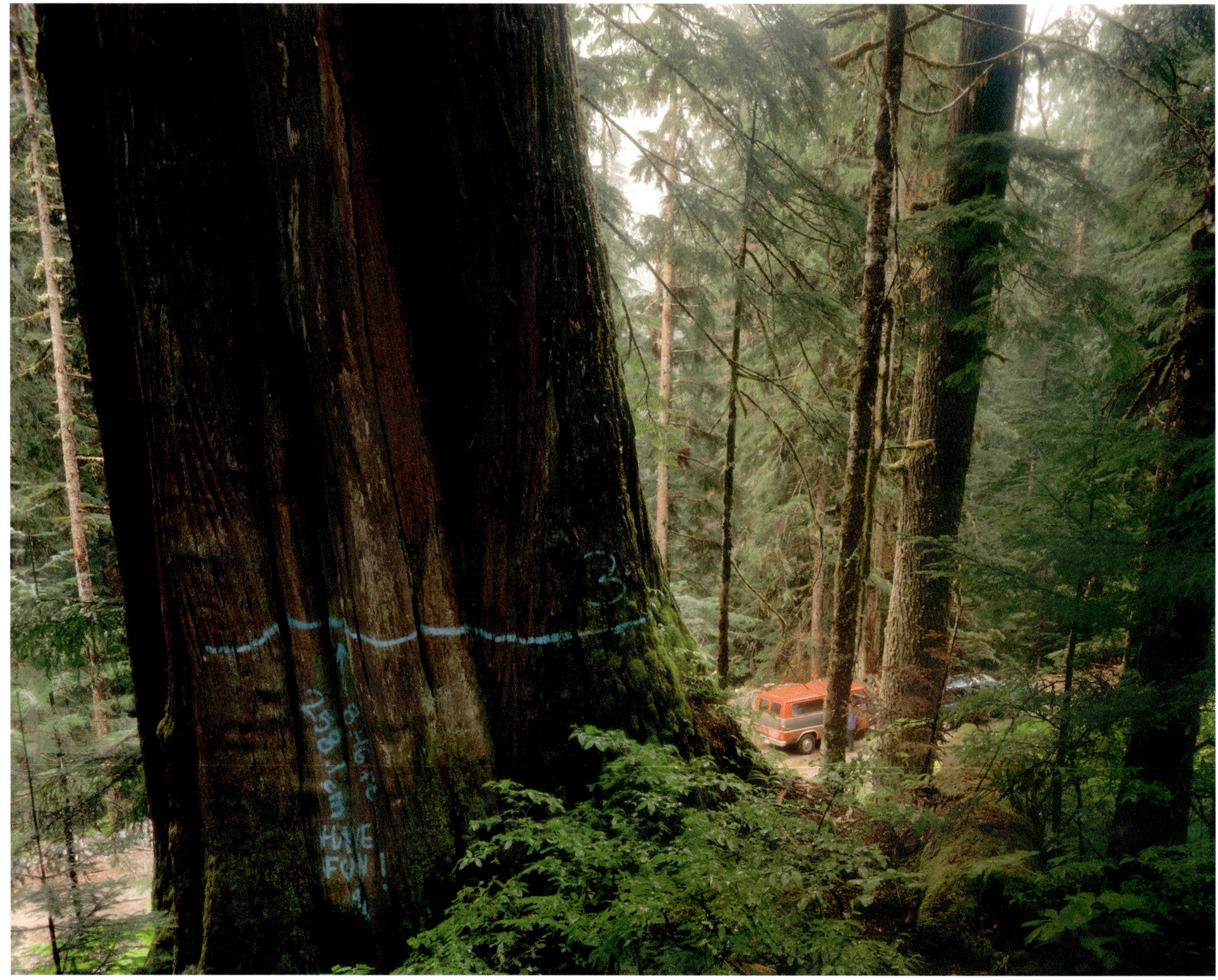
3
238.1cm
HAVE FUN!

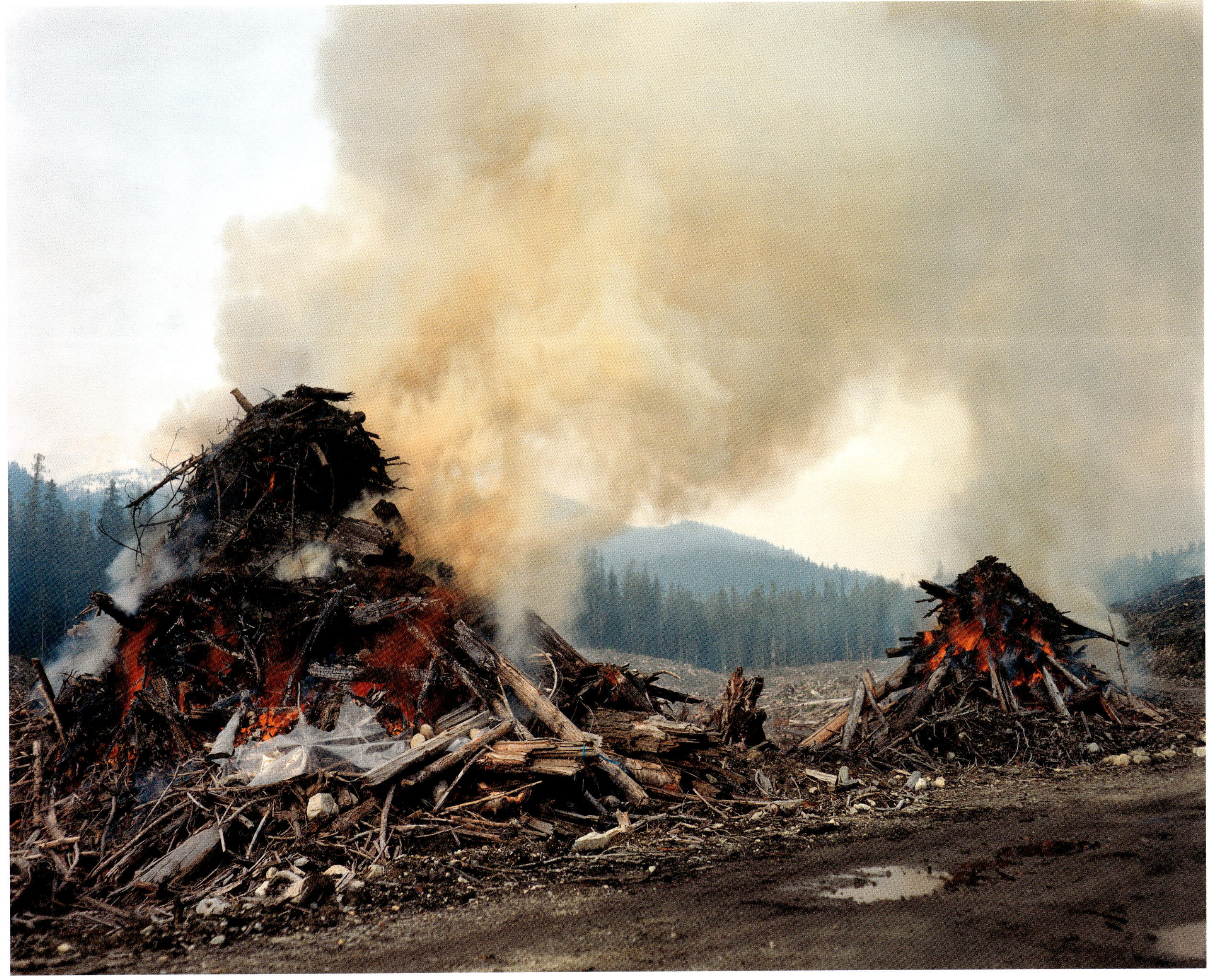

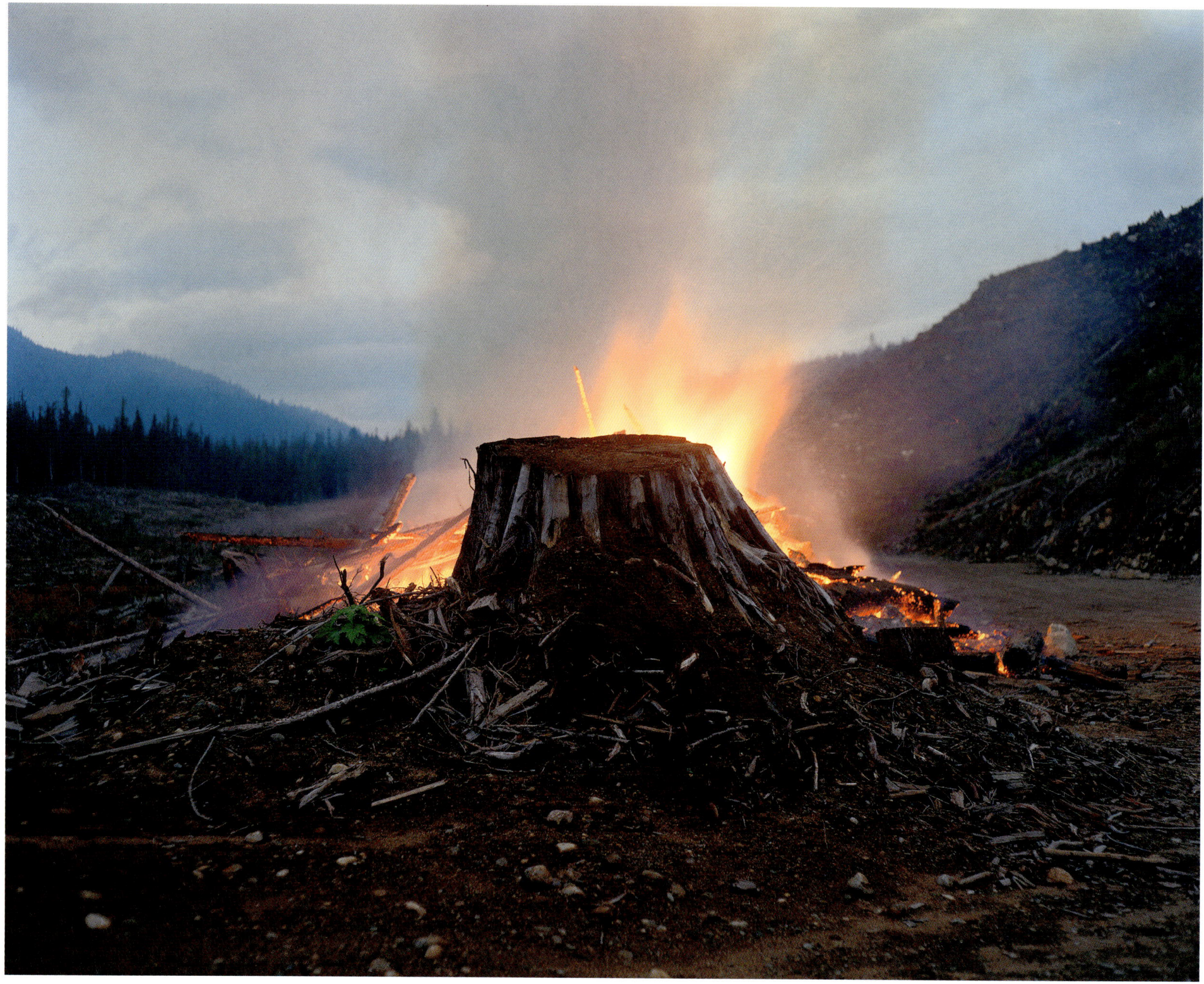

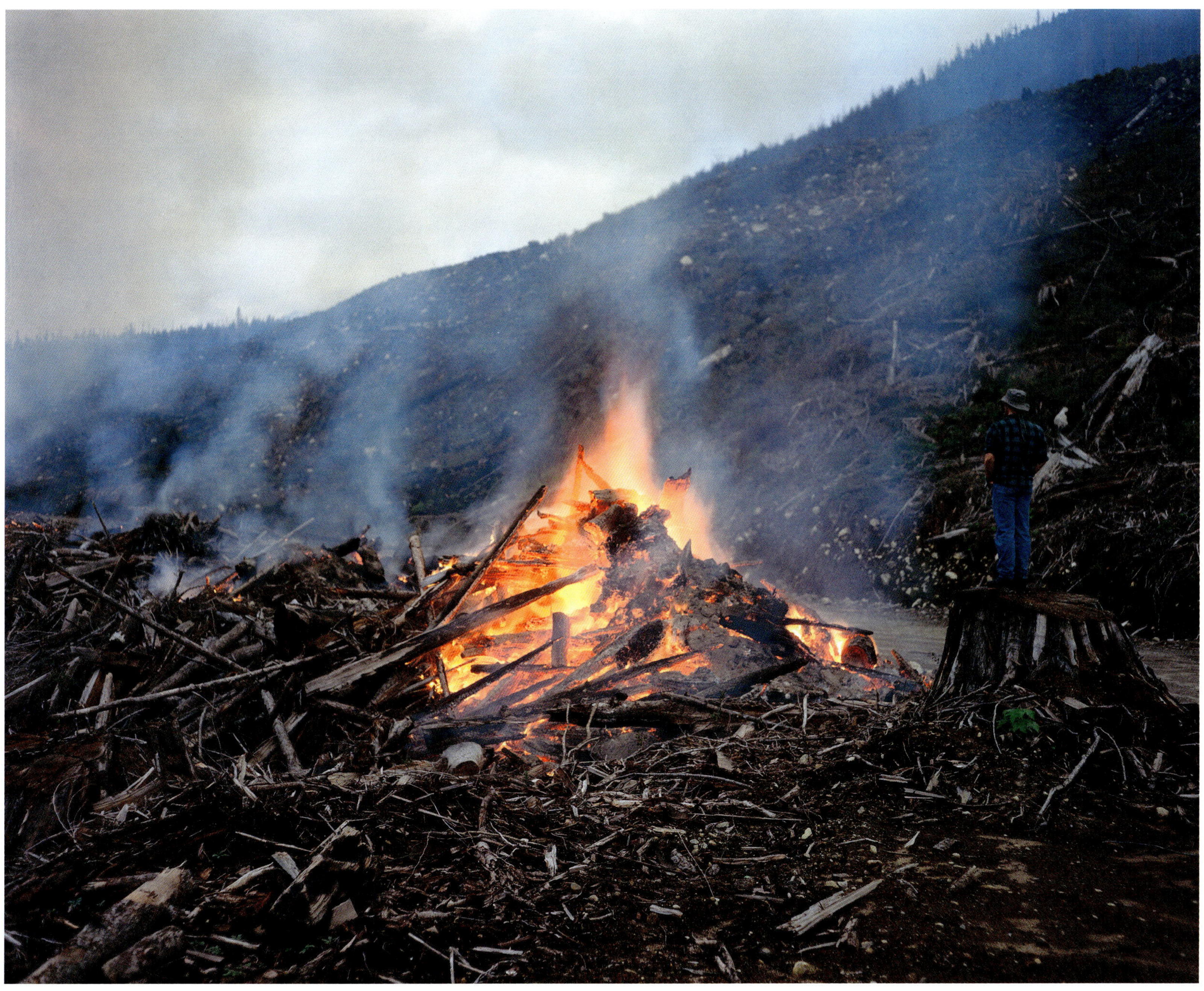

The three of us were just sitting by the water, and it was very empowering just to be there. And then we looked up and we just saw this fleet of logging trucks driving by with the largest cedar, and we just grabbed our hearts. Ohhhh. Senaqwila was just standing by the river, just looking around, and she looked over her shoulder and said: “Where are they taking our grandmothers?” And I just thought: the work we’re doing here is so important, we cannot allow this to continue; if my two-year-old daughter can understand that her grandmothers are being taken away from her home, we can never give up this fight.

CEASE WYSS / T’UY̓TANAT

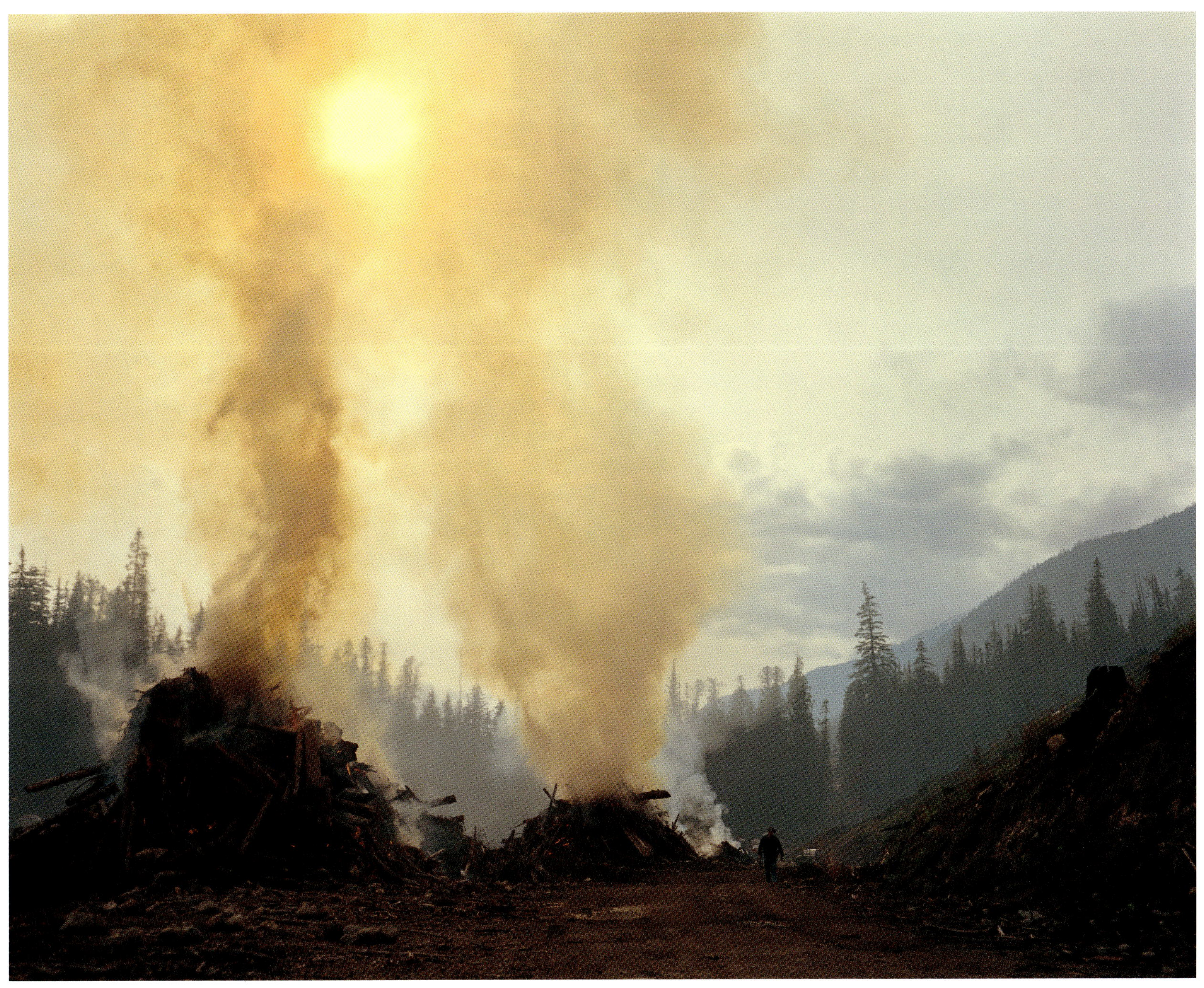

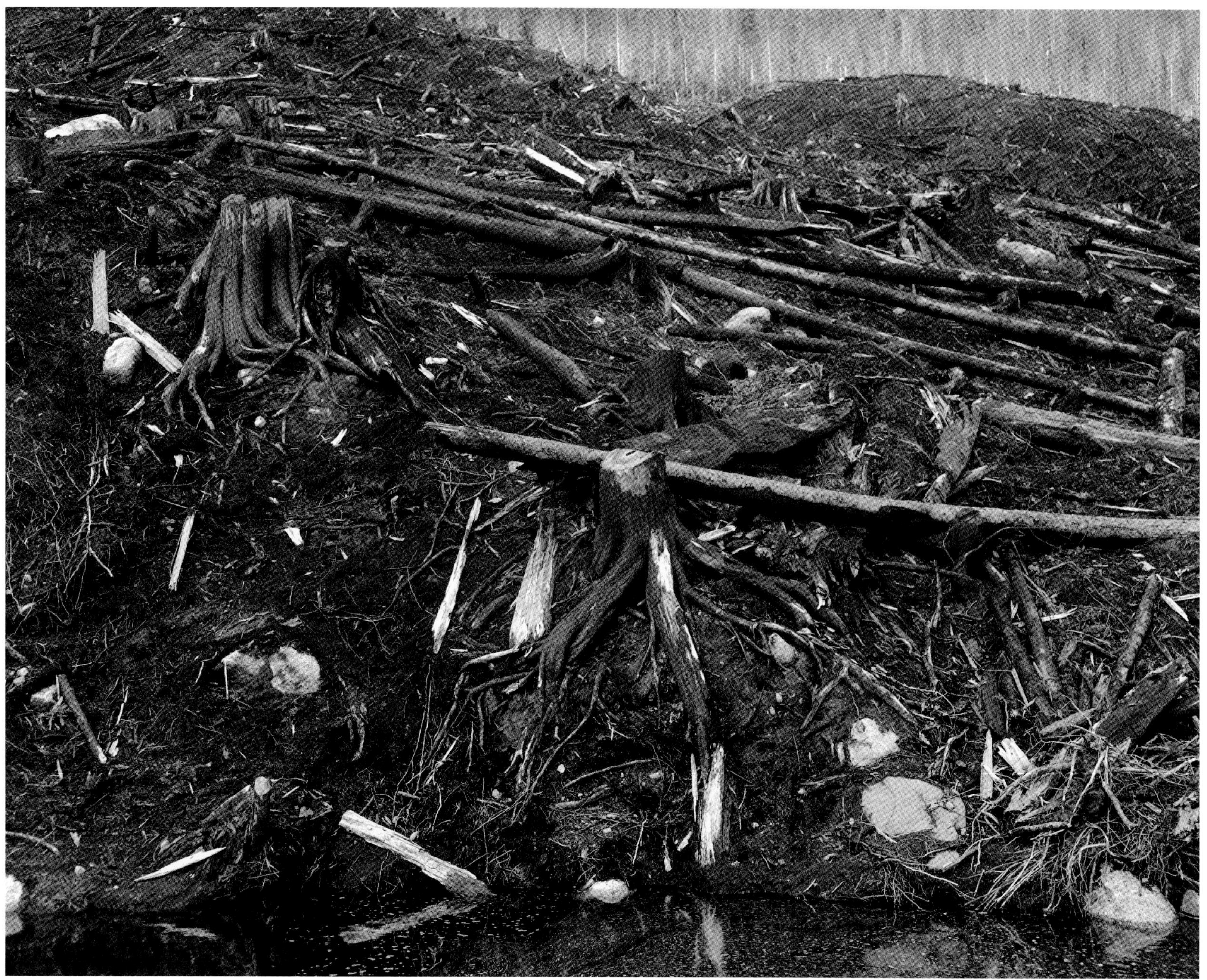

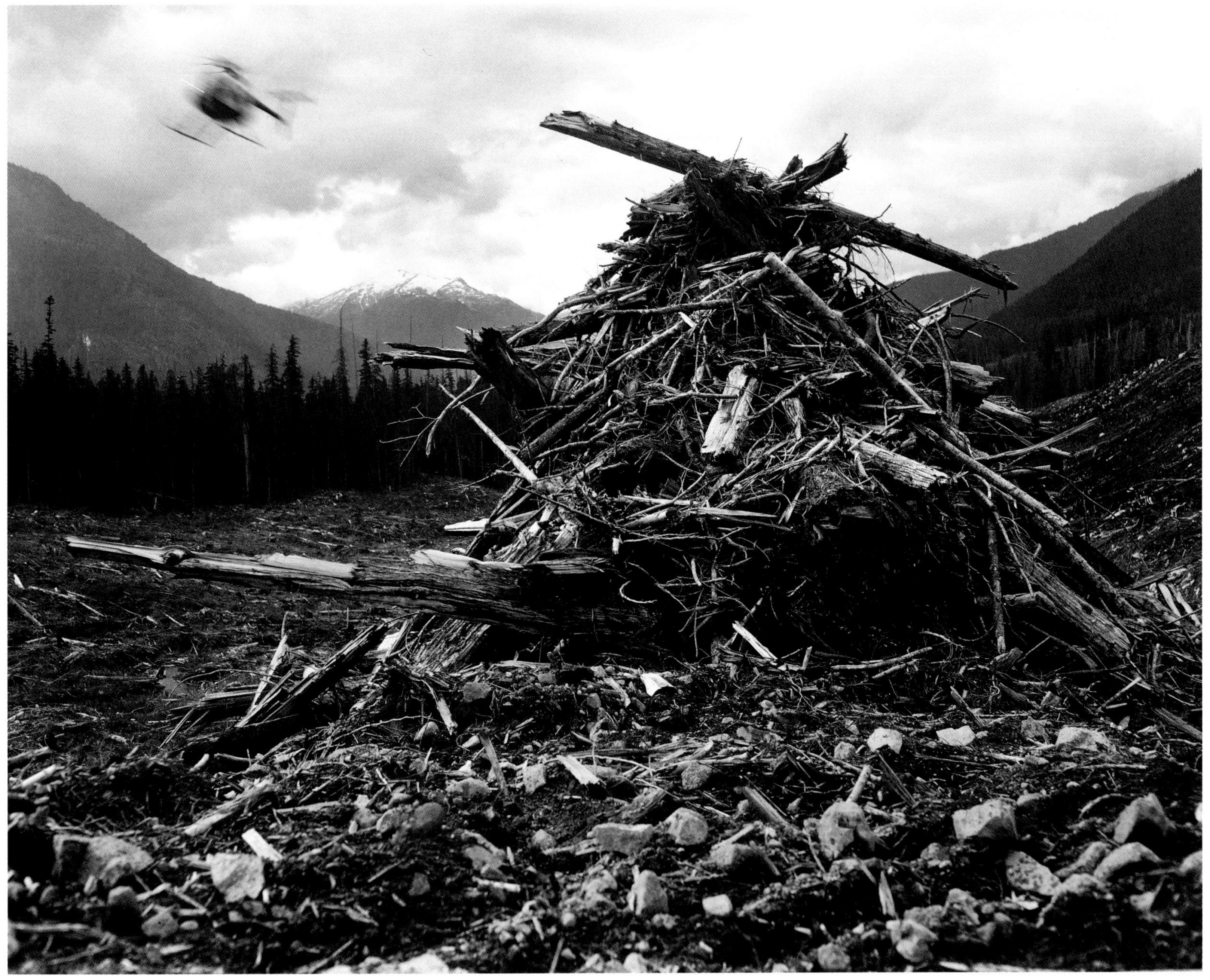

Many people here had spirit helpers
who spoke to them, and not just
bears and wolves but trees and
rocks and water and moss.
In order to hear them, a Squamish
person would go away from other
humans and simply sit still and listen.
After days or weeks or even years they
would let themselves hear what had
been around them the whole time.
The sound of the world.

AARON NELSON-MOODY / TAWX'SIN YEXWULLA / PÚLXTN

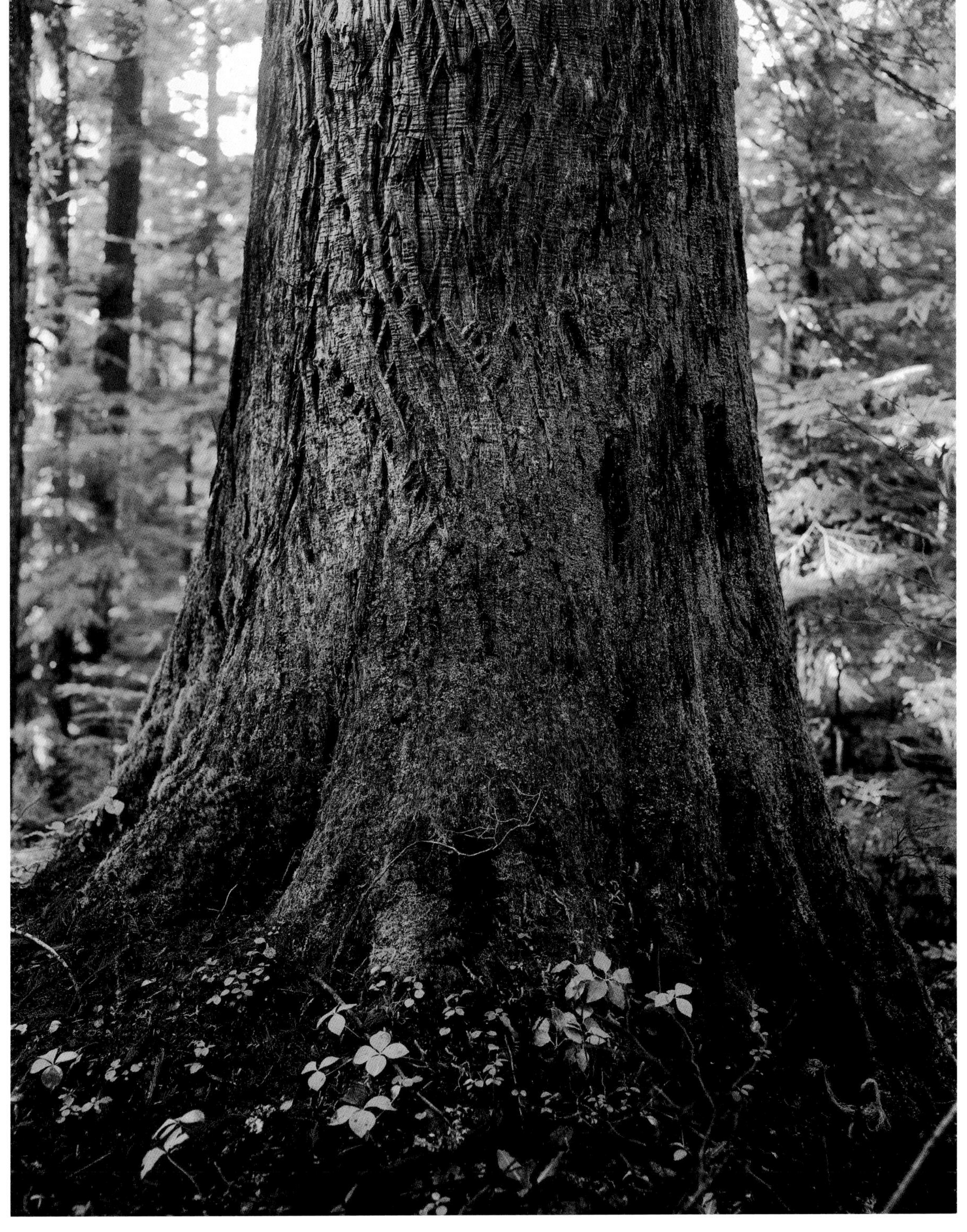

What we call “Ut’sám̓” we ask you to witness, to be the ones to watch and listen to what is about to take place, and that is an ancient custom that still is adhered to today in our ceremonies and in many of our gatherings. It’s a way of acknowledging our visiting dignitaries, as well as our local “siy̓am̓,” matriarchs and patriarchs, to ask them to be the ones to validate the significance of any particular ceremony or changes in one’s life.

CHIEF IAN CAMPBELL / X̱ÁLEḴ / SEḴYÚ SIY̓ÁM̓

PROLOGUE
PICTURING TRANSFORMATION NEXW-ÁYANTSUT

UTSÁM WITNESS

Rainforest mist, or it could be smoke from a burning slash, rises from a roadway that cuts across what was pristine old-growth forest. This is not a welcoming site. Yet the panoramic image of this logging road, juxtaposed with the photo of William Nahanee/*Kwelánexw*, Coast Salish Speaker in the Longhouse tradition, in his regalia is eerily beautiful. And deeply sad. Many of Nancy Bleck's artworks unflinchingly reveal the scars that business as usual, and clear-cut logging in particular, have wrought upon British Columbia's woods.

Once upon a moment in time immemorial, during a decade from 1997 to 2007, a particular piece of land witnessed a transformation. At first known simply as the Witness Project, a community formed around an "invitation to witness" during camping weekends on the sandbar at Sims Creek, deep in the northern part of the Squamish Nation's traditional territory. A sandbar became a longhouse, and a sandbar, as sandbars in the wild are known to do, disappeared. What reappeared was the rich traditional history of this special place. A new space of collaboration was opened up, and the public was invited in to witness.

Being called to "witness"
in the Coast Salish tradition
is a sacred honour.

Bearing witness by a "hired" Speaker
carries responsibilities and duty.
As a witness, they are to listen and watch
the "work" that is going to take place.
They are to carry the message back
to their home community.

If, in the future, or at any time in their life,
there is a concern over what took place, they,
as witnesses, have to recall what they have heard
and seen with regard to the event.

FROM THE SQUAMISH NATION
Assertion of Aboriginal Title

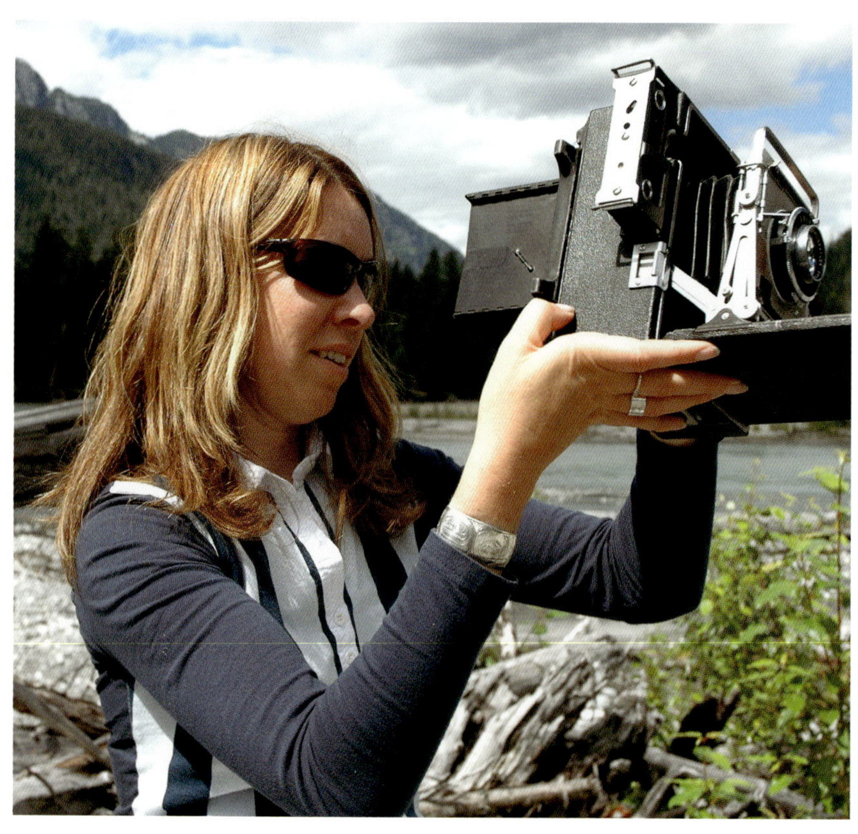

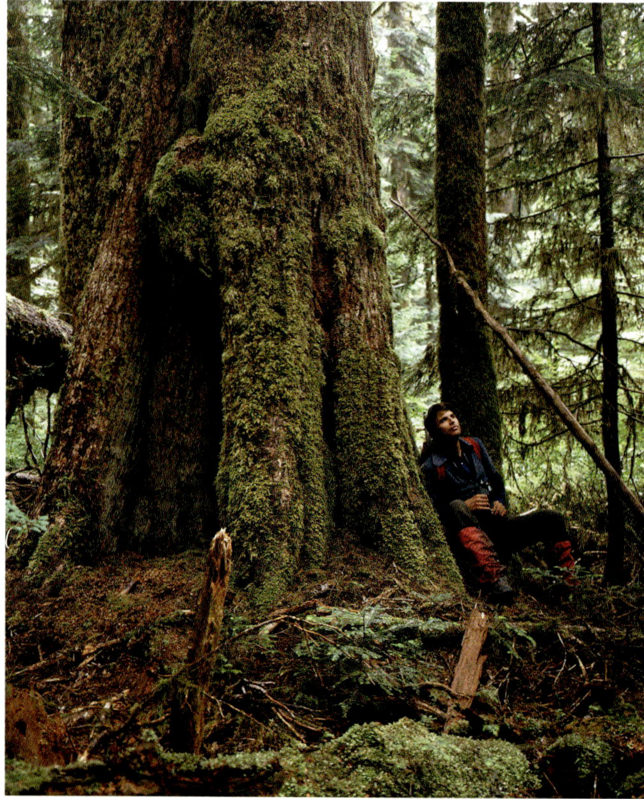

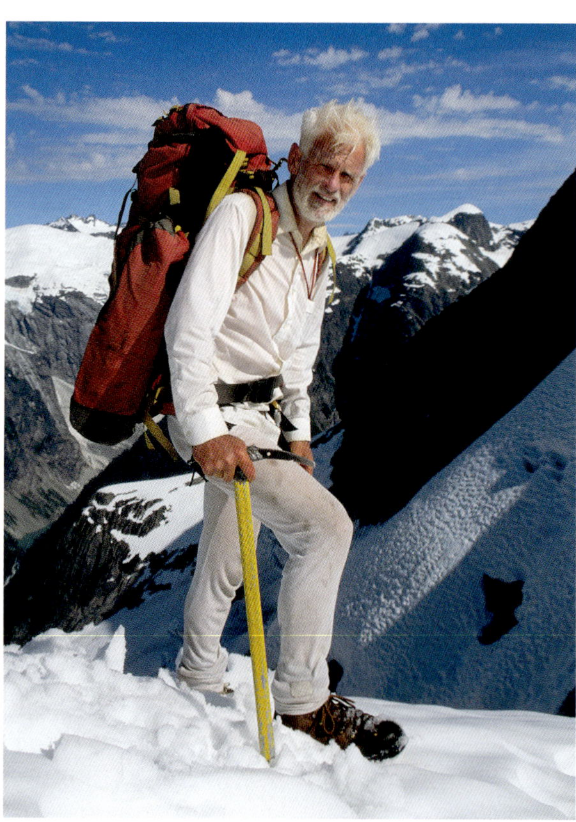

ONE

BREACHING PROTOCOL

Originally from German-immigrant roots in Mississauga, Ontario, Nancy Bleck first came west when she won the photo contest at Expo 86, and she discovered an unexpected feeling of kinship with B.C.'s forests. She was still a high-school student then, but she knew she'd be back. And when she returned in 1989, she got involved with the conservation groups. Her first guide to this world of West Coast wilderness was the well-known conservationist Randy Stoltmann. While hiking with Randy in the Carmanah Valley on Vancouver Island, Nancy had her own wilderness epiphany when she felt, in a deeper, more profound way than mere rational knowing, that it was greatly important to protect these last remaining old-growth forests.

Nancy started going out into the bush with her 4 × 5 camera, getting to know the land through her lens, and the Western Canada Wilderness Committee (WCWC), the environmental advocacy organization known to most people as WC², used some of her images on its posters around that time. Nancy describes getting to know the forests so intimately that the trees felt like family—and losing them to logging felt just as devastating to her as a death in the community.

When Randy died in an avalanche on May 24, 1994, in the Kitlope region of the Coast Mountains, Nancy felt even more drawn to the forests and determined to protect them. She sought out an area that Randy, with the precision of a skilled cartographer, had highlighted on a map as holding valuable bio-rich species of old-growth cedar, Douglas-fir, hemlock and white pine forests. "Of anyone I've ever known, Randy knew his trees," she recalls. So when Nancy happened to meet world-famous mountaineer John Clarke in 1995 in the Elaho Valley northwest of Squamish, it was not exactly by accident that they were in the same place at the same time. Randy was why John came down from the mountains.

John was leading the traverse when Randy died. The loss of such a close friend shook him, and he felt compelled to take up Randy's conservation legacy. This spot where Nancy and John both chose to be in the summer of '95 had previously been identified by Randy as the next hot spot for wilderness conservationists. In fact, the Wilderness Committee had just declared it the Randy Stoltmann Wilderness Area.

facing left: **Nancy Bleck**, photo by Beth Carruthers, 2006

facing centre: **Randy Stoltmann**, photo by Nancy Bleck, 1990

facing right: **John Clarke**, photo by Greg Mauer, 2000

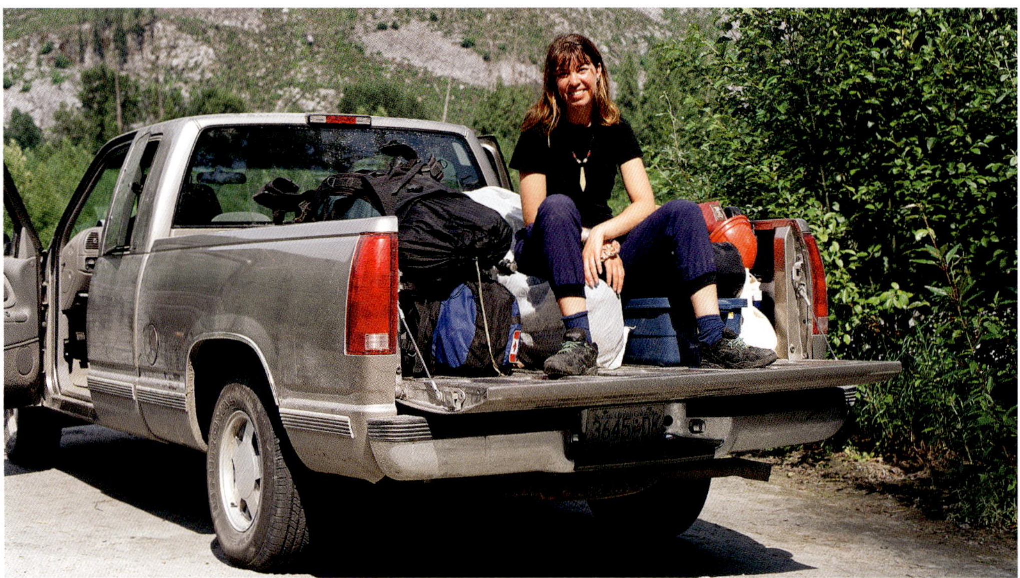

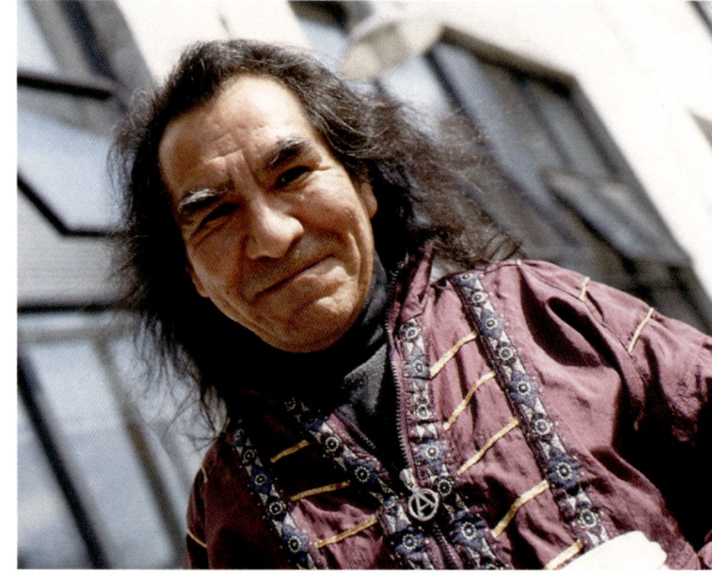

above: **Nancy Bleck**,
photo by Shel Neufeld, 1999

right: **James Nicholas**,
photo by Nancy Bleck, 1999

Nancy had long been identified as a photographer, but now as a student at the Emily Carr Institute of Design in Vancouver her journeys into the woods were also evolving into a more interesting process than photojournalism. It was truly an artistic inquiry she was beginning, and her own aesthetic was influencing how she wanted the images used. The forests were becoming her focus, and art-making the medium she wanted to explore. She recalls that working in this manner was a way of listening to the land speaking.

At the time, Nancy started questioning what was behind the word "wilderness," a word being used by environmentalists as if no one had been there before the land was "discovered" by settlers. She reframed this idea using the Western artist's idea of "landscape" and the concept of "territory," which is where living things—animals and, of course, people—belong. These thoughts began to shape the way John referred to his own photos, which he shared publicly in slideshows. And in spite of their deep affection for Randy, they were not of the opinion that the area should be named after him; they were sensing that the land did not belong to them, even if this struggle to save it might.

Joe Foy, of the Wilderness Committee, also a friend of Randy's, was hanging out with John and Nancy and remembers their conversations and Nancy's insistence that a new peaceful model of activism was needed. A "non-confrontational space," as he recalled her describing it. And Joe, being "up to his eyeballs trying to move forward using confrontation," thought the idea would be worth a try. It was no accident, then, that their campfire conversations became the new salon for these ideas.

For John, experiencing the land was always key to conservation. As he put it, "There is no substitute for getting out there, swatting bugs and sitting around a campfire under the stars." Nancy didn't need to be convinced of this. So in 1995, Nancy and John, along with a group of like-minded volunteers, formed an informal "group with no name" and began taking the public to the headwaters of the Upper Lillooet, between Pemberton and Lillooet. They believed that to protect the area from logging, people needed to care about it. The following summer, they shifted locations from the Upper Lillooet to Sims Creek in the Elaho Valley.

Around this same time, Chief Bill Williams/*telálsemk̲in siỷám̓*, one of sixteen hereditary chiefs of the Squamish Nation, was observing what was going on. He is, like his father was before him, a watchman, with a mandate to take care of the northern part of the Nation's territory. He had been keeping an eye on what the Wilderness Committee was up to, as well as what the logging company Interfor was doing. He had seen Nancy and John's notice about the camping weekends in Vancouver's free weekly newspaper, the *Georgia Straight*. On September 28, 1996, ironically Randy Stoltmann's birthday, Chief Bill headed to Squamish.

At Barney's PetroCan, the last pit stop before heading out on the logging road, Nancy borrowed Chief Bill's cell phone, though she didn't realize who he was at the time. So when she met Chief Bill again a few hours later on a sandbar at Sims Creek, and he handed her his business card, Nancy was not sure they should be there at all. Nancy, like John and Randy, hadn't really been engaged with the First Nations people who had a claim on this land. Until now, for the group of volunteers that had been trying to protect the area, it had been a battle over resources, or a deep love for the forests, but not home. However, Nancy had been engaging with these issues in her art practice, and she had been working with artist and Emily Carr associate professor Sandra Semchuk and the late James Nicholas, a Cree actor and writer. She understood enough about First Nations culture to realize it would be a big faux pas to fail to acknowledge the chief, in whose living room they had been squatting that summer. It would literally be adding insult to injury. She practised saying his traditional name, pronounced Ta-LALL-sum-cane, See-YAHM. She asked him for permission to be there.

"We were being arrogant white people even though we didn't want to be. And I had no idea who Chief Bill was until Nancy was smart enough to realize, oh my god, it's Chief Bill!" describes Lisa Baile, a friend of John's who was originally from England and co-founder with him of the Wilderness Education Program. She was there that weekend and remembers the incredible energy that happened when John, Nancy and the Chief joined forces.

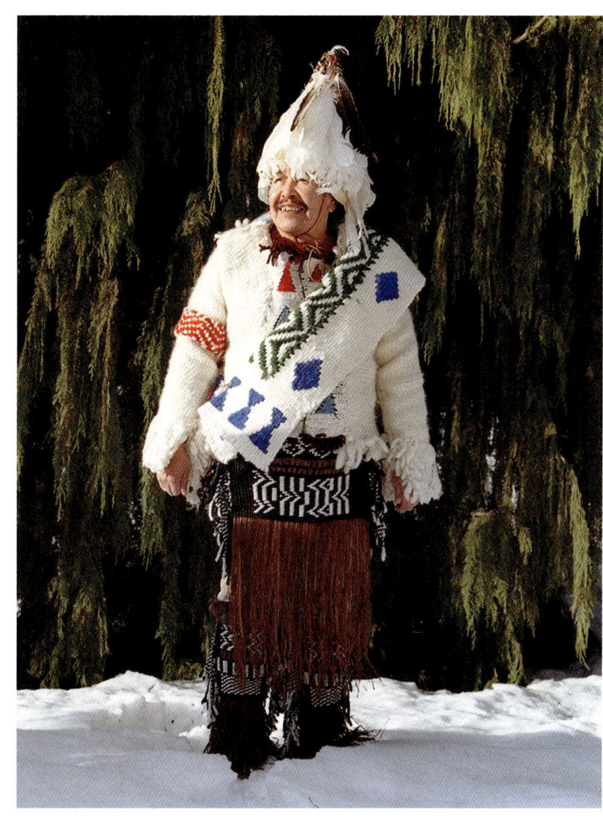

Chief Bill Williams,
photo by Nancy Bleck, 2009

By now Chief Bill knew a bit more about what Nancy and John were up to. "I wish I could welcome you to this northern part of our territory formally," he replied, "but the protocol has already been breached." Protocol is an old-fashioned word, used more often in the modern context for legal jargon, to describe high-level diplomatic etiquette. Geekier types use it to define how computers talk to each other. And literary critics see it as a word that has a richly nuanced lineage. Protocol is not a word that has typically been top of mind for ecologists and environmentalists. But let's not mince our words: this land was a territory under attack with violence on all sides. The loggers who built the road had not asked permission. The group of camping environmentalists had used the logging road to get to where they were, on the sandbar of Sims Creek, at mile 54. Through no fault of their own, they were in a place where all was not as it should be.

In spite of the breach of protocol, Chief Bill expressed support for what Nancy and John were doing and joined their gathering. It was the end of camping for that summer, and gifts were being exchanged. Nancy realized she must not leave out Chief Bill. Searching through her tent, she found the feather that had been given to her only a few weeks earlier by Sandra and James for completing a vision quest. As much as she valued this eagle feather, she knew she had to give it away to the chief. Gift giving is a cornerstone of Squamish Nation (and many First Nations') protocol: the true power of the gift is to give away that which is held most dear.

Chief Bill Wiliams and Lisa Baile,
photo by Nancy Bleck, 2009

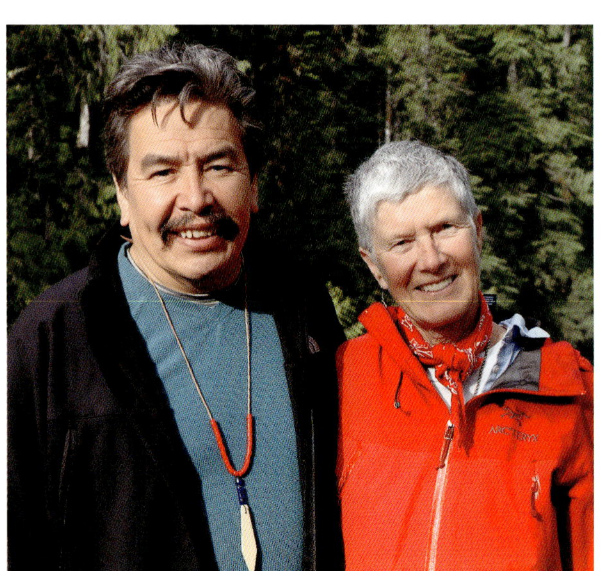

The gift of an eagle feather was the key that unlocked the door. In that moment, Chief Bill decided that he could possibly work with this white girl and white-haired man. He became part of the unofficial group with no name. Right away, John bounded into that opening and invited Chief Bill on a journey through his own territory, to places the chief had never been before.

BY WAY OF WATER TO THE ROUNDHOUSE

The Witness Project began as an elaborate book-like document, which Nancy had been up all night copying at Kinko's. It landed on the desk of Amir Alibhai, the brand-new arts programmer at the brand-new Roundhouse Community Centre. Begun as an assignment for Susan Schuppli's class in public art at Emily Carr, the document included a centrefold art piece and a cover mapping the waterways connecting the Roundhouse to Sims Creek. Amir recalls, "This really quite brilliant proposal from Nancy had in it writings and ideas and offers for partnership with Chief Bill Williams and John Clarke as well."

By proposing a six-month project showcasing elements of traditional Squamish culture within the public art context of the community centre, and taking anyone who wanted to wilderness camping at the sandbar on Sims Creek, the proposal was a perfect fit for the Roundhouse's mandate to offer programs that link recreation, the arts, the environment and culture. The community centre offered some infrastructure to help run the project and made Nancy its first artist-in-residence.

Nancy had imbued the proposal with an aesthetic appeal and an artistic vision that was not typical of most environmental projects at the time, and this visual approach carried over to the design of all the brochures promoting the project. Drawn by the image of the ocean-going canoe on the cover, Cease Wyss picked up one of the very first Witness Project brochures while hanging around the Roundhouse. Inside were numerous photos and an "Invitation to Witness." Being Coast Salish, Cease was familiar with the witness ceremony and was glad to see it being shared through an outreach project. As she says, "Witness felt like something I had been waiting my whole life to see, something so exciting between different communities."

It was also a chance to be in the forest.

On a Saturday in July 1997, an unsuspecting group of about a hundred gathered at the Roundhouse at 8 AM for the three-hour journey to Sims Creek, to camp, to do some hiking and to participate in the first public Witness ceremony. Young and old, coffee cups in hand, they were travellers, young parents, an entire multi-generation Asian family and their tiny dog, even a couple who had lived in downtown Vancouver for more than twenty-five years but never yet set foot in an ancient rainforest. Most of them didn't realize that their convoy of cars going up the dusty logging road was setting a precedent.

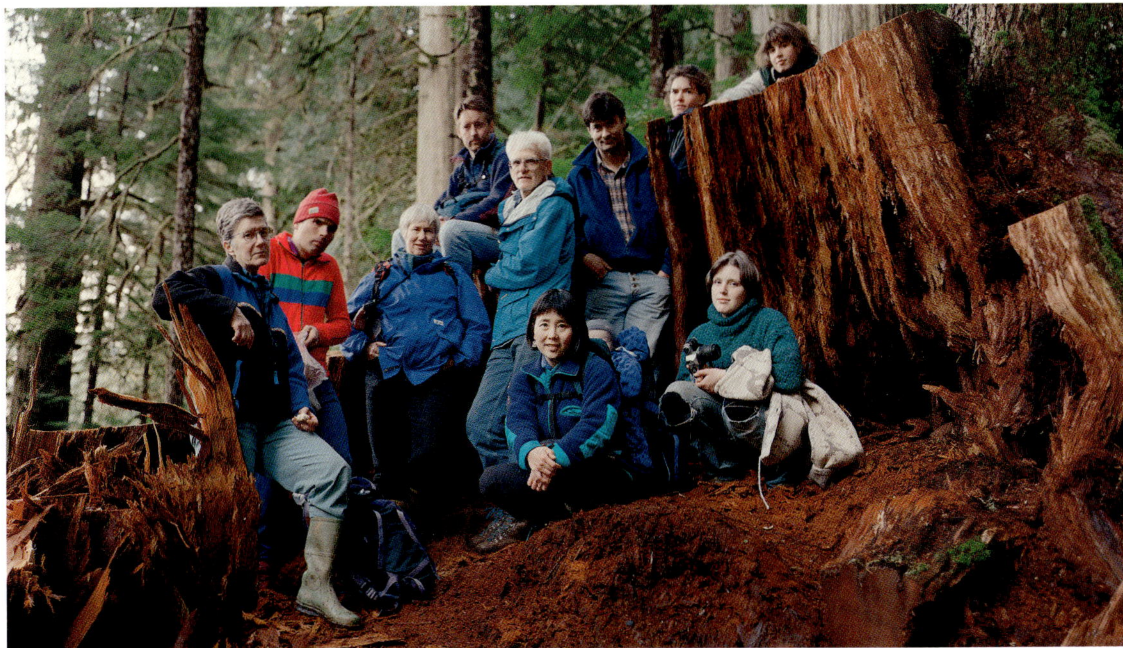

At the hollow tree by Sims Creek, photo by Nancy Bleck, 1998

Their destination was the sandbar on Sims Creek at mile 53 on the G Main logging road, in the northwest part of the Squamish Nation territory. Only the organizers knew that the loggers at mile 21 had decided to blockade the environmentalists and that Chief Bill had called in the Squamish Nation Peacekeepers to escort the convoy through the Nation's territory. Nancy had just returned the day before from working with a filmmaker photographing the reunification of Hong Kong with China, and when John met her at the airport, he announced: "We've got a problem; it's the very first weekend and there is a logger's blockade!" Even so, Nancy quickly pulled together her tent and camping equipment, and they were off. But John, thanks to his white hair, public declarations about protecting the environment and

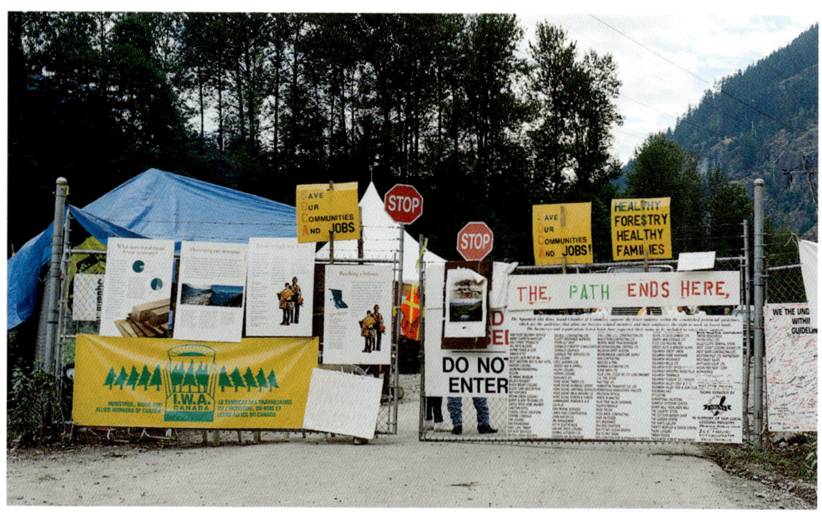

Logger's Blockade, photo by Nancy Bleck, 1997

a wave of publicity about him just before the project started, had become a visible target for the loggers. So, on that first Witness journey up the logging road, Chief Ian Campbell/*X̱álek̲/Sek̲yú siy̓ám̓*, one of the young Squamish Nation hereditary chiefs, though he was meeting John for the first time, offered to hide him under some blankets in his truck.

The battle between loggers and environmentalists was raging at this time, and logging in this area was slated to begin very soon. During the first few weeks of that first summer of the Witness Project, the loggers kept up their own blockade, which was a pre-emptive tactic to prevent any environmental groups from blockading them. Only the Witness participants, with their Squamish Nation Peacekeeper escorts, made it through. No other eco-activists got near the place.

Witness took the idea of summer camp to a whole new level. Although every weekend was a bit different, what stayed the same was the journey from the Roundhouse to the land and a Witness ceremony at the centre of it all. A complex, organic process emerged out of this very simple concept: from the individual and collective experiences of the many different witnesses each weekend was forged a human knowledge bank akin to the ecosystem of an old-growth forest, where the forest floor and the tree tops are a living library and a laboratory for natural innovation and vision.

For Cease, as an artist, herbalist and single mother, it was not easy getting onto the land. "At the time I started with Witness I did not yet have my traditional name, but I had some teachings and that passion and drive to go there and I really wanted to participate." The project made the land more accessible for her, and provided a community. She started giving workshops during Witness weekends on traditional medicines that could be gathered from the forest. And many others joined her in offering up their own skills—whether traditional like drum making, scientific like geology tours or even contemporary like a media literacy workshop—to whomever had come that weekend.

Witness unfolded in even deeper directions than Nancy could have imagined when she first submitted her proposal to the Roundhouse. What was occurring during those weekends was a literal confluence of wild and urban, nature and culture, and the need to both honour the past and protect the future. The arts, First Nations' culture, ecology, science, politics and economics were all flowing in a new direction. Out of this confluence a new space emerged, uniting past, present and future through a passion for the land, the pain of loss and the pleasure of process.

CALLING WITNESSES

The witness ceremony, a traditional Coast Salish practice, was opened up to all who came on the camping weekends.

For most non-indigenous participants, it was the first time they had ever experienced Squamish culture, and for many members of the Nation it was the first time they had been to this part of their own territory and experienced a witness ceremony on the land.

Nancy noted that for Chief Bill to invite the public into a ceremonial circle was an extremely generous act: "He was showing us, not telling us, another way of seeing, hearing and feeling the world, and given the historical injustices that First Nations people have gone through and continue to experience in Canada, for him to make this process inclusive was itself part of the uniqueness of Witness."

During the first Witness weekend, the Squamish Nation *Assertion of Aboriginal Title* was handed out in photocopied form, and Chief Bill spoke of his people's desire to reclaim their territory and expressed hope that the Witness Project would light a spark and start the flow of information.

He described the witness ceremony as "protocol that we as Coast Salish, or Squamish people, have been doing for well over ten thousand years. This protocol is established in oral history by passing down names and passing down information that is important to the family, that needs to be publicly displayed to other members of the community and, as such, to the family. As family, we hire Speakers to speak for us."

Drew Leathem was one of the many non-indigenous people drawn to Witness and the simple elegance of the ceremony itself: "The witness ceremony unified people in terms of how they connected with the project, how they became involved and how information was shared. Because the protocol was there."

Chief Bill, Nancy and John all had a very deep love for this place, but for Chief Bill, it was home.

And while the happy group of Witness founders and volunteers were rediscovering protocol, Interfor was gathering steam. There was a lot at stake. Although few actually noticed the *Assertion of Aboriginal Title* document on that initial weekend, what was witnessed in that very first year of the project's formation was significant. After that original Witness summer in 1997, the forest above Sims Creek was logged.

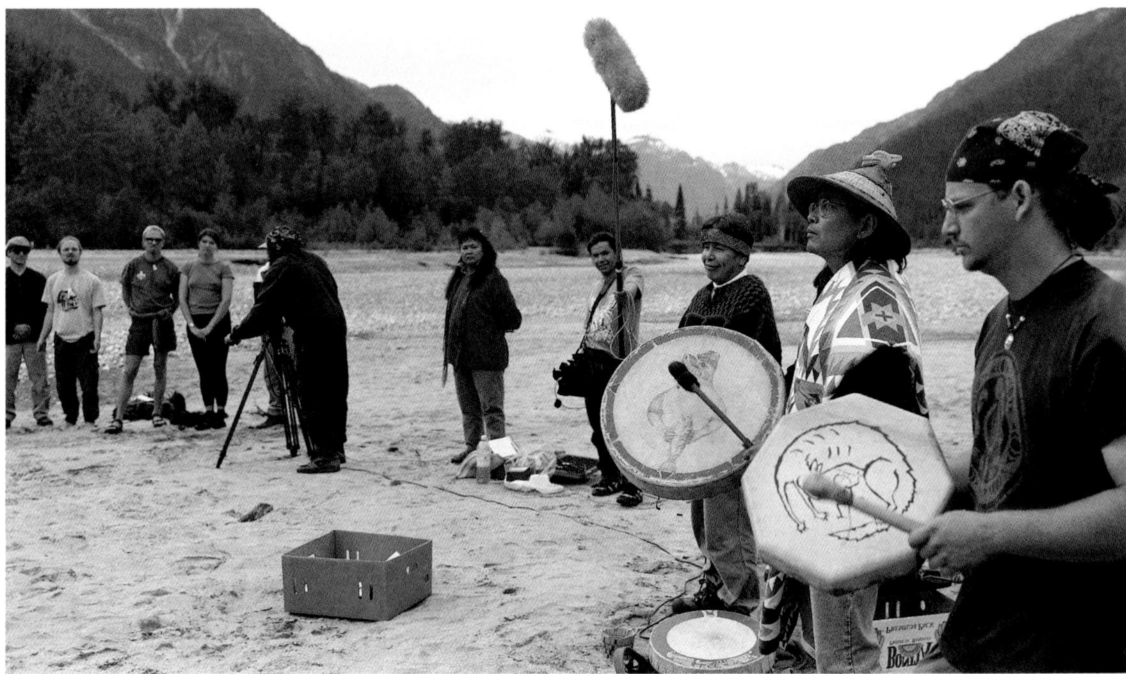

Witness Ceremony at Sims Creek,
photo by Nancy Bleck, 1997

CALL TO WITNESS

1997

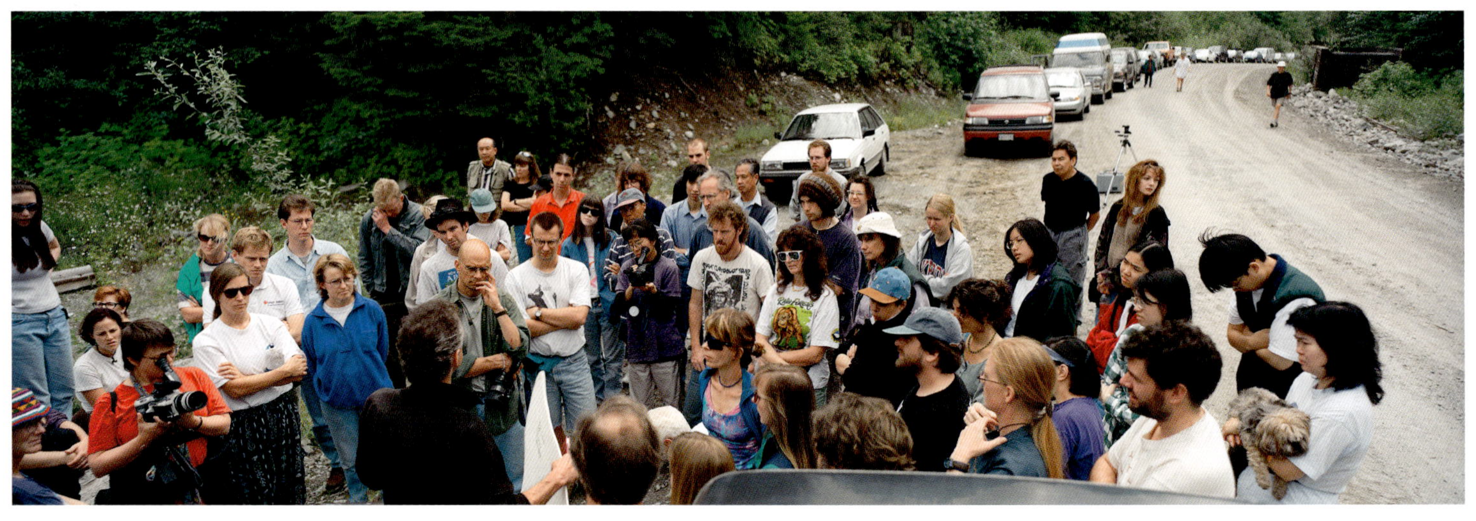

The land bears ***witness*** to the settlements, resource sites, and spiritual and ritual places of our ancestors.

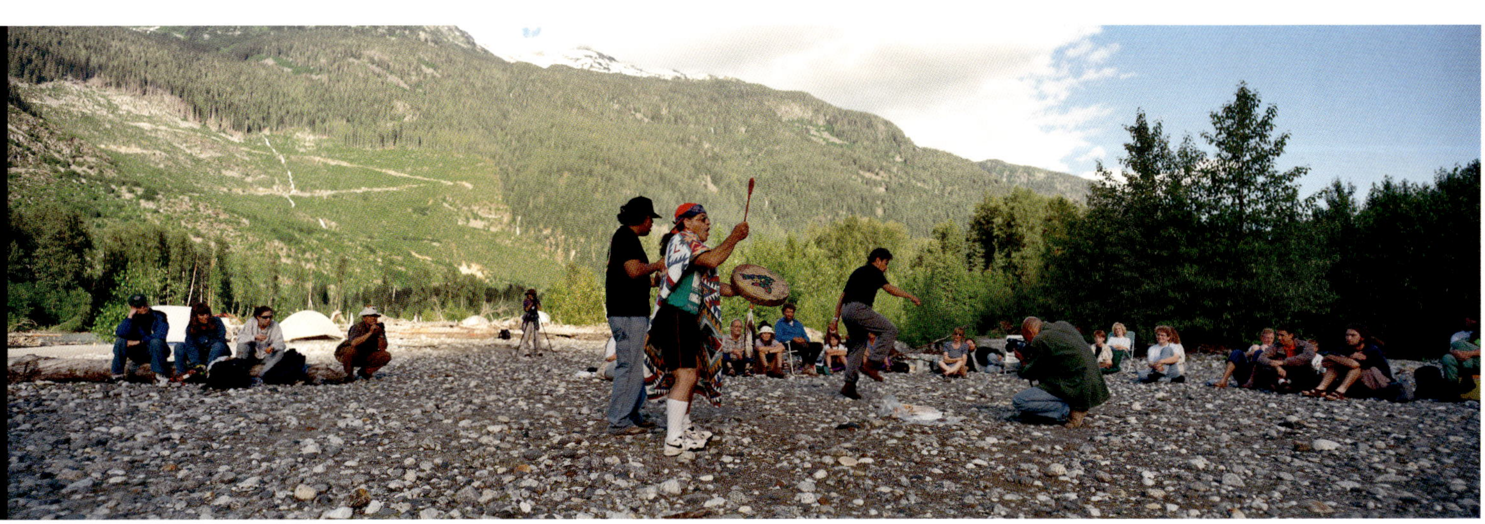

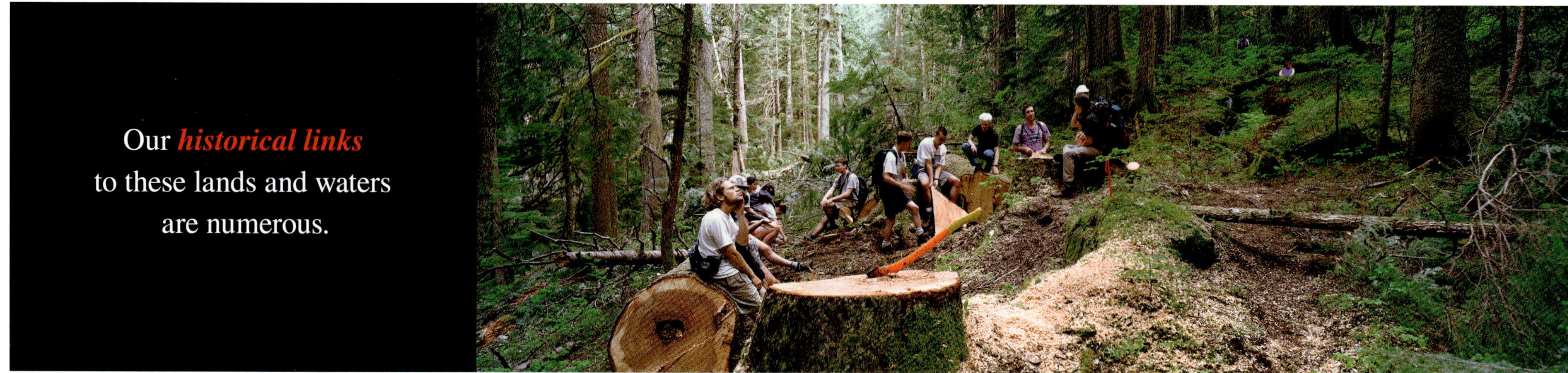

Our ***historical links*** to these lands and waters are numerous.

We have never ceded or surrendered title to our lands, rights to our resources or the power to make decisions within our ***territory***.

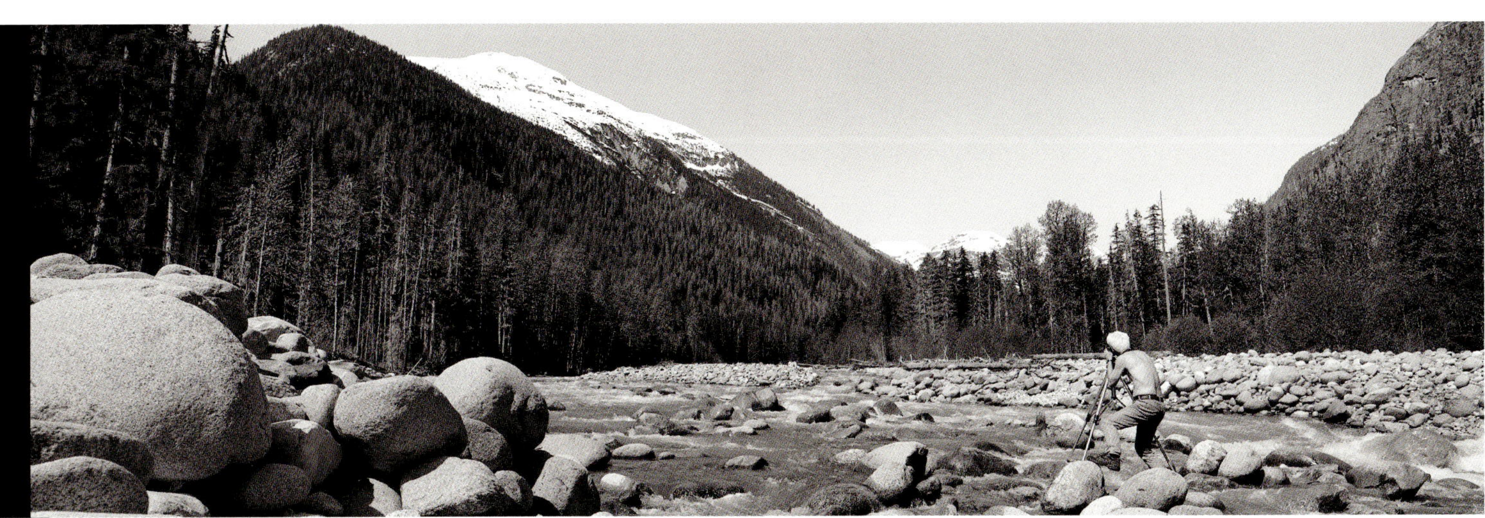

Because of the bounty
of our land and our unique
relationship to the land,
we were economically
self-sufficient.

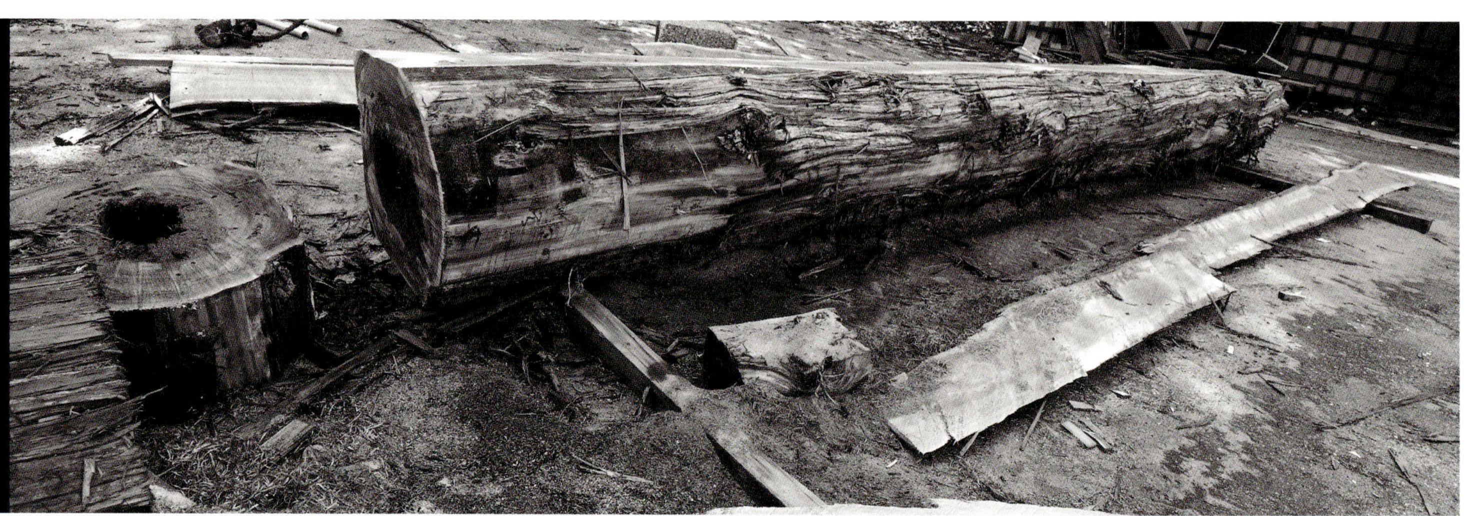

The Squamish nation has existed and prospered within our traditional territory since *time immemorial.*

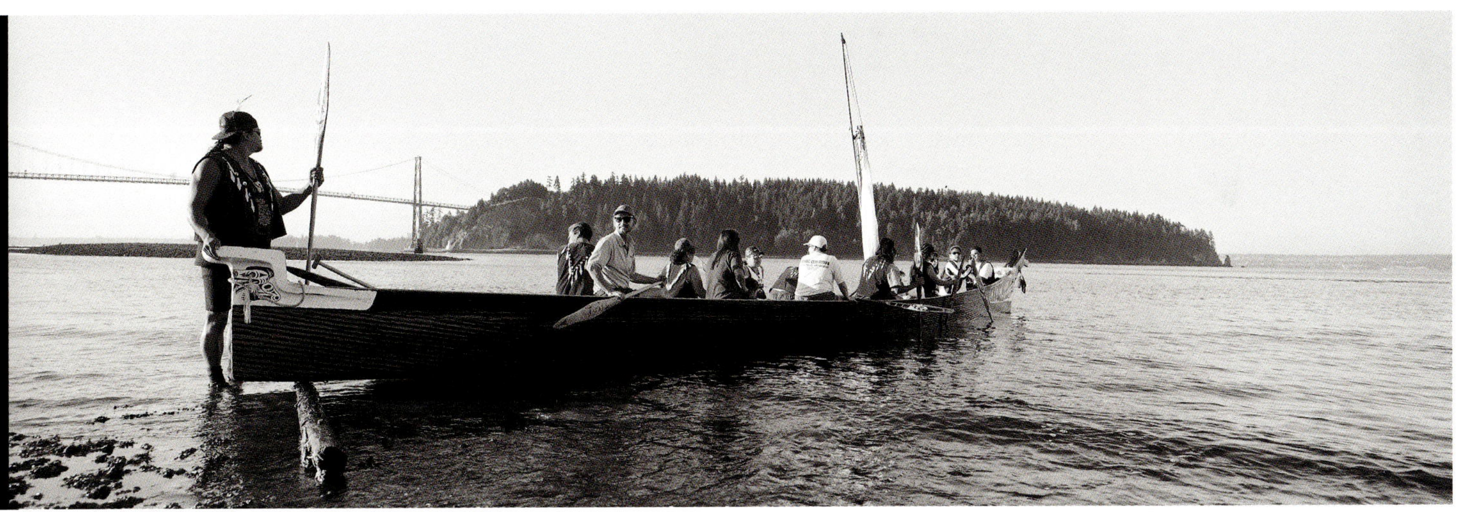

PANORAMA DOCUMENTS

1996–2005

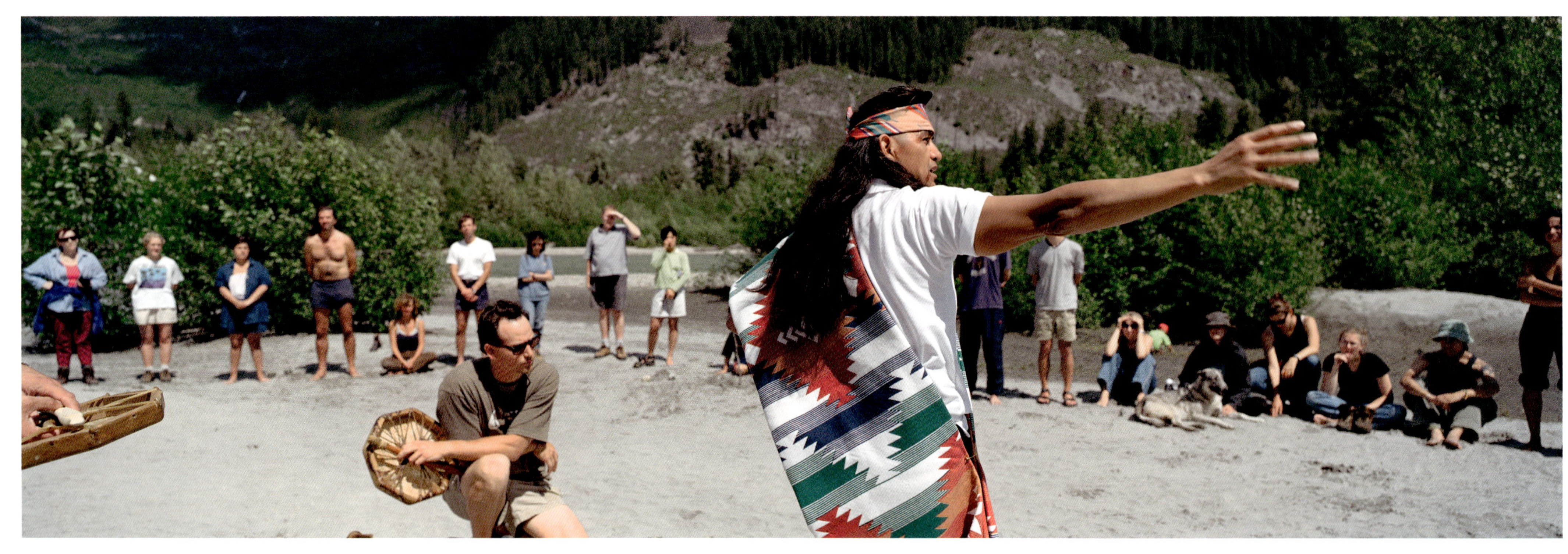

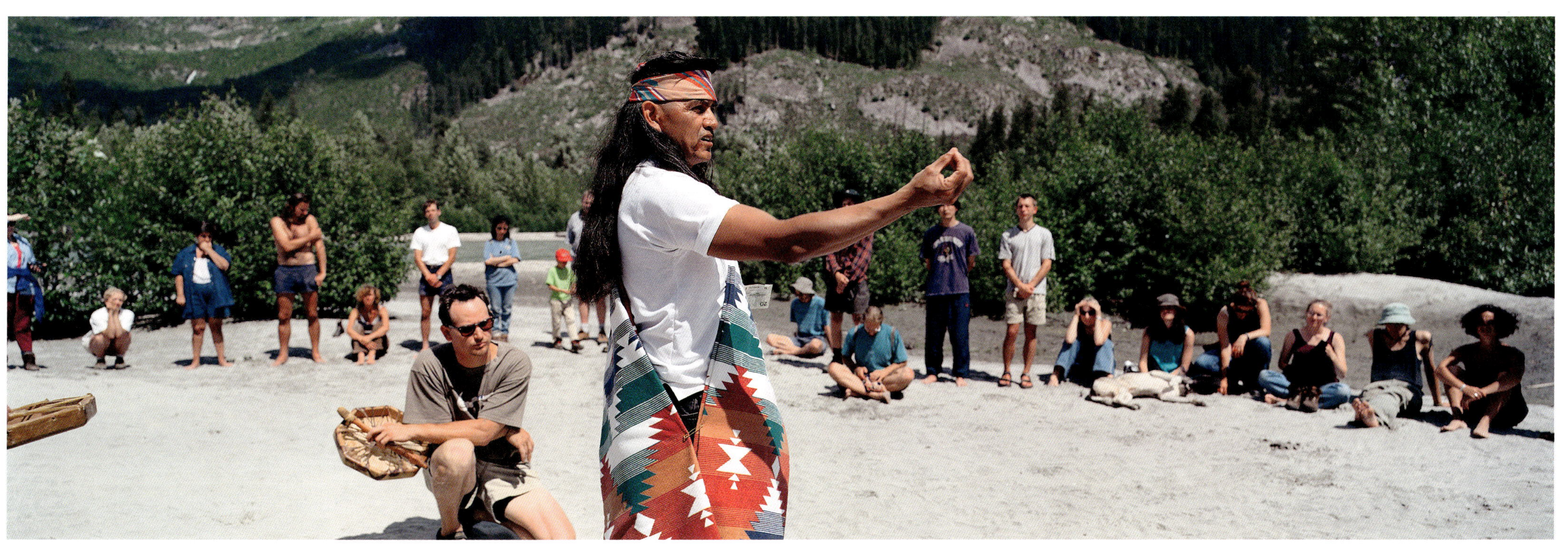

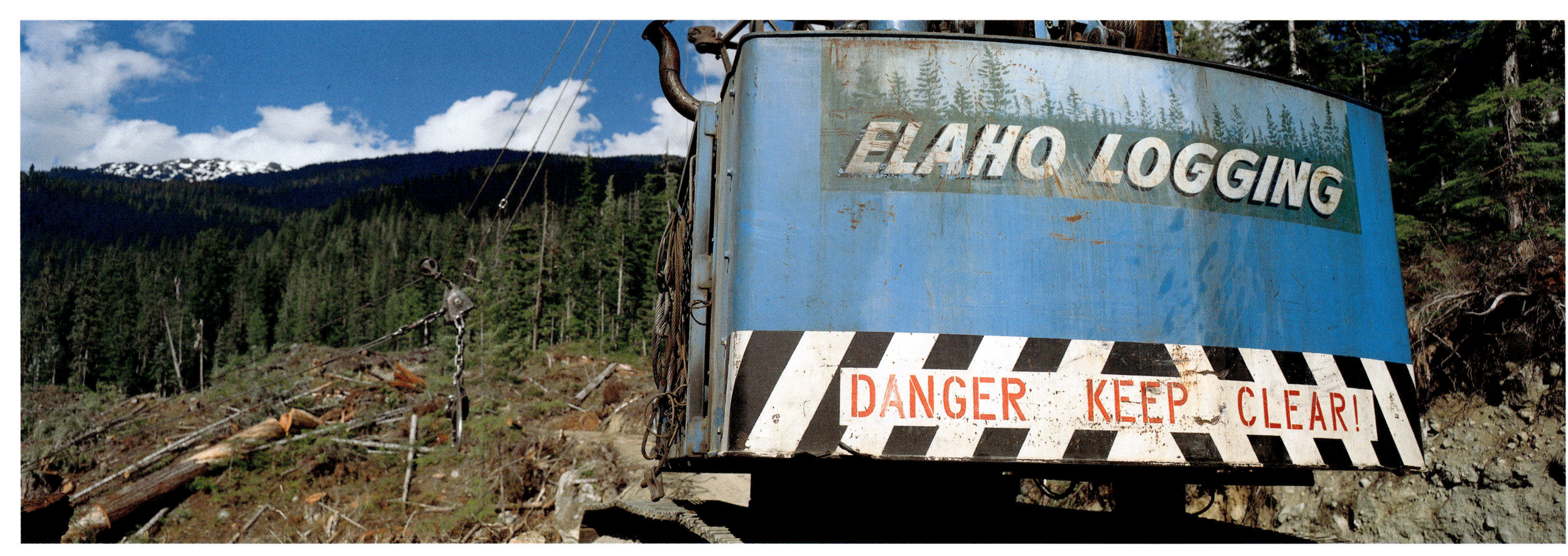
ELAHO LOGGING
DANGER KEEP CLEAR!

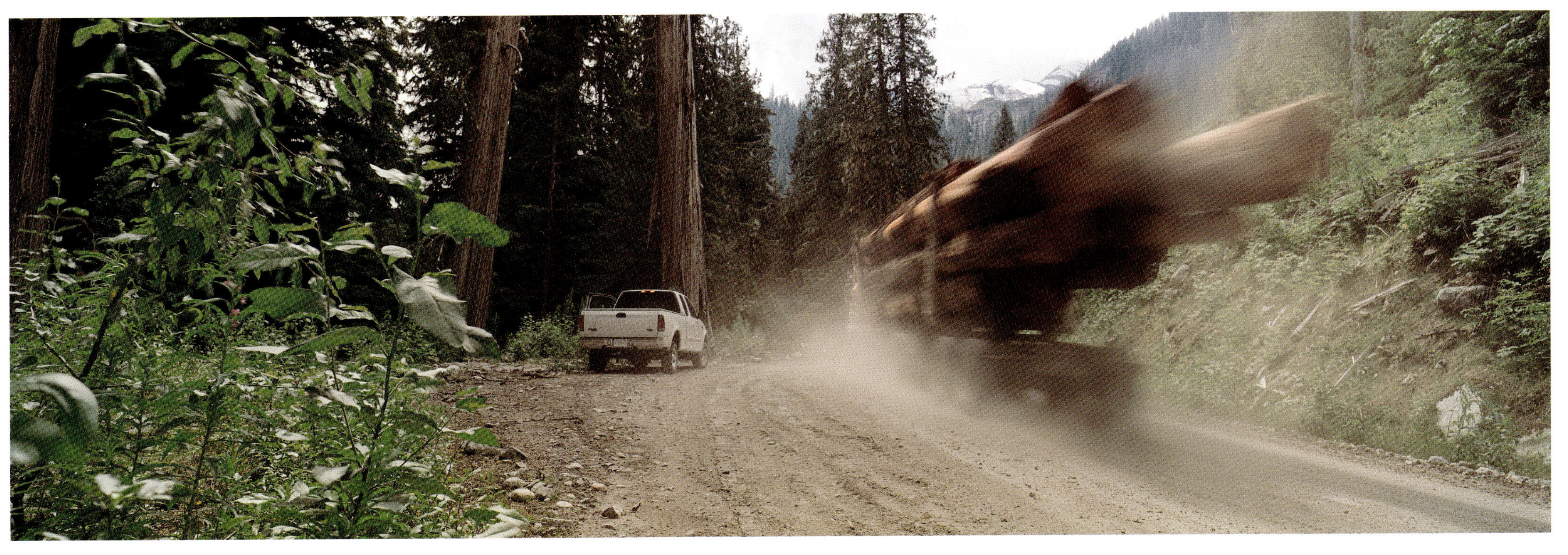

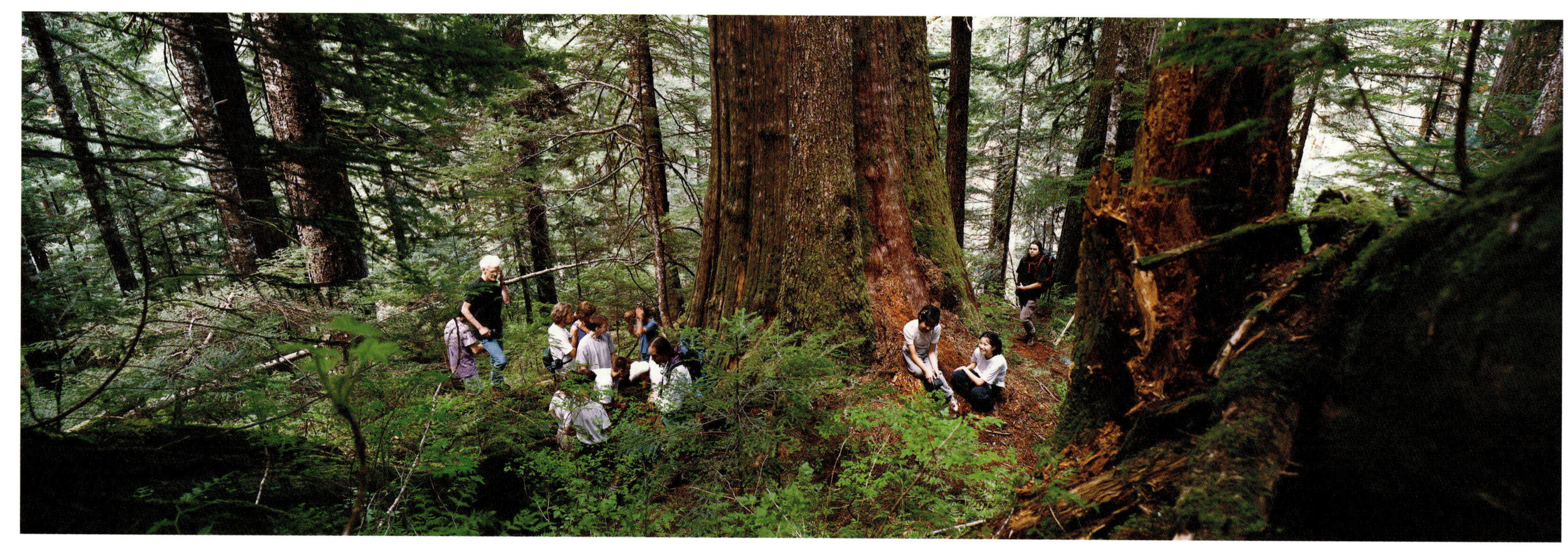

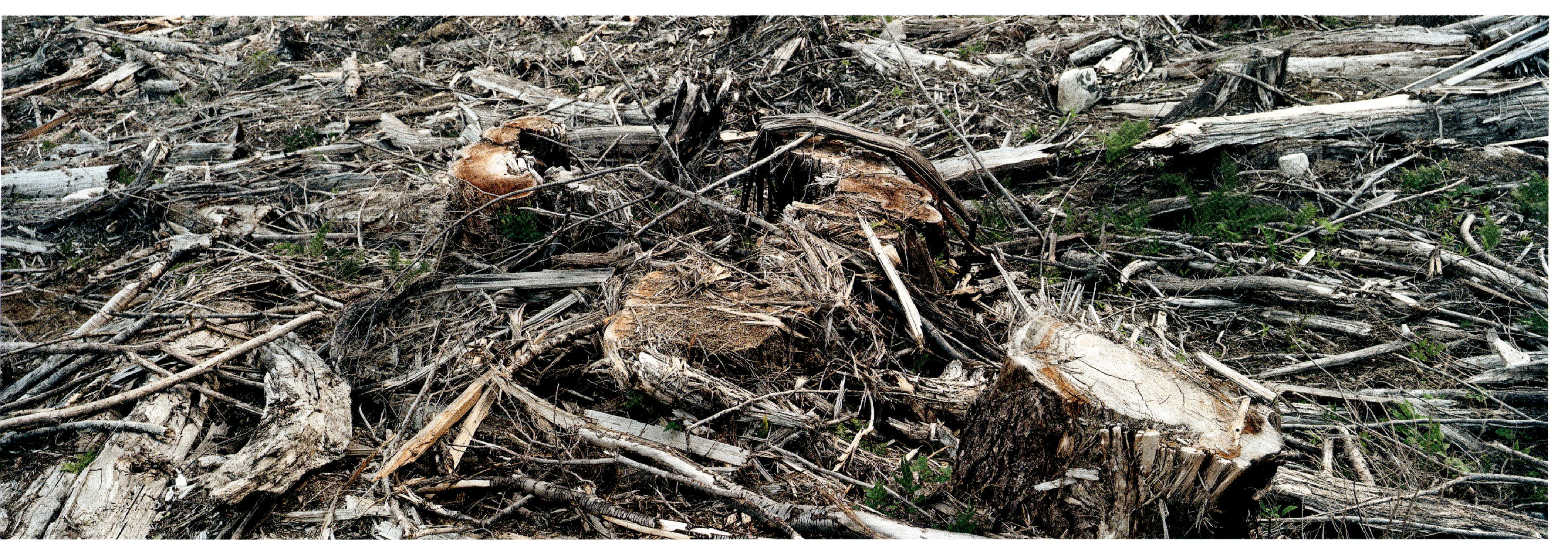

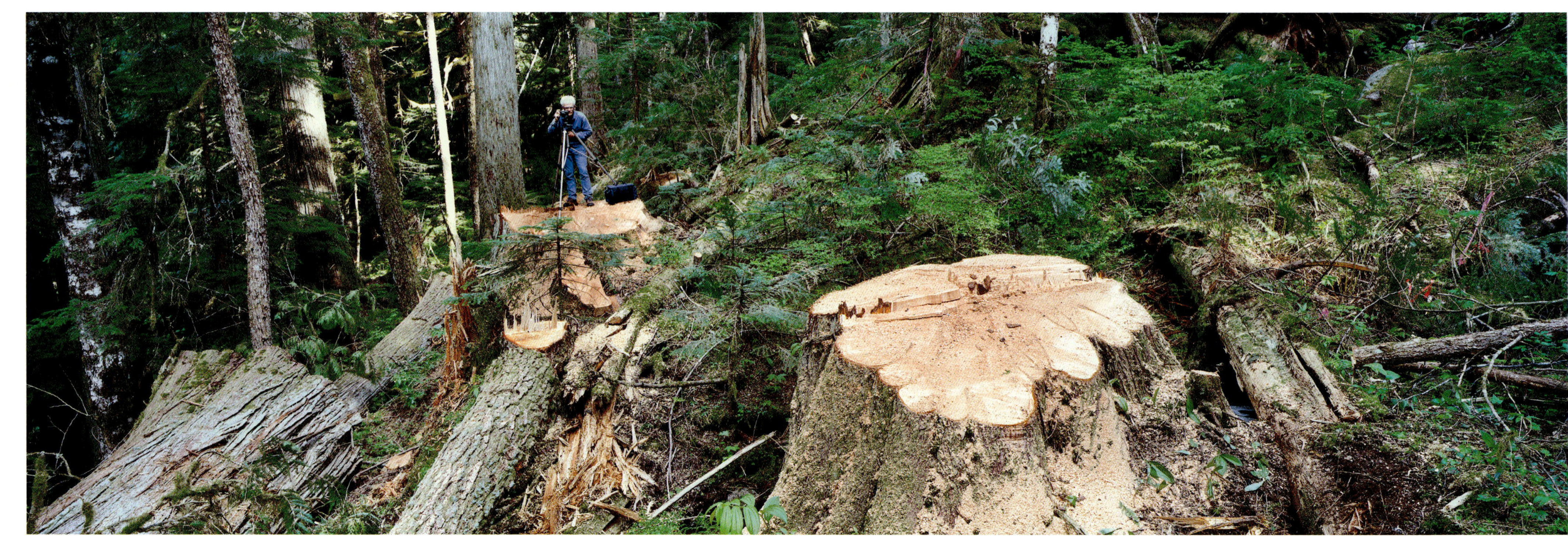

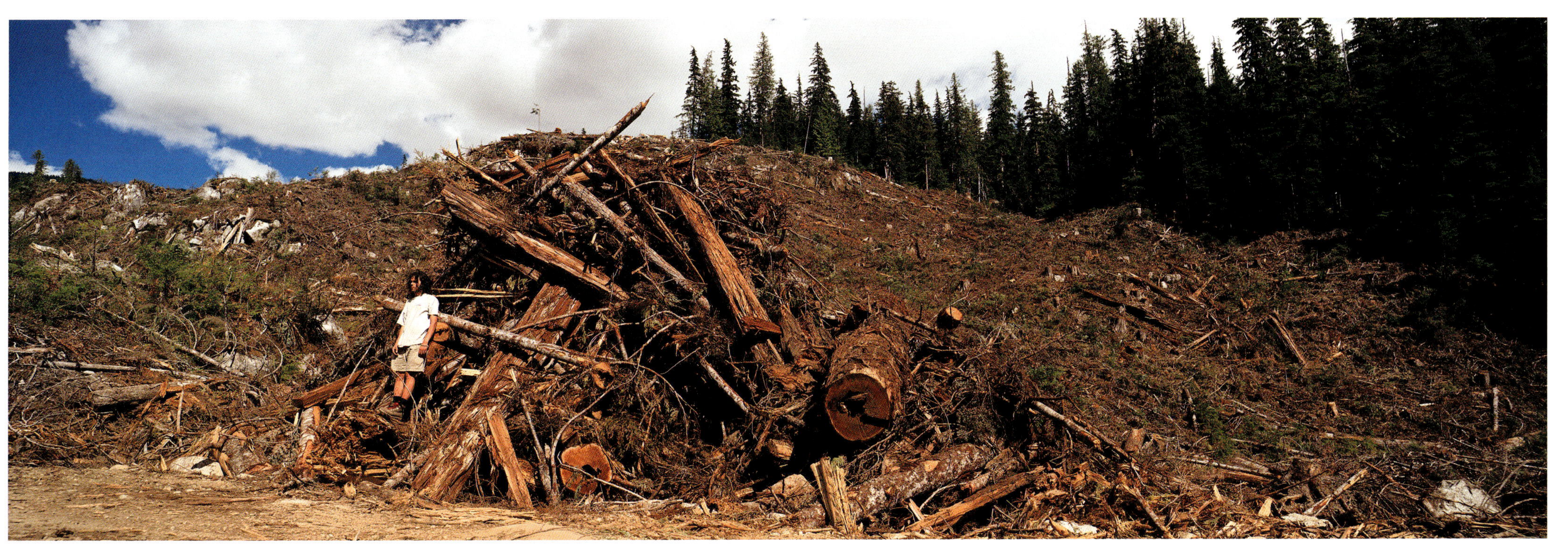

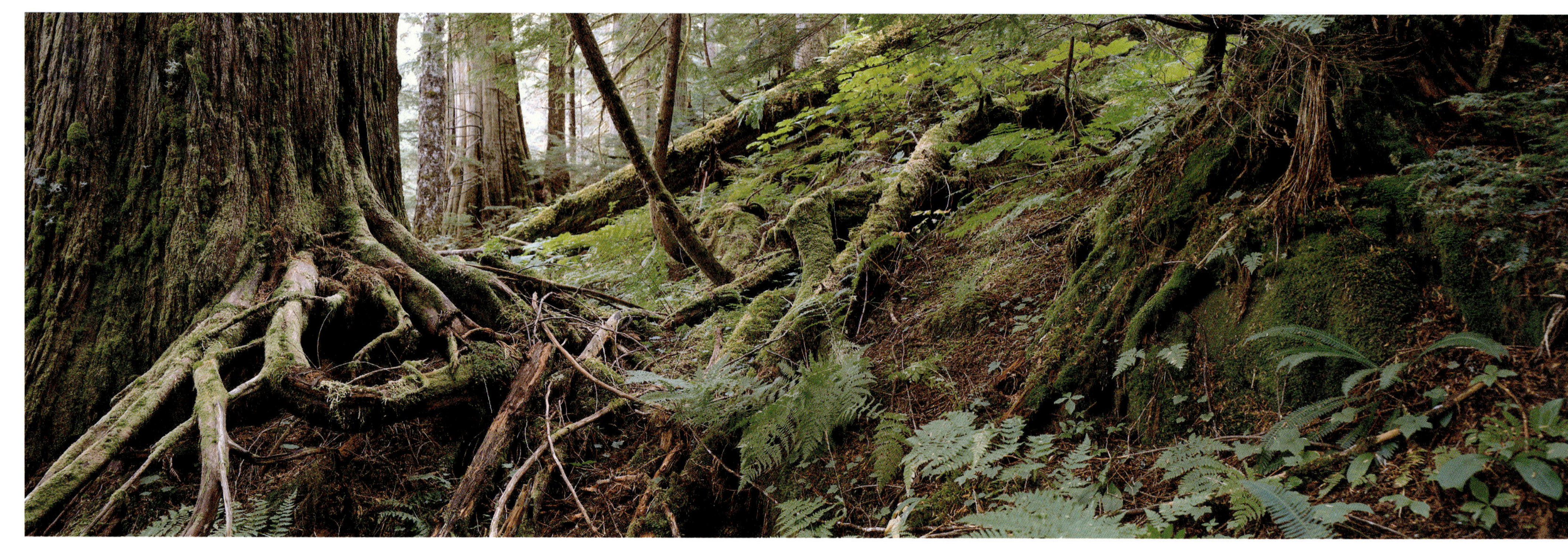

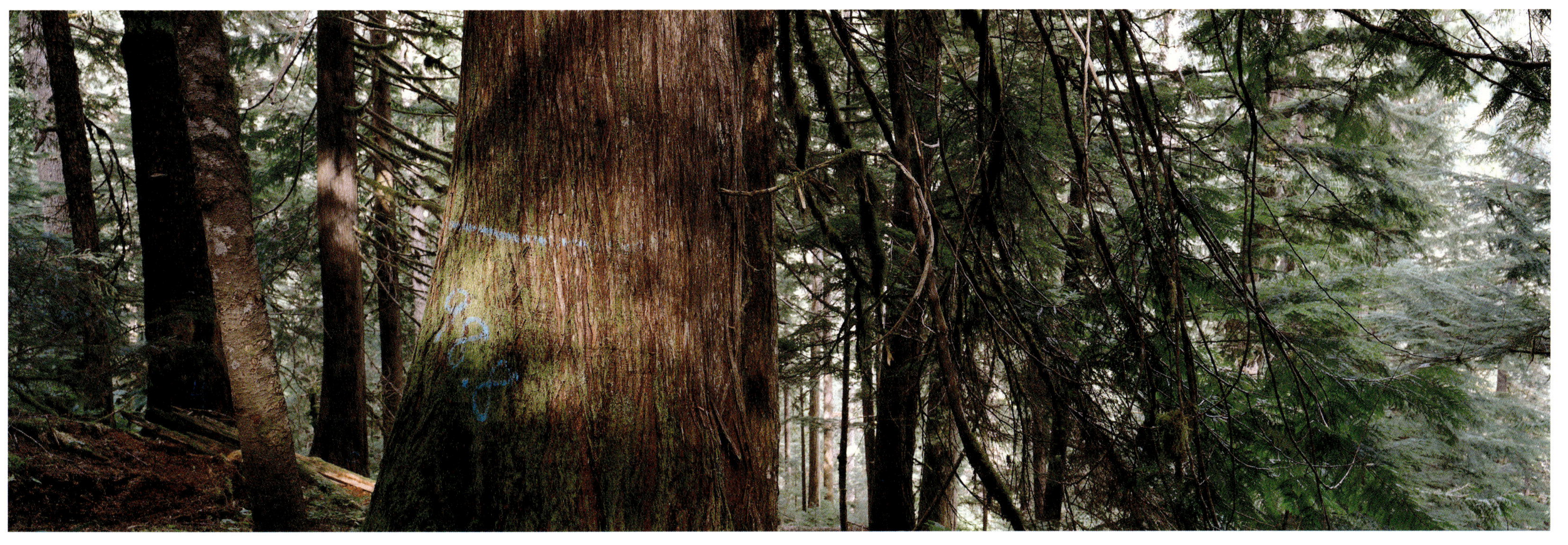

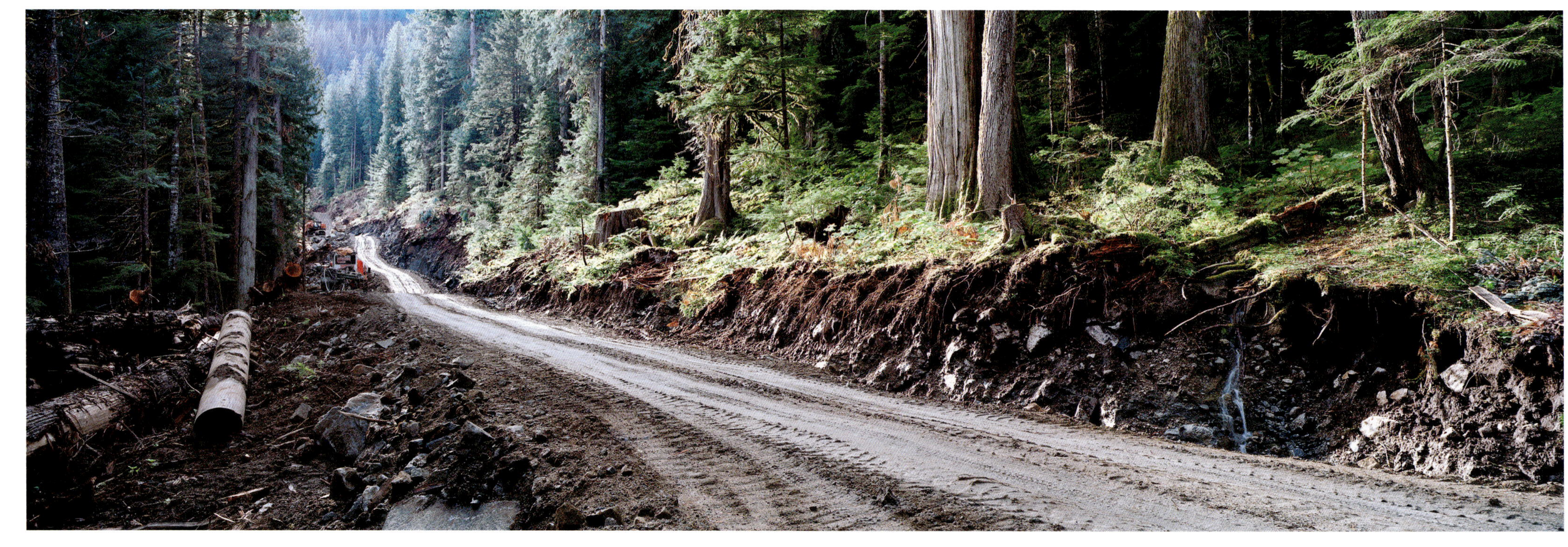

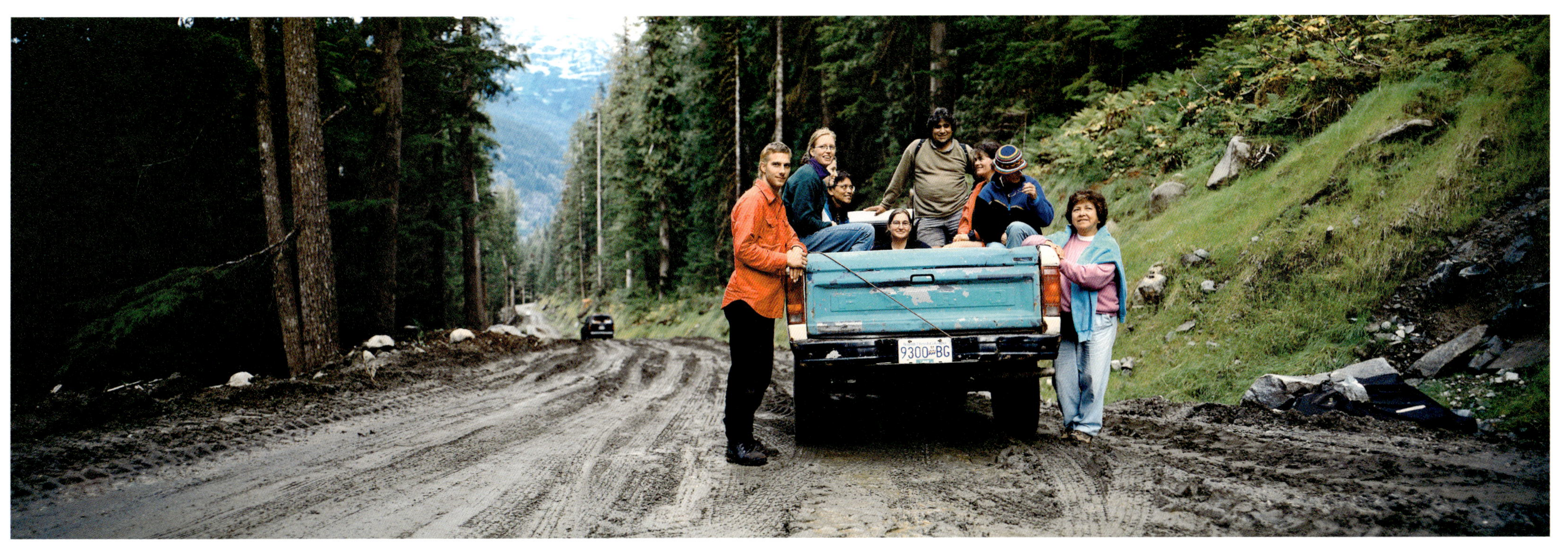
9300 BG

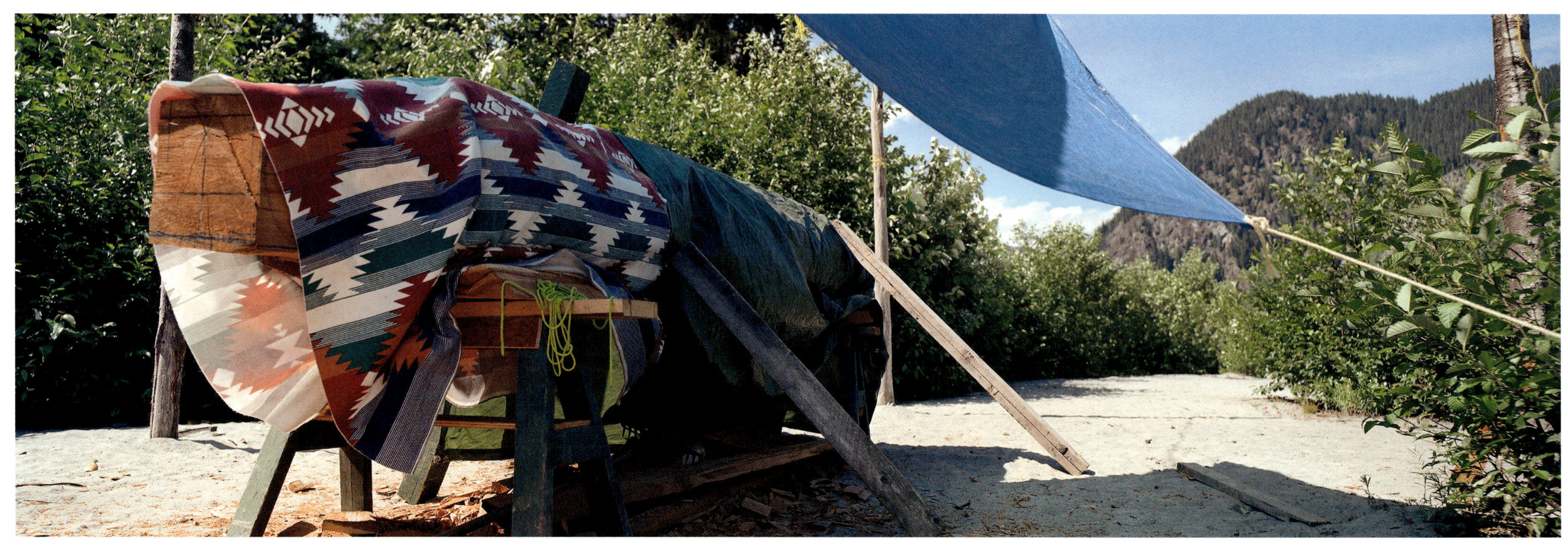

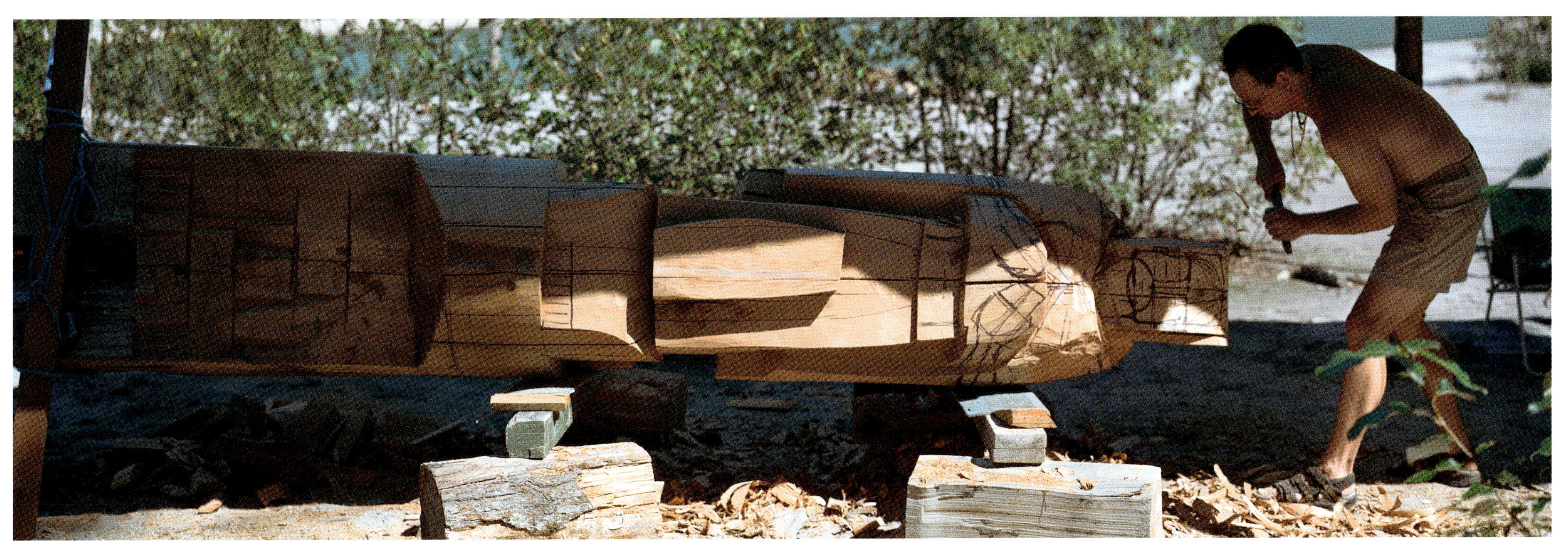

I was amused sometimes, because one of our most spiritual people, or one of our most significant leaders would show up, and they would be dressed in jeans, pull up in an old car, and no one would know who they were and then they would start to run a ceremony! And you would see peoples' mouths dropping; you could see that people were so amazed by some of the words and song and ceremony that ordinary people were carrying around with them.

AARON NELSON-MOODY / TAWX'SIN YEXWULLA / PÚLXTN

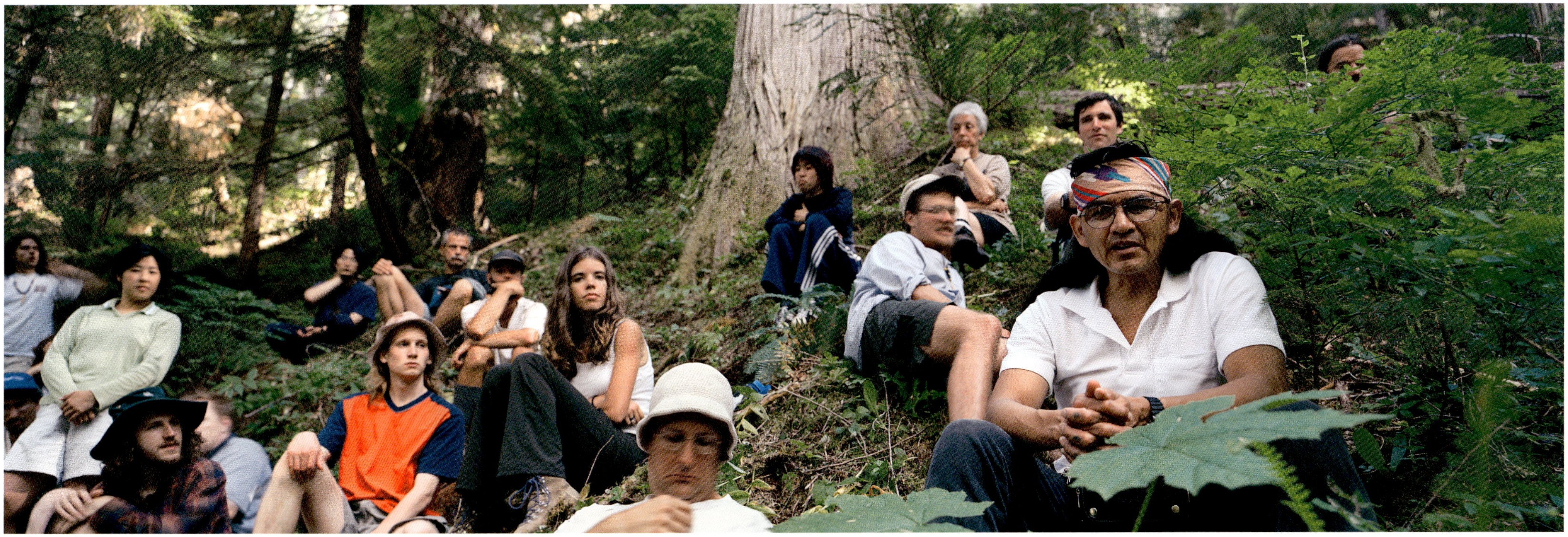

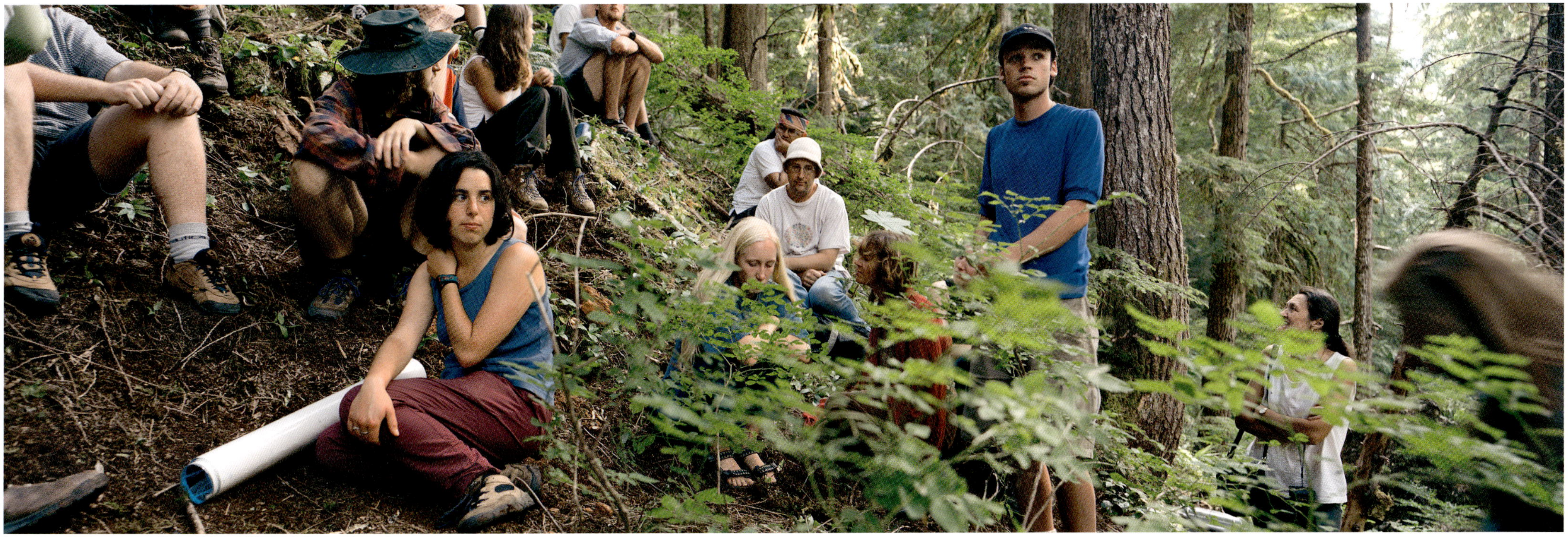

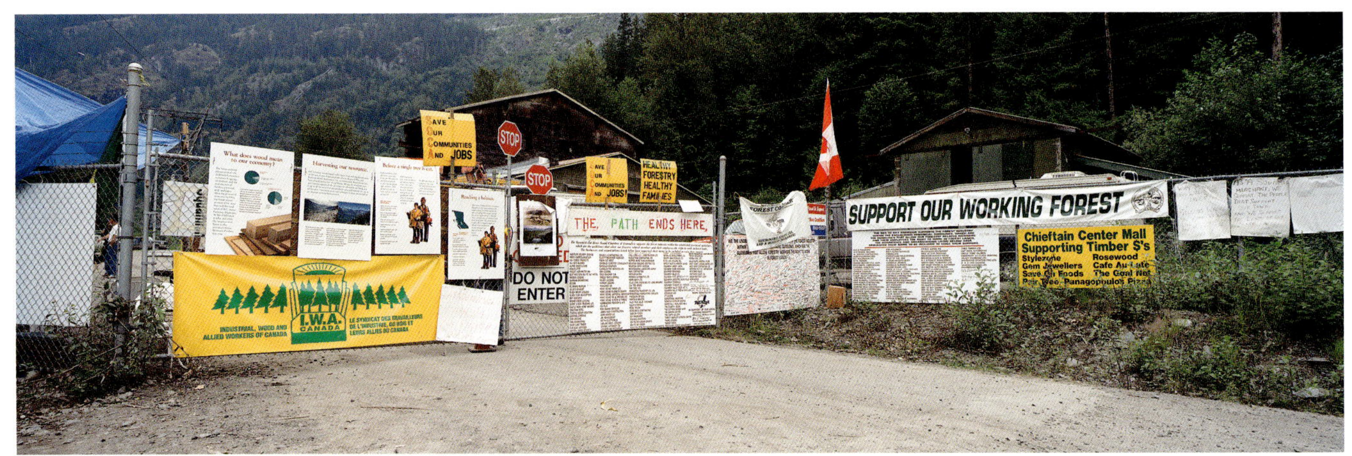
STOP
HEALTHY FORESTRY HEALTHY FAMILIES
THE PATH ENDS HERE.
DO NOT ENTER
I.W.A. CANADA
INDUSTRIAL, WOOD AND ALLIED WORKERS OF CANADA
SUPPORT OUR WORKING FOREST
Chieftain Center Mall
Supporting Timber S's

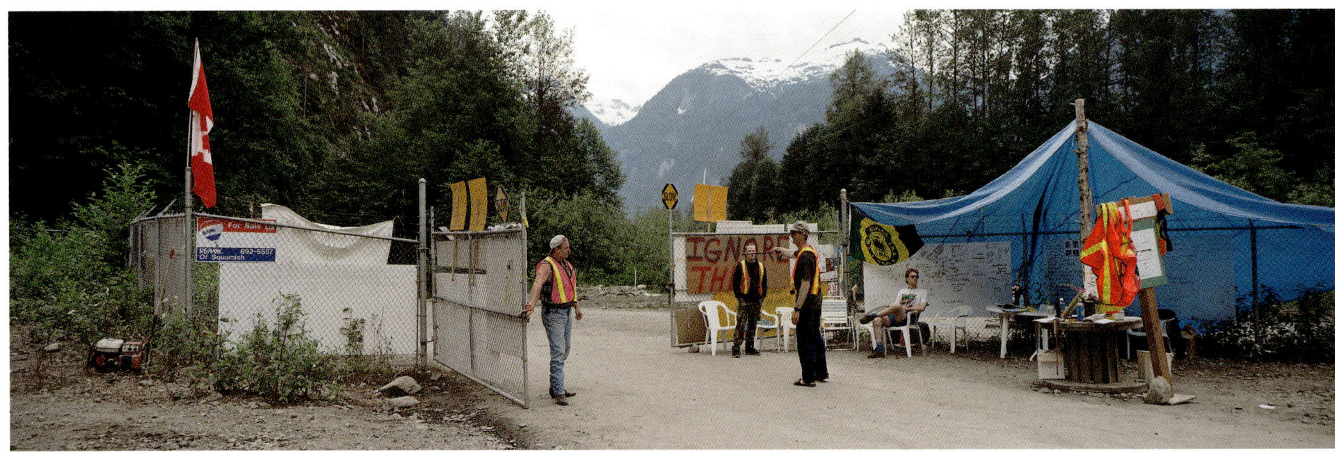
For Sale
SLOW

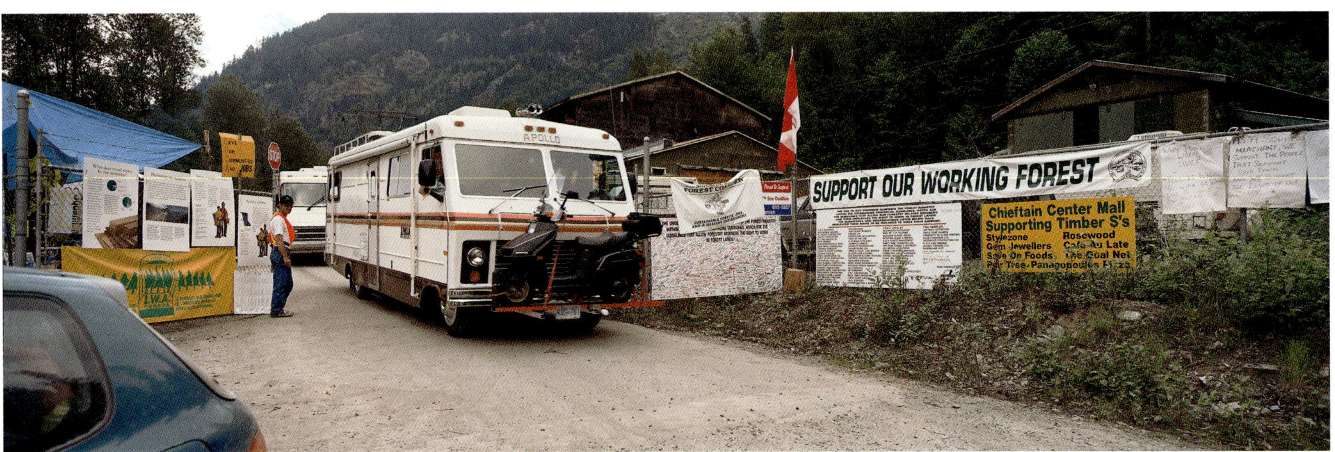
APOLLO
STOP
SUPPORT OUR WORKING FOREST
Chieftain Center Mall
Supporting Timber S's

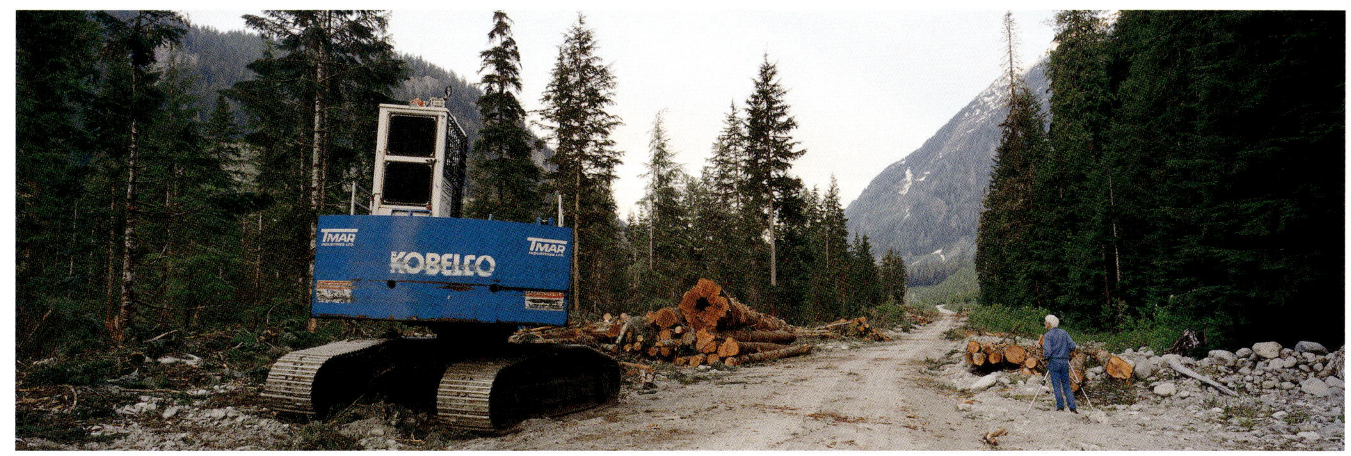
TMAR
KOBELCO
TMAR

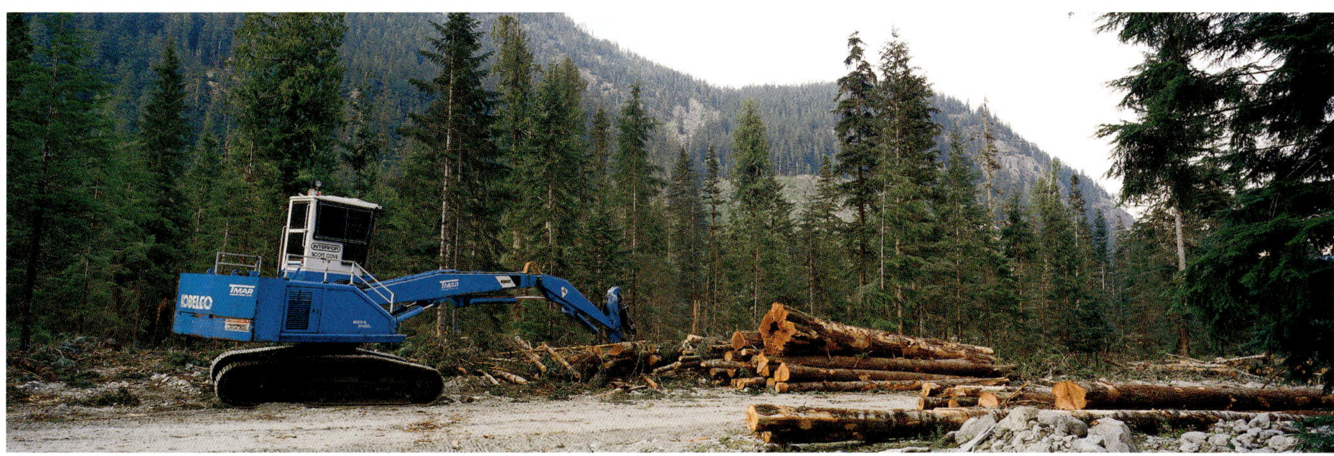
KOBELCO
TMAR

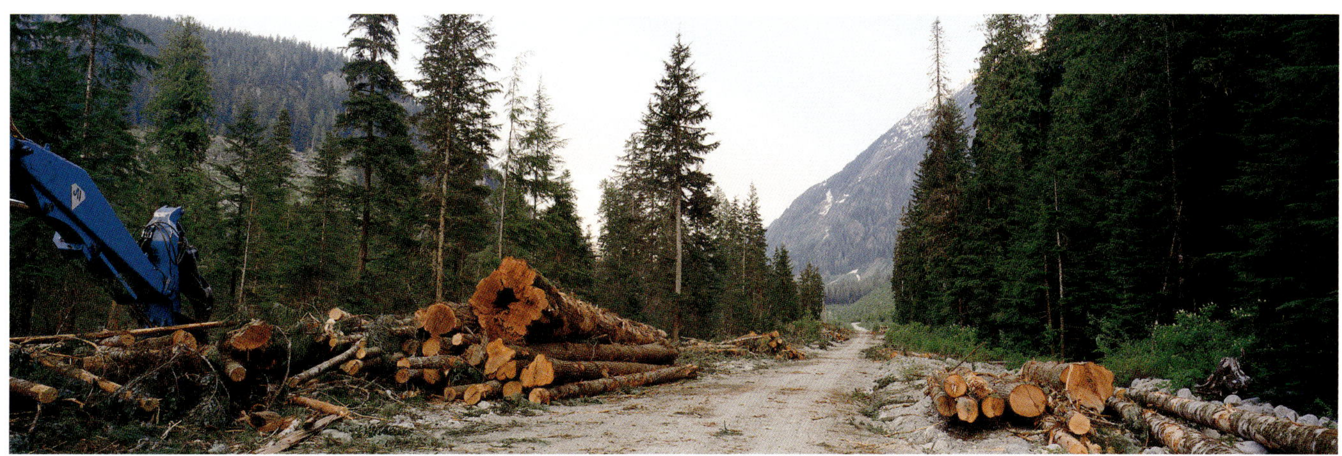

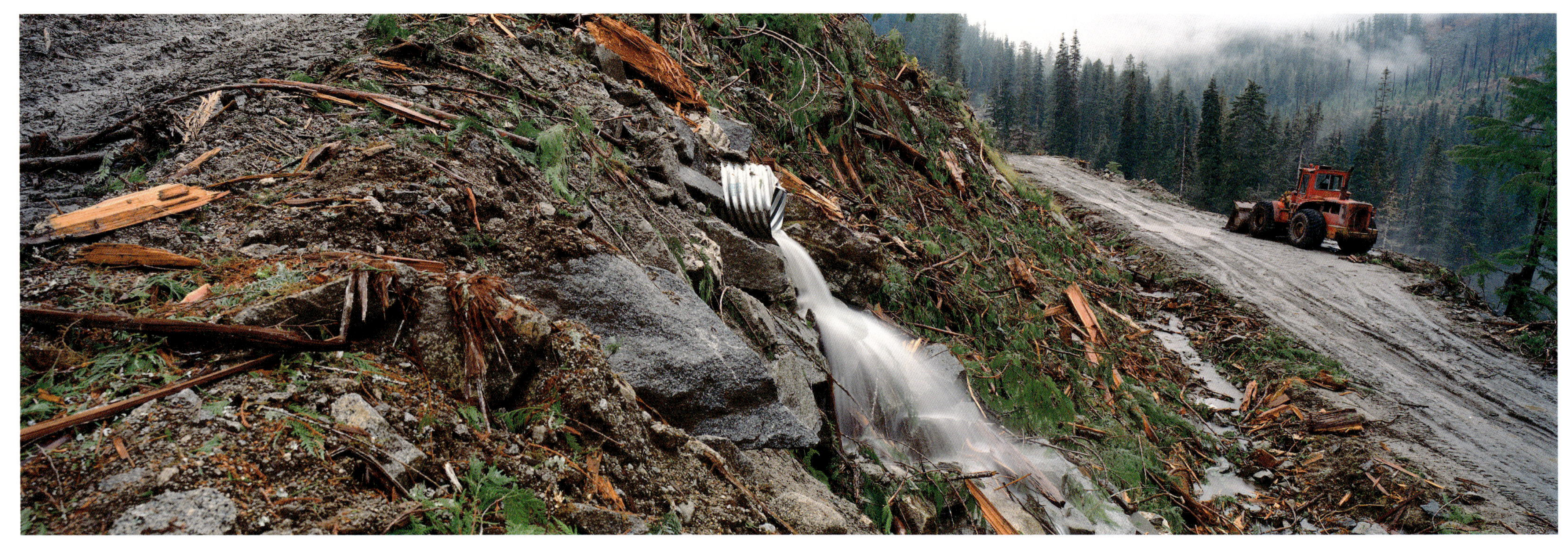

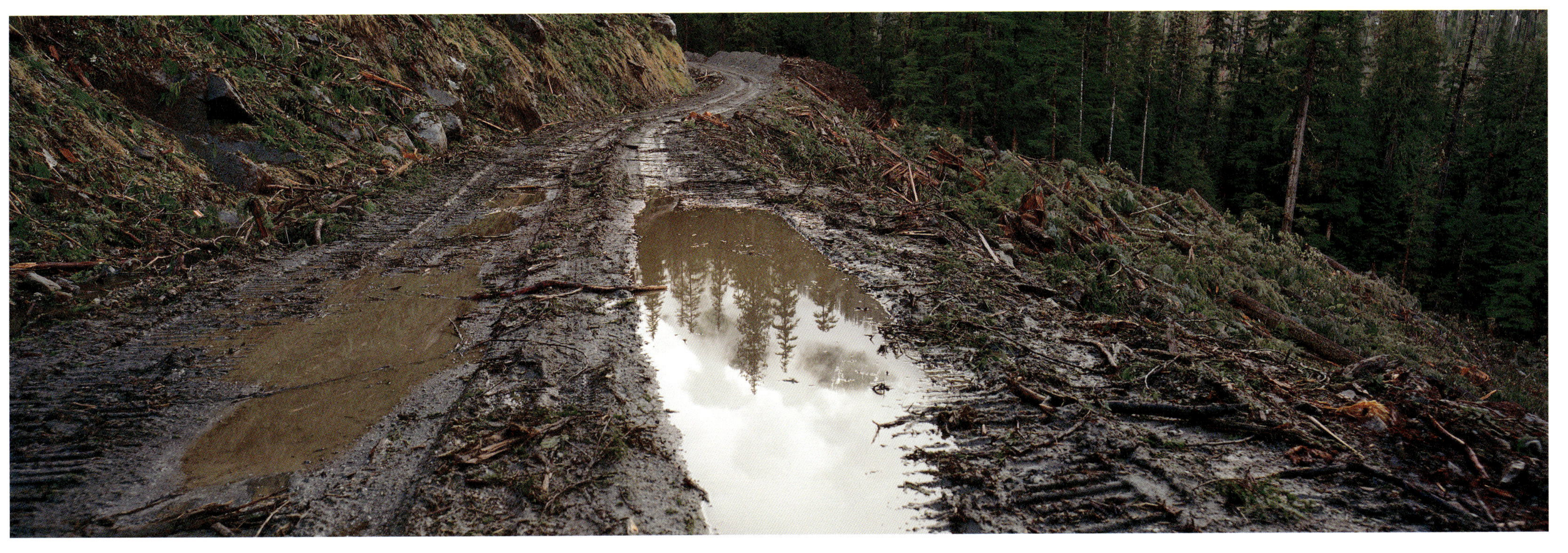

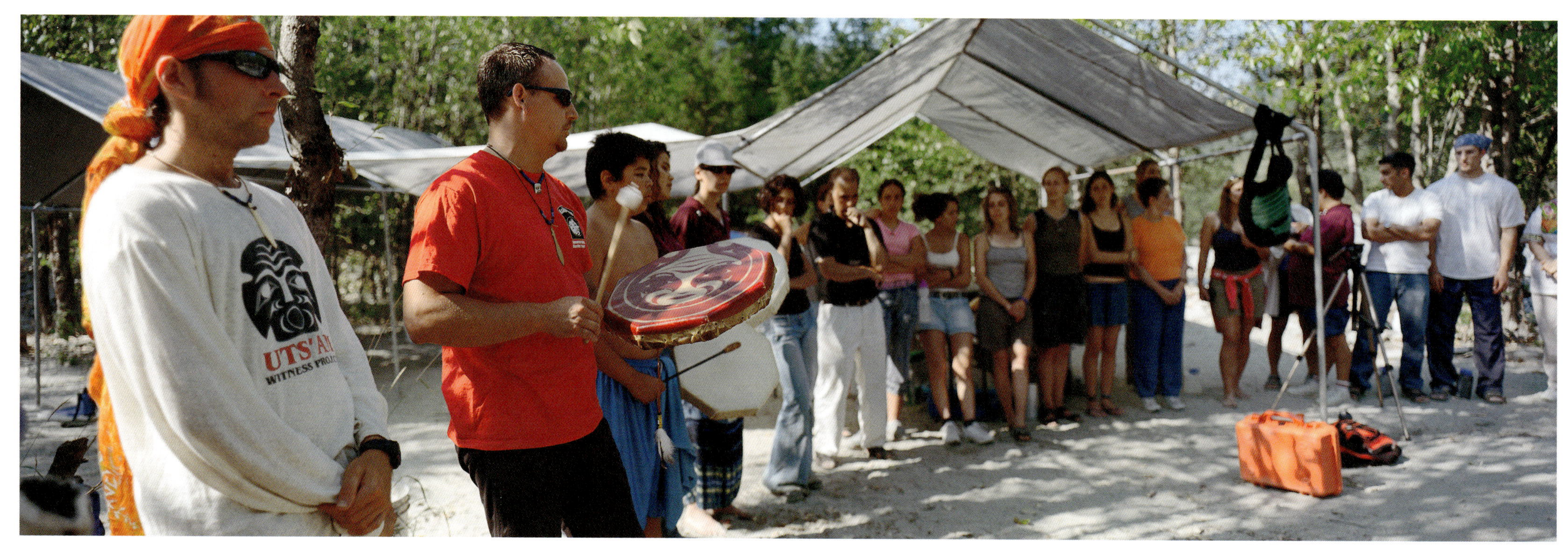

To be called to witness is the actual cornerstone of our Longhouse tradition of what we call *chìy̓áxw;* it is the foundation of our law, of how things get done. And in order to verify our law, we need people not just within our family, our community, but people from outside our community to come in and to verify the event that is taking place.

CHIEF BILL WILLIAMS/TELÁLSEMK̲IN SIY̓ÁM̓

We write not on paper or stone, but on the hearts of the people who come.

AARON NELSON-MOODY/
TAWX'SIN YEXWULLA/PÚLXTN

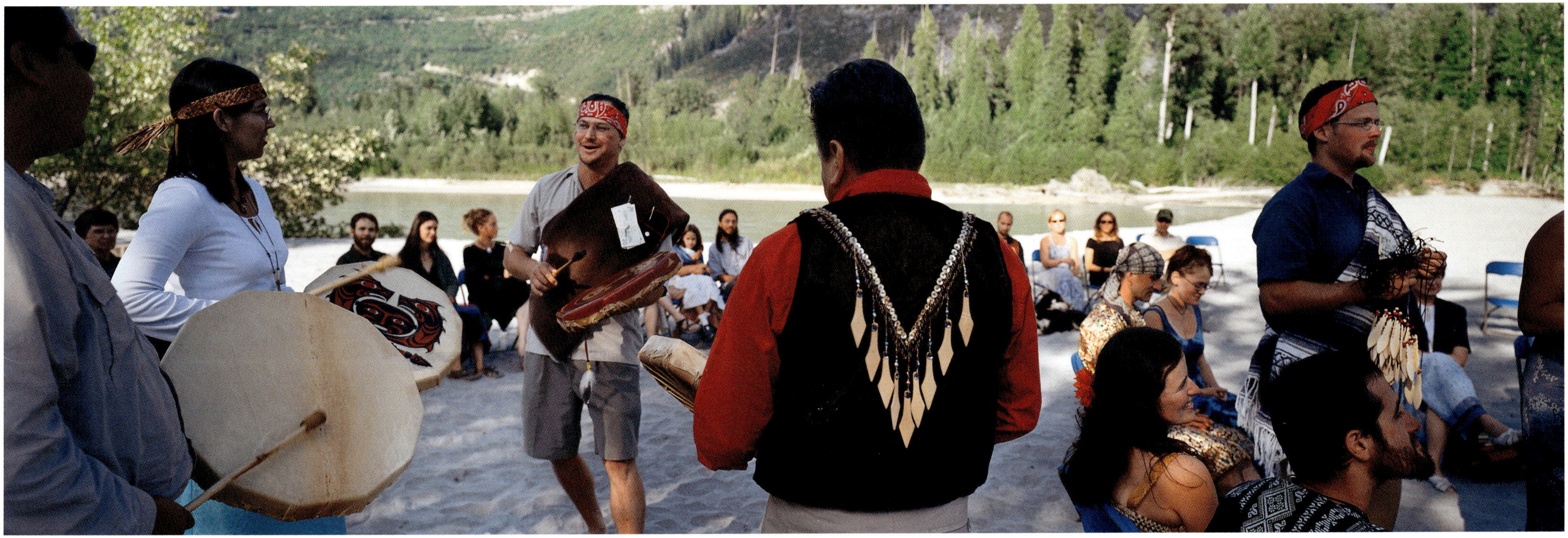

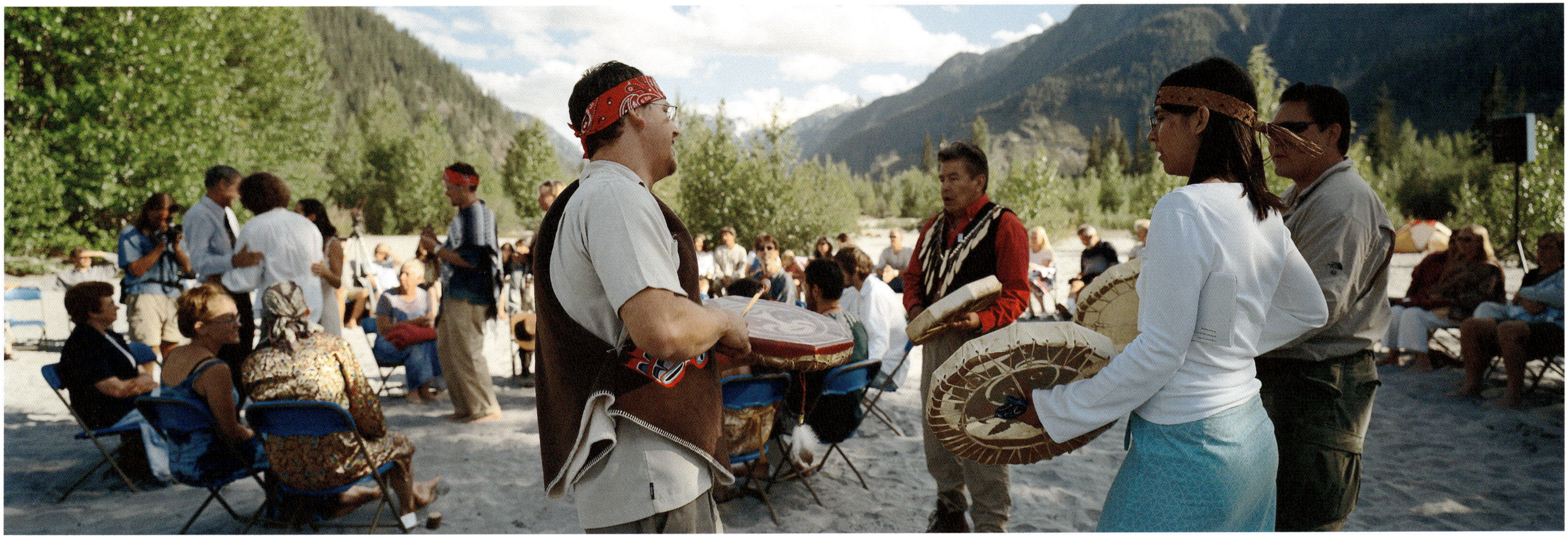

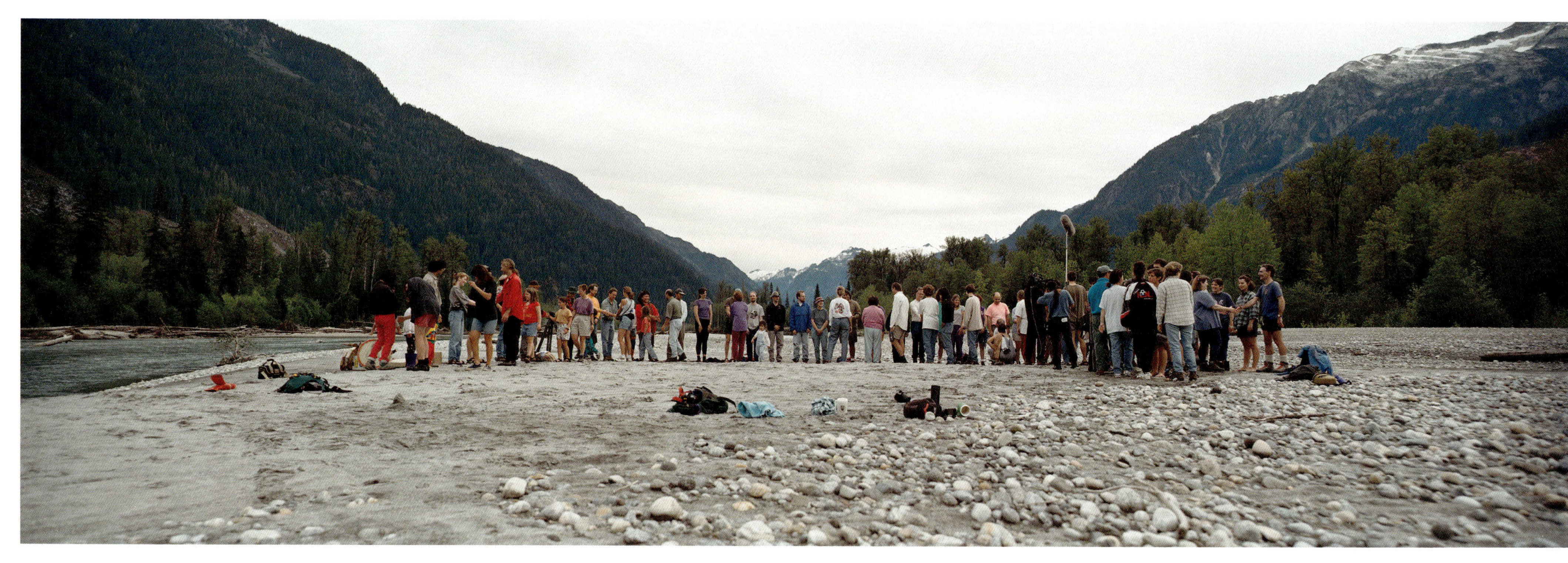

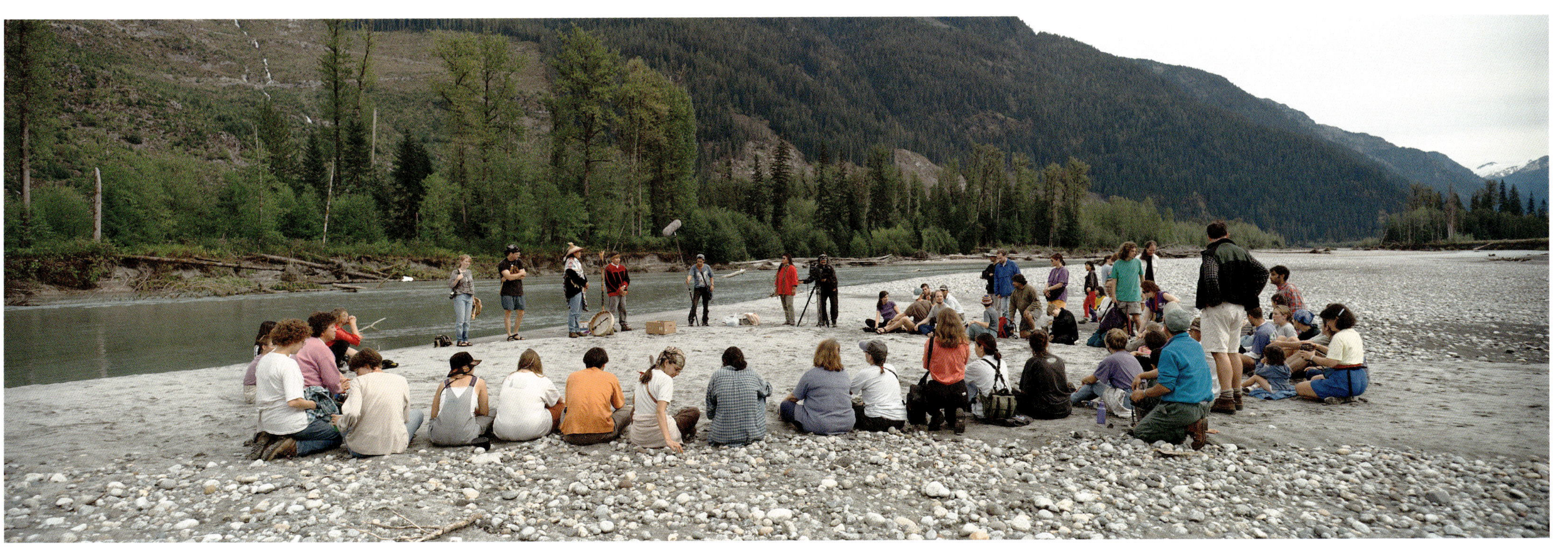

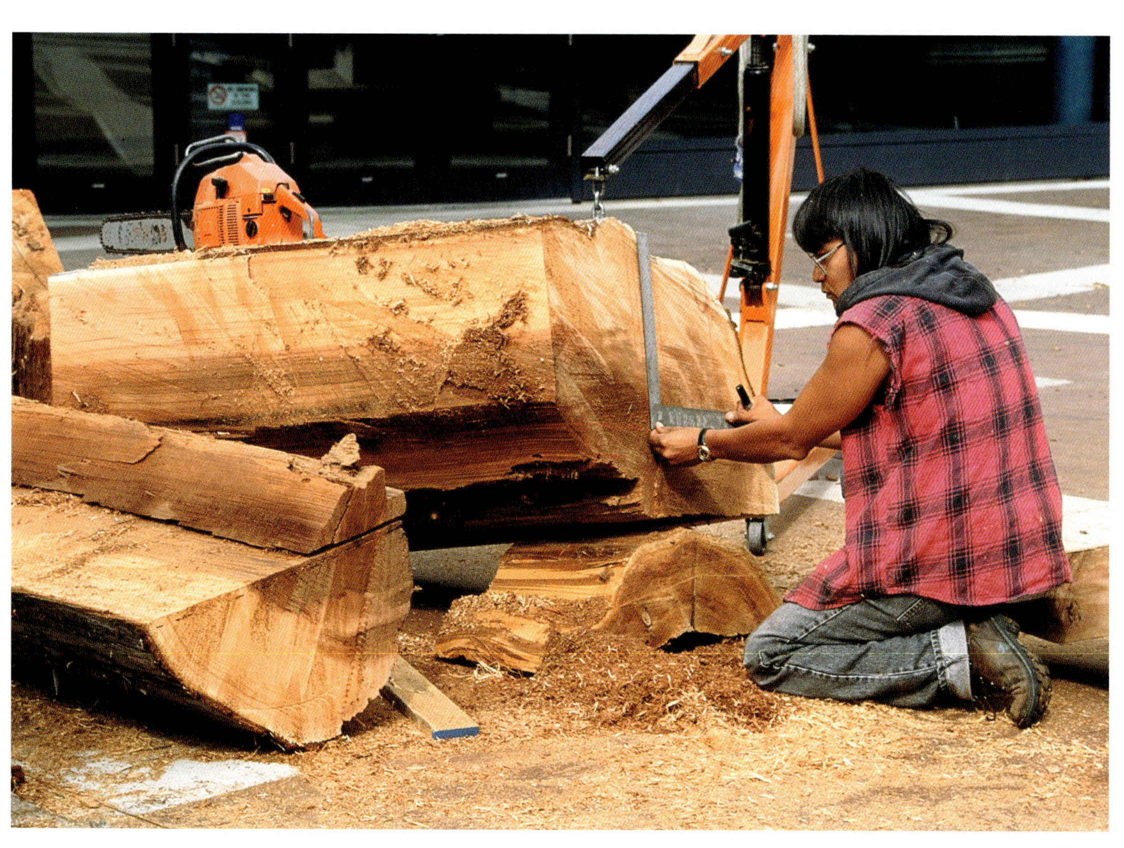

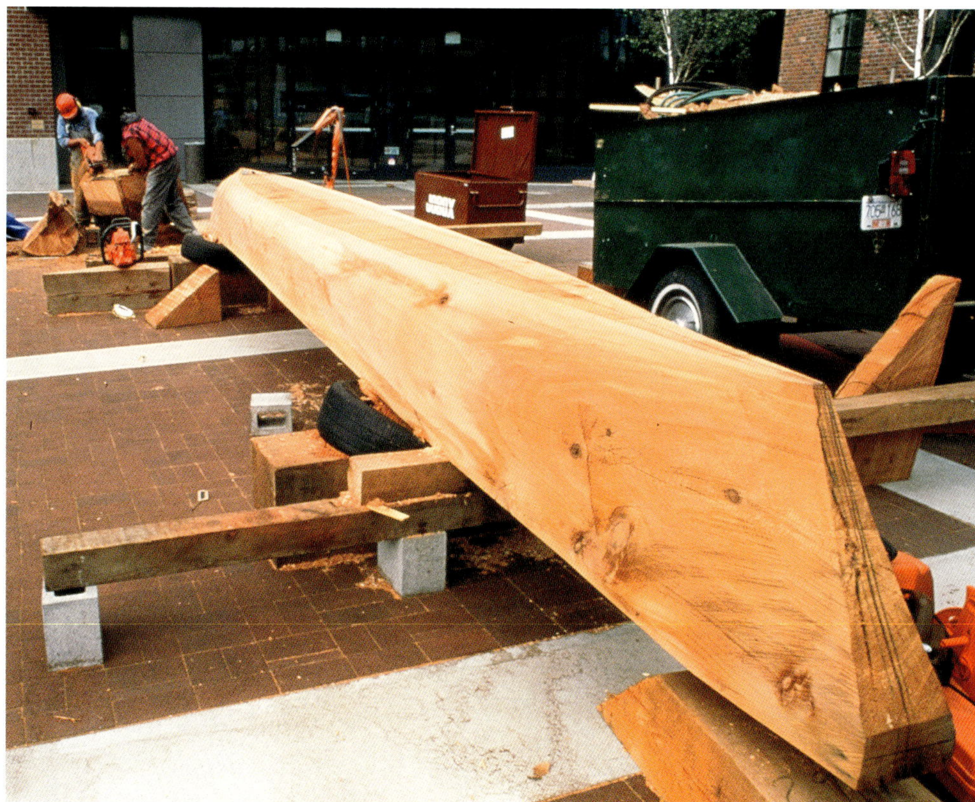

TWO

WORK: ART AND CEREMONY

While the camping weekends were giving people the chance to experience the land firsthand, many artists and participants were also bringing the stories of the land to people in the city through the *Witness Art Exhibition* at the Roundhouse Community Centre. This show, which followed the first summer of Witness, was B.C.'s largest-ever exhibition on themes of environmental practice, First Nations culture and political engagement: 175 people—professional, emerging and non-artists—all exhibited work.

From the outset, this community-based project was hugely attended. Outside the community centre, Squamish carver Rick Harry/*Xwelá̲ktn* carved an ocean-going canoe, ten metres long as is traditional, out of a single log. Inside, just a window away, Nancy's work started a conversation between traditional canoe carving and contemporary photography. Her banner, made of image and text, was the same length as Rick's canoe carving and contained text from the Squamish Nation *Assertion of Aboriginal Title* document that had been witnessed during the first camping weekend. What was unique about it as an art show was the way the "work" of becoming the eyes and ears of the land was taken up in so many different ways. It is unusual for one show to embrace populist folk art along with contemporary high art, but the exhibition that arose around Witness literally did it all. There is a very real sense that the participants all want to communicate: Experience. Urgency. Beauty. Devastation. History. Culture. Community. For many of those who exhibited, this was the one and only time they made art around the subject. But for others, it was the beginning of a way of working and thinking that had many creative offshoots.

The exhibition at the Roundhouse made more than a fleeting impression. The media, including MuchMusic, picked up the story. The Witness Project was nominated for an Ethics in Action Award in 1998 and was the national winner of the Best Cultural Event Award from Tourism Canada in 2002. Amir Alibhai, an arts programmer at the Roundhouse, made the project the subject of his master's thesis. Significantly, it transformed his own views of nature, art and culture.

There has never been a seamless flow among traditional art based in Indigenous culture, contemporary art from a theoretical Eurocentric modernist lineage or naïve

facing left: **Xwelá̲ktn, Rick Harry**, photo by Nancy Bleck, 1997

facing right: **Canoe carving**, photo by Nancy Bleck, 1997

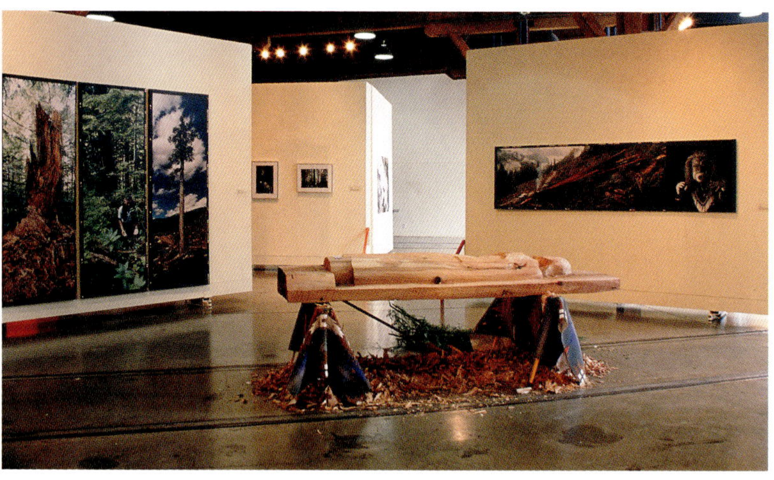

Witness Exhibition at the Roundhouse Community Centre, photo by Nancy Bleck, 2001

experience-based folk roots, and activist "art from the heart"—and it wasn't seamless with Witness either—but there was a pretty sweet confluence of all these artistic forces of nature/culture around the project. As Amir explained, "It was the first time that I saw this land that we were on as more than just a biological resource, or you know I didn't see it as wilderness anymore. I saw it as a cultural space and site—as powerful, as important, as relevant, as a cathedral—and feeling that it had somehow been tended for many, many centuries. There was a sense that there was a culture here, there was a people, there was a practice, there was a way of being here, that I was really excited about."

Nancy's photographs also reflected this cultural element in the landscapes and this idea of the larger "work" involved in artmaking. By this time she was exploring a new approach to the land and to trees, photographing them with a panoramic camera. This panoramic approach felt like the only way to treat the vastness of the landscape, an idea that came to her after a lecture by artist Ian Wallace at Emily Carr, who commented that you actually can't photograph an entire tree on the West Coast, you can only photograph its parts. Challenged by this notion, Nancy started experimenting. What resulted was a *mise-en-scène* still image of the ongoing performance project that was the whole of Witness. In other words, each panorama created a visual stage that was large enough to fit the whole group engaged in a Witness ceremony inside the frame, making them part of the land, not keeping their distance from it.

DIALOGUE

The conversations questioning the very settler notion of "wilderness" that Nancy had started first with James Nicholas, then continued with John, were being carried on by the Witness Project. In its own way, Witness was becoming a laboratory in a participatory primary research project. The body of work Nancy produced around Witness was an exploration in deconstructing stereotypes of people, of culture, of nature. As Nancy sometimes says, she, Chief Bill and John embodied the categories of "otherness" under Western, corporate-driven society: women, Natives and those who speak for the intrinsic value of the earth and who bear the brunt of sexism, racism and disregard for the environment. Together, the trio demonstrated how different communities can come together to work on a common project without having to merge their identities or their agendas into one.

Amir points out that in fact Witness didn't even take place at only one site, let alone involve only one community: "We learned from the perspective of Chief Williams and from the cultural knowledge about the land. We started to learn that there were also the interests of the people who make their living off the land, in different ways. There were the loggers that were involved, and they became part of the conversation." Nancy continued, "The work was always about sitting together and getting down to some very important conversations, cross-cultural and intergenerational—children allowed to have their opinions and elders and forest workers, everybody. A place to speak with meaningful dialogue is a very hard thing to actually try to set up, but if you think about it, that's what culture is. It's what art practice is."

Nancy felt that with Witness it was often hard to tell where the art starts. And where it stops. As she said, "When creating an art object, it's often not the object itself that has the resonance but what happens around it. It's the dialogue that gets created around it: when there is something precious, you almost can't speak *about* it but you can speak *around* it." According to Amir, "There was a lot of curiosity and exchange of ideas and techniques and skills, people interested in making drums, people interested in learning how to take photographs, people wanting to make drawings and paintings as well, so there seemed to be all these nodes where there seemed to be interest in this idea of cross-cultural sharing. And also getting to the land. That was the thing that bound all these groups together."

The art world is a breeding ground for theory, so it's also no surprise that the project started spawning theoretical essays and philosophical ponderings from many of its participants. Often "artspeak," and even a lot of artworks, have a reputation for belonging only for insiders who "get it." The writing around this project strived to explore, and to understand, what was going on. What was this magic ingredient that seemed to be working here? What place does experience have in art and wilderness? In social justice? Attempts to situate the work of Witness in contemporary theory do not fit it entirely. As James Nicholas often said: "There was no wilderness until the white man came." But there was no art theory either. An emerging way of writing around theory, and a hybrid use of multiple voices, has been one theoretical legacy.

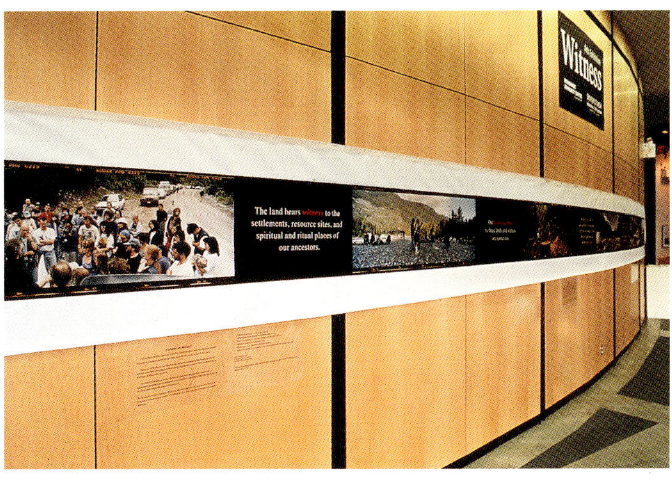

Witness banner, detail,
photo by Nancy Bleck, 1997

From Amir's perspective, "All this energy seemed to have gathered on the weekends, and people were brought together, and it was the land that brought them there. And what I found very interesting was that this perspective included folks who were really familiar with going out and being in the land, and those folks who had never been out there ever before. It was almost a collision at times that led to innovative solutions to some of the issues that were being discussed." Wrapped up in ceremony and stories, these dialogues took place in the face of simple survival on the land, with real conversations and the clear and present danger of losing it all.

GOING DEEPER

By the second year of the Witness Project, the program was drawing more people and greater support from a wide

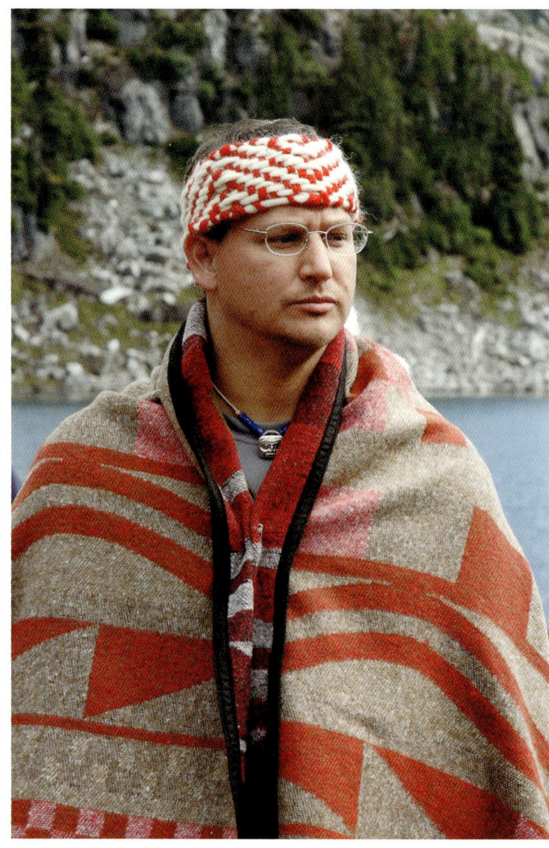

Honouring Splash,
photo by Nancy Bleck, 2005

variety of people. Aaron Nelson-Moody/*Tawx'sin Yexwulla/Púlxtn*, a Squamish Nation artist and writer most often known as Splash, remembers at first wondering "what his chief was up to in this part of their northern territory... Some of us had seen a brochure that had an image of our 56-foot sea-going canoe on it, and rumours around the rez were that Bill had formed a company with an eco-tour operation and was taking non-Native people on canoe rides and hikes for big money. It turned out he was doing something completely different and a little more interesting than that." He adds, "I didn't know what I was getting into!"

At the time, Aaron was still young in his artistic journey and in his practice as a Speaker. One of his early mentors was Rick Harry/*Xwelá<u>k</u>tn*, who was one of the first members of the Squamish Nation to use his traditional name publicly and to take up traditional practices to expose the non-indigenous public to these traditions. It was fitting, then, that Witness began with Rick's canoe carving at the Roundhouse and it also seems predestined that Aaron would take up this work during the decade of Witness. He credits Rick for helping him to understand the significance of Chief Bill's actions opening up the witness ceremony and setting him on this path, but working with Chief Bill and Witness really gave him the chance to become comfortable engaging with traditional practices on the land.

Aaron had observed on his first Witness weekend that when people met Chief Bill, they thought he was the leader, but he actually wasn't. And he points out that in Squamish culture, there is no word for leader, or boss. "If you were to be our Speaker," Aaron explained, "you would listen to everyone. If you wanted to speak for us, you would have had to talk to us, and know what we were thinking, and you'd have to sum it up. So we'd trust those people to sum up what we felt, so they weren't actually our bosses, they weren't actually our leaders, but by the time that they spoke, we realized that if we trusted them enough to say what everyone thought, not just what I thought, so their word was kind of like law." He continues, "When Bill wanted to take action, he had to listen to people, not just our own people, he had to listen to everyone. So it wasn't so much that he had a vision when he started, he had faith in the process—get people to sit down together to talk and by the end, and in his mind, ten to twelve years, by the end of the conversation he'll know what people think, so he just knows that if we sit long enough and talk long enough and laugh long enough and tell stories long enough we'll get to the bottom of things."

What is clear is that Chief Bill realized there were now people eager to work with him to assert the title to Squamish land. And he found many willing volunteers among the Witness community. It was Chief Bill who encouraged Aaron to do his traditional carving on the land, not formally as part of the Witness weekends but so there would be a reason for people of the Squamish Nation, and youth in particular, to engage in ceremony on their territory and to feel like it was their birthright. Aaron points out that in the Squamish language there is no word for "art" or "artist," so his work carving, teaching drumming and simply participating in the witness ceremony is all part of his journey as a Squamish man. Through the process of Witness he became more versed in and prepared to take on a leadership role, and he became an ambassador for his people's culture in the settler community.

Aaron knew there was increasing controversy about how the land should be used in that area and recognized how important this project could be. He says, "Chief Bill joined with other people to involve Squamish Nation in that debate, because until then our voice wasn't really being heard." However, Aaron also recognized how valuable the process was to open up to the public: "From our communities' perspective, having a forum where we had a chance to train our youth how to speak to the outside world about some of the most important issues that we have, to run our ceremonies in our way, on our territory, I thought that it was an amazing opportunity."

Like Aaron, Drew Leathem is the first to admit that Witness turned out to be way more than he ever expected. He and pal Shel Neufeld, who were both in their early twenties at the time, were looking for some outdoor recreation with an environmental focus, where perhaps they might meet "young women with similar interests." Soon Drew and Shel were hiking regularly with John during camping weekends and on several longer, more difficult treks, and they took to wearing a white dress shirt, the signature piece of clothing John used while trekking. Drew was learning more and more about the Squamish culture through these weekends, getting to know more members of the community. Pretty soon he was deeply hooked in and asking Chief Bill for more ways he could help the Nation.

Drew was studying cultural geography at university, and Chief Bill started by assigning him a simple mapping exercise designed to see how he would do and to test how useful he might be to the Nation. He was asked to follow the flags that marked the end of the cutblock and to make sure that Interfor did not cut beyond that. When Drew proved successful at this, Chief Bill asked him to explore ways to get the Nation's youth out onto the land, which he set out to do.

Meanwhile, Drew's friend Shel introduced his roommate, Melanie Rivers/*7imlamelwet*, to Witness. At first it was her keen interest in the environment that attracted her, and she went up to Sims Creek four or five

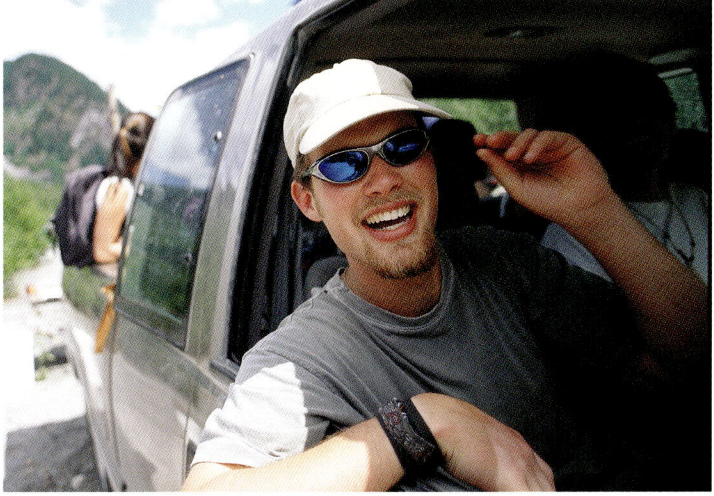

Drew Leathem,
photo by Nancy Bleck, 1999

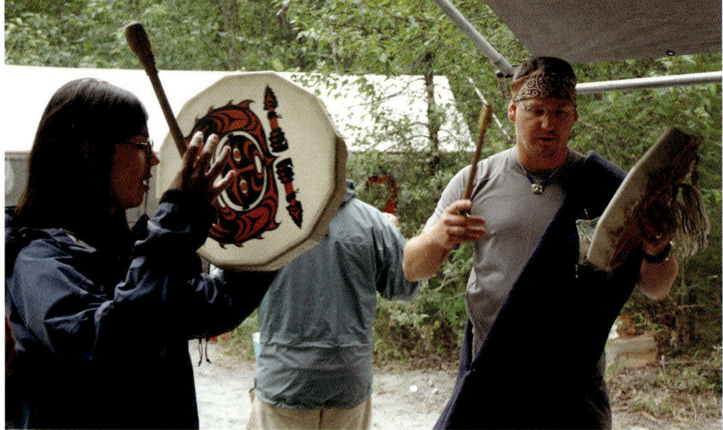

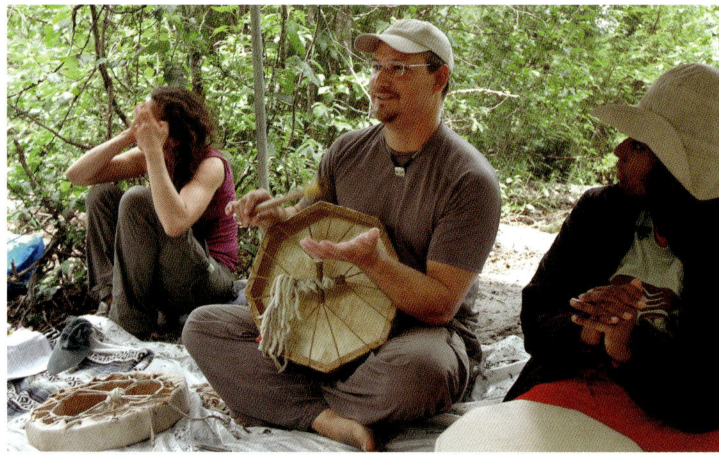

top: **Melanie and Splash**, photo by Nancy Bleck, 2006

bottom: **Drum-making workshop**, photo by Nancy Bleck, 2006

times that season. She was working as an HIV educator for Chee Mamuk, the Aboriginal program of the BC Centre for Disease Control's STI/HIV Prevention and Control Division, and as she learned more about her own Squamish traditions, she began to develop a deeper understanding of her own Squamish identity through taking part in the Witness ceremonies. And Witness became a much bigger journey than she could have imagined: it was there that she would meet her future husband, Aaron, and that she would become a Speaker. She explains, "It was the last weekend of one of the summers, which was the biggest weekend in terms of the number of people that came up. The Speaker who was supposed to come wasn't able to, so Chief Bill Williams turned to me and asked me if I could be the Speaker. For me, it was very challenging because women don't traditionally take on the role of being a Speaker; I had never done it before and I consider myself very young in terms of learning our traditional teachings. I decided to be brave, step forward and speak in my Longhouse voice across the circle of a hundred and twenty people and share the words that Chief Bill Williams wanted me to share." In this, and in so many ways, the Witness Project was reflecting contemporary times, using tradition in brand new ways to do things differently.

So although Utsám̓ Witness had founders, it didn't have one leader. No one was being asked to become a follower. Those who visited Sims Creek, witnessed a ceremony and engaged in dialogue around issues of the land were left with the experience and the responsibility. Witness led itself through a process akin to a true participatory democracy.

WAR IN THE WOODS

When the Witness Project launched in 1997, *Delgamuukw*, the court decision that raised the constitutional question of Aboriginal title to land, had just happened, and no one knew yet what it might mean for land disputes.

Throughout the '90s, environmental activism was increasingly defined by a confrontation in B.C.'s forests. There were death threats. Tensions were high. In 1993, twelve thousand protestors had blockaded the logging at Clayoquot Sound on Vancouver Island, gaining international attention. That area was later declared a biosphere reserve by UNESCO, but at the time 856 activists were arrested, the largest mass arrest in Canadian history (until June 2010, when nine hundred protestors were arrested at the G20 Summit in Toronto). Increasingly, First Nations people all over Canada were turning to blockades to protect areas of their territory from logging, mining and, in the case of the violent conflict in 1990 between federal and provincial governments and the Mohawk people of Kanesatake in

Oka, Quebec, to prevent a golf course from being built on sacred burial grounds.

Witness was trying to do things differently, non-violently. Organizers and participants were even entering into dialogue with loggers, with Interfor, but as the logging escalated, the group's sense of urgency grew. Nancy recalls, "Things were scary and things were ugly. Violence was being done to the land, and it really was becoming war in the woods." In those first years, Nancy experienced harassment from loggers, and on September 15, 1999, a camp of environmental activists was brutally assaulted by 100 loggers employed by Interfor. Joe Foy agrees that it really was a battleground at that time, but he credits the combative model with creating the desire for change. He also acknowledges that this approach likely would not have created a solution in the case of Sims Creek. He notes that Witness was operating in a different mode, and that it managed over time to stay face-to-face and personal was one of its unique, transformative qualities.

Melanie Rivers reiterates that Witness was using an innovative way and that it was at its heart non-violent. This kind of deep collaboration was very unusual. The success of the Witness Project was how it tapped into the longing of so many different people—including people from other artistic communities, like Montreal-based artists Scott McLeod and Dana Velan—who were moved by supporting the project and forged connections in other places such as universities, art galleries and colleges in eastern Canada and with the people of Kanesatake. Witness was rooted in the land, but it was never about only one thing. Without prescribing a precise path, the process provided a way to connect at the level of love and desire: for land, for community, for ceremony, for art and for justice. Cease Wyss put it very eloquently: "I think that considering there was so much negativity surrounding the protection of the land, there was nothing else to do but engage in ceremony. This was how the land was going to be taken back."

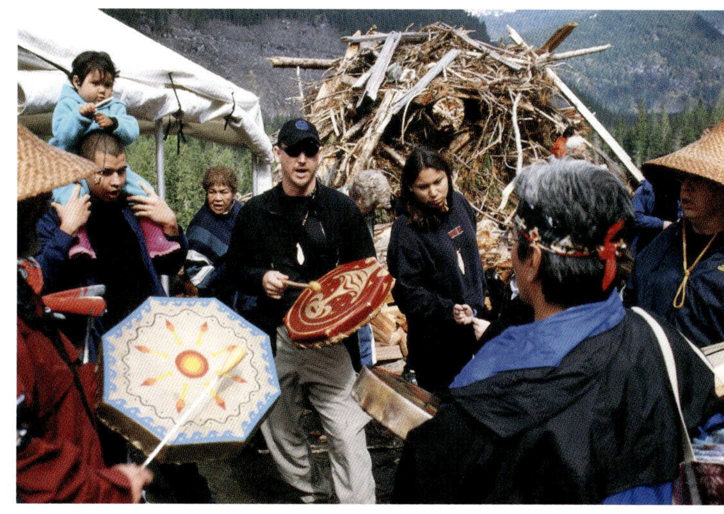

Verification Ceremony,
photo by Nancy Bleck, 2001

As more and more cut-blocks were slated for the chainsaw, the witnesses were witnessing a lot of logging. The urgency to do something more was gathering momentum.

CEDAR

Ten years is not that long. But three thousand years is quite a while. That's how long it takes a cedar tree to grow to maturity, die and decay to the point where it becomes what is known in the Squamish language as *temlh*, literally a cedar pigment used to paint the body for spiritual protection, as part of regalia.

It was the summer of 1999. In an area not far from the place the Witness camping weekends took place, Squamish Nation anthropologist Rudy Reimer/*Yemk̲s* made

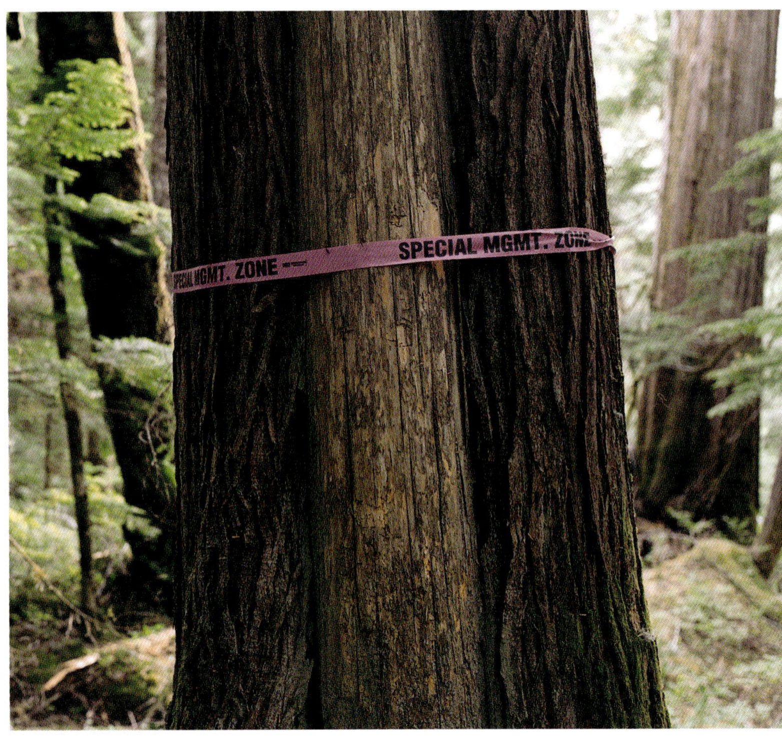

Special Management, CMT,
photo by Nancy Bleck, 1999

a significant discovery. While doing fieldwork in the northern area of the Squamish Nation territory, he had found culturally modified markings on the outer bark of cedar trees. A culturally modified tree (CMT) is a red cedar tree whose bark has been peeled to expose the inner bark and which was used by Coast Salish people to create traditional goods for their family, such as mats, clothing and regalia. These culturally modified trees Reimer had located were proof that this was a Squamish historical site, likely thousands of years old. But this sacred site was slated for logging—and soon.

Chief Bill knew he had to move quickly. Evidence of these markings would give the Squamish Nation ammunition to stay the logging until a land claim treaty could be agreed upon. He wanted Nancy to photograph the site, but first she had to prepare.

Chief Bill Williams/*telálsemḵin siy̓ám̓* asked Aaron Nelson-Moody to do the work of conducting the songs and ceremonies that would prepare Nancy to take on a photographic project. As Chief Bill pointed out to Nancy, there is a lack of photographs showing Squamish Nation people doing ceremonies and other evidence of their everyday culture and history. Historically, the photos taken were of nicely dressed kids lined up in front of a residential school. These were colonized images taken with the colonizer's technology.

Nancy remembers not feeling at all ready to take on a responsibility this important, but as Aaron acknowledged, "witnessing is a very important idea for photographers too." This mission was an evolution from Nancy's solo explorations of the land to a community-sanctioned journey Squamish Nation–style.

She recalls, "Before I entered the sacred site, Aaron applied the *temlh* to my face, and I said to him, 'I don't feel it's appropriate that I return here by myself.'" He replied, "Don't think of yourself as walking behind us, think of yourself as walking beside us." The work that Aaron did with Nancy was to acknowledge to the ancestors her presence in the forest. She spent several days alone, camping and fasting and recording images of the culturally modified trees with a panoramic camera. Witness was always about the land, but it was never about only one way of doing things. And the very act of photography in this context confuses completely the nice, neat division Western Eurocentric society likes to place between nature and culture, subject and object. The entire process is as much a part of the work as the photograph itself; in other words, it is not made by one artist and the artwork is not the end result.

Just as Aaron prepared Nancy for this journey, she photographed him preparing to begin the first of four Cedar

Women to be carved in the housepost tradition. In a piece made for a gallery setting, Nancy's composite panoramic photo shows the first Cedar Woman etched in a large cedar log just as the carving has begun. Beside Cedar Woman is a square-format portrait of her carver, Aaron Nelson-Moody/ *Tawx'sin Yexwulla/Púlxtn*, in regalia, face painted with *temlh*, cedar bark hat on his head. He is a modern man at work in a traditional way.

Each carving in Aaron's Cedar Women series is loosely based on a specific woman. Aaron describes how Theresa Nahanee told him he would create four houseposts: "She was not a carver but a friend and mentor for me. She worked in community health and healing and was also very involved in our spiritual practices." In so many ways, her teachings and influence affected his process of both what he carved and how he approached it. For example, when Aaron was carving his first figure, the log suddenly split. At first Aaron thought the carving was ruined, but the fact that the central figure emerged whole made it unique, and he completed the carving in a style more like a welcome figure than a typical housepost.

For him, this carving took on a poignancy when Theresa passed away just after it was completed. He explains: "The welcome figure is carved to depict a society within our society, a group of women raised from birth to act as leaders in our stewardship of the land. There is no equivalent in non-Native society, as the women were as much medicinal doctors as they were environmental lawyers, as much librarians as they were land managers." After Theresa passed away, Aaron began to create his carvings for Chief Bill and considered them part of the work he was doing with Witness.

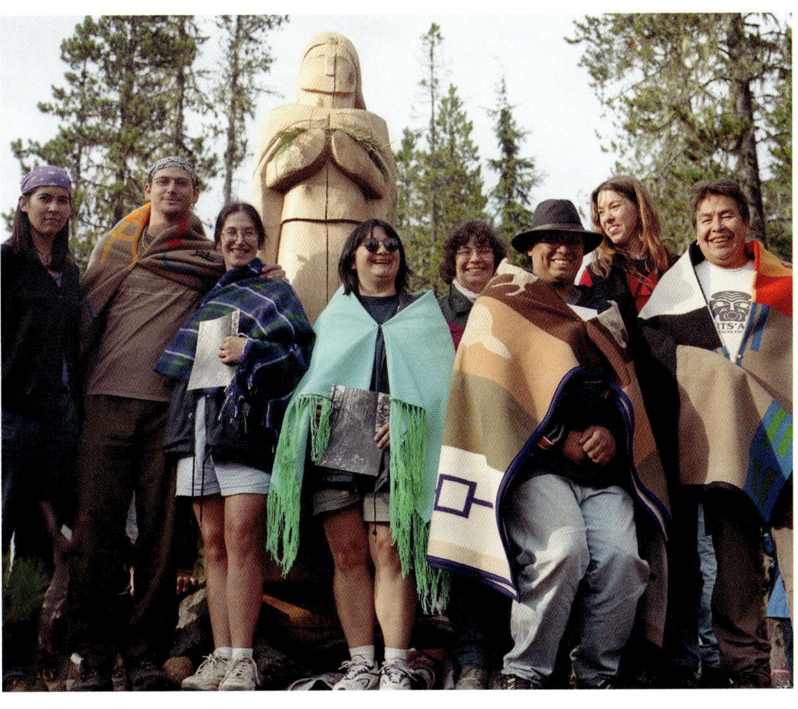

Honouring guests from Oka-Kanesatake in stewardship of the land, photo by Nancy Bleck, 2000

Traditionally the carver lays the completed carving at the feet of the community, which decides where it will be placed and arranges the ceremony. Chief Bill saw the need not only to record evidence of his people on the territory but also to make sure the land was being used. Together, Chief Bill, Nancy and John decided to place the first figure of Aaron's Cedar Women series at Bear Bluffs, located at the end of the logging road. It's where they decide to "draw the line," as the figure, facing south with arms upraised, welcomes people to the beginning of the old-growth forest but also warns that there will be no more logging here. Now settler and First Nations people who happen upon Splash's carvings on the land will see evidence of history and tradition. This is not ancient history but a contemporary reflection of living people: placing poles on the land is a way of taking back the space and reasserting a cultural claim that was removed when, in the past, settler culture cleared the land of poles—the evidence of "other"—and placed them in museums.

CEDAR PEOPLE

1999–2007

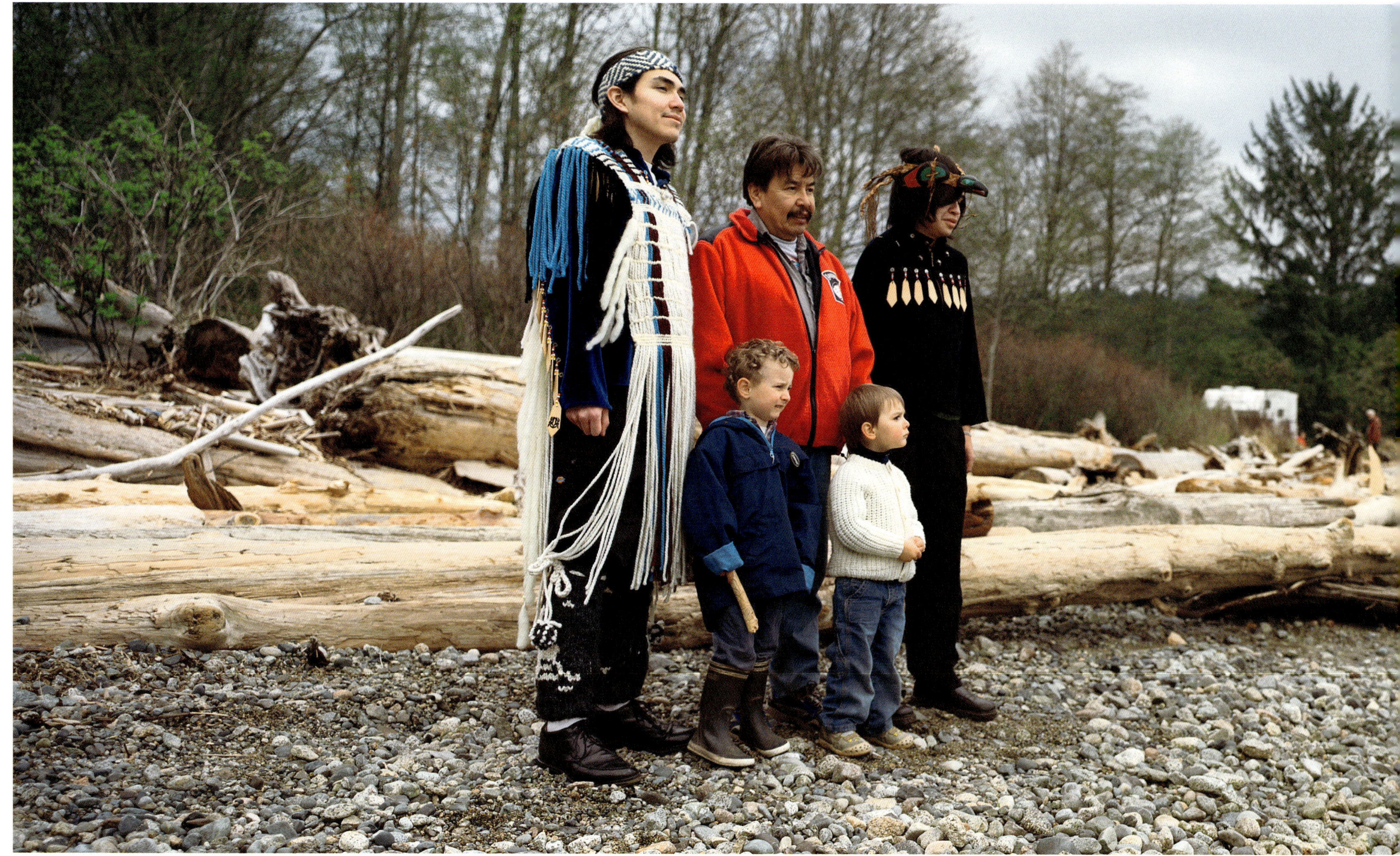

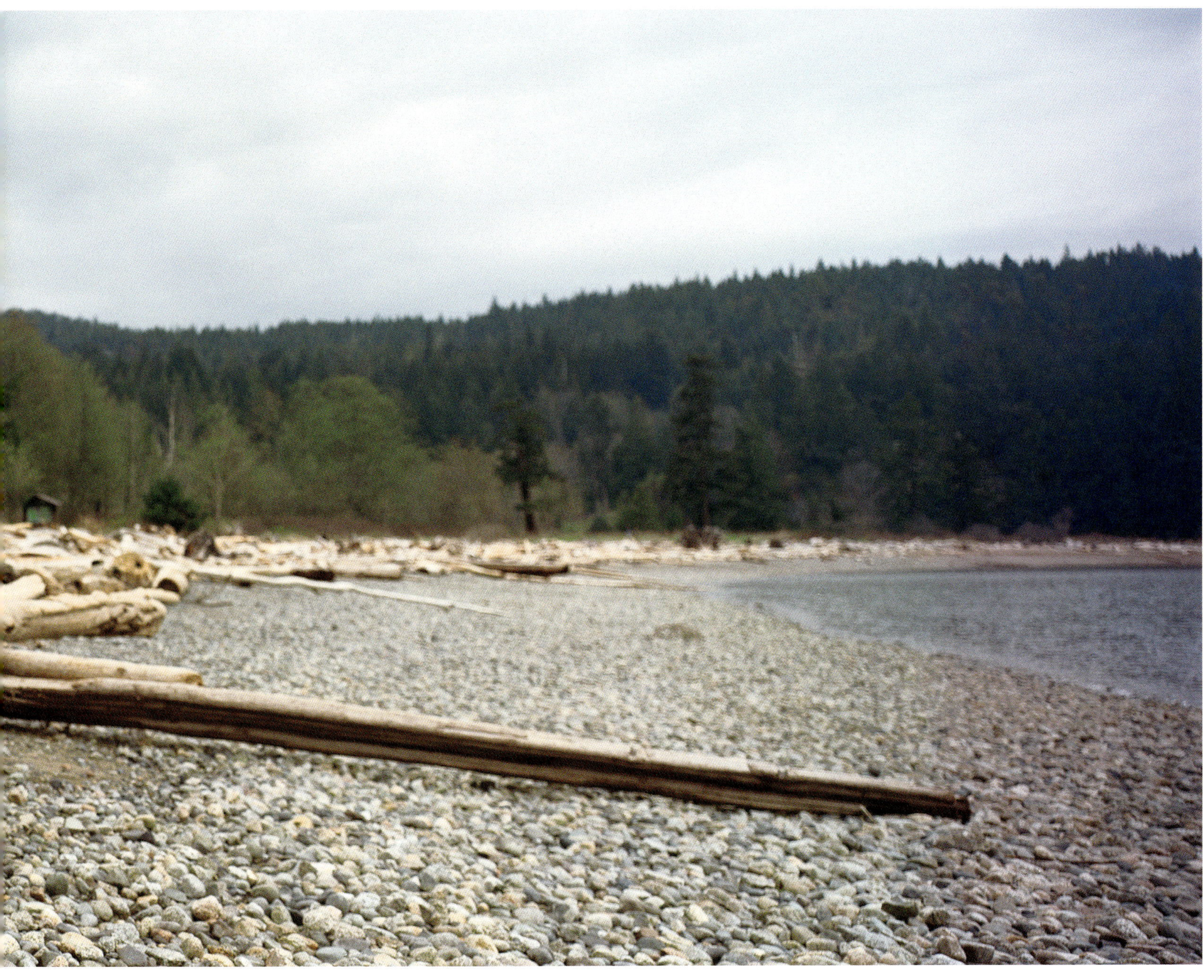

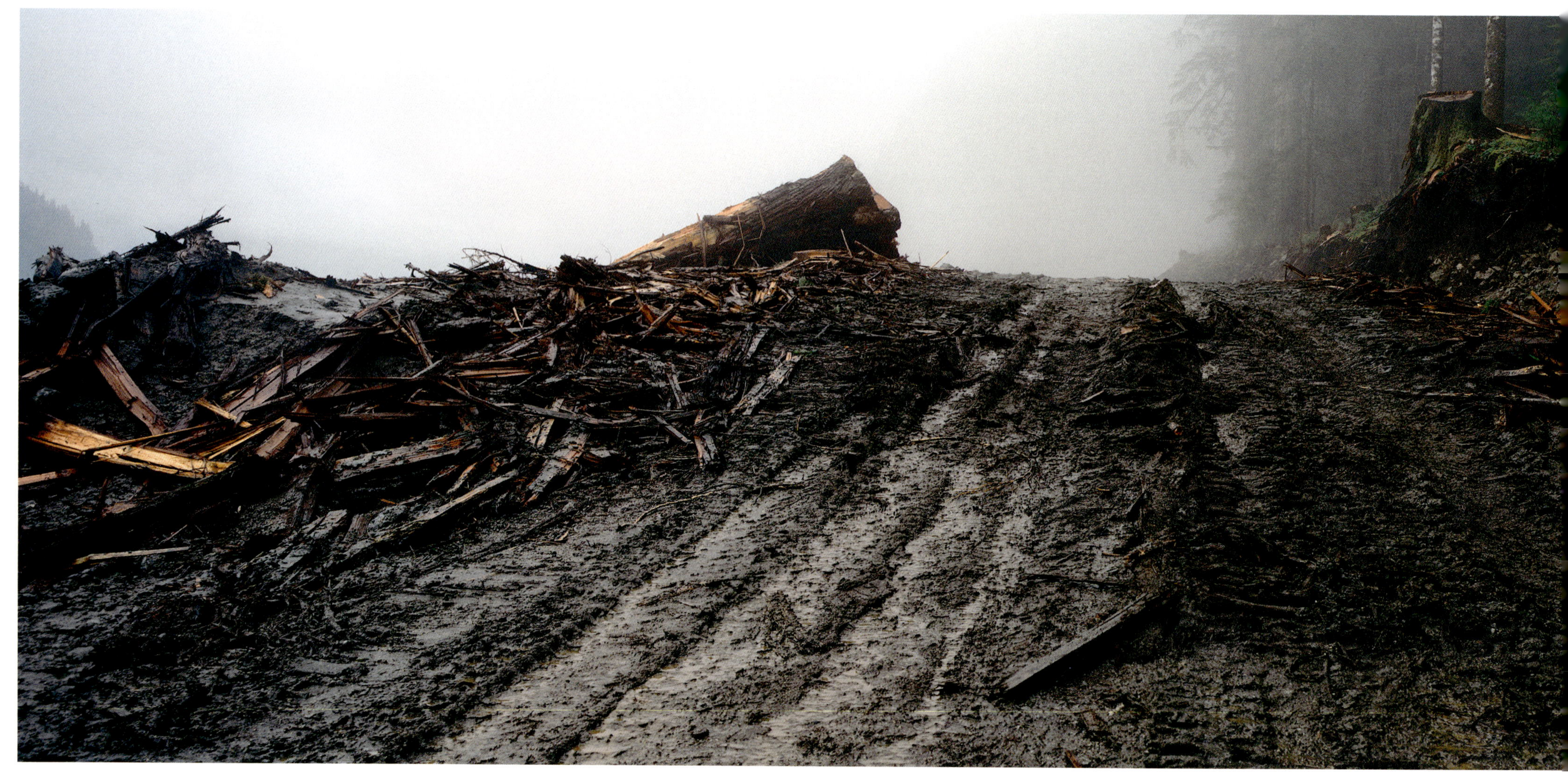

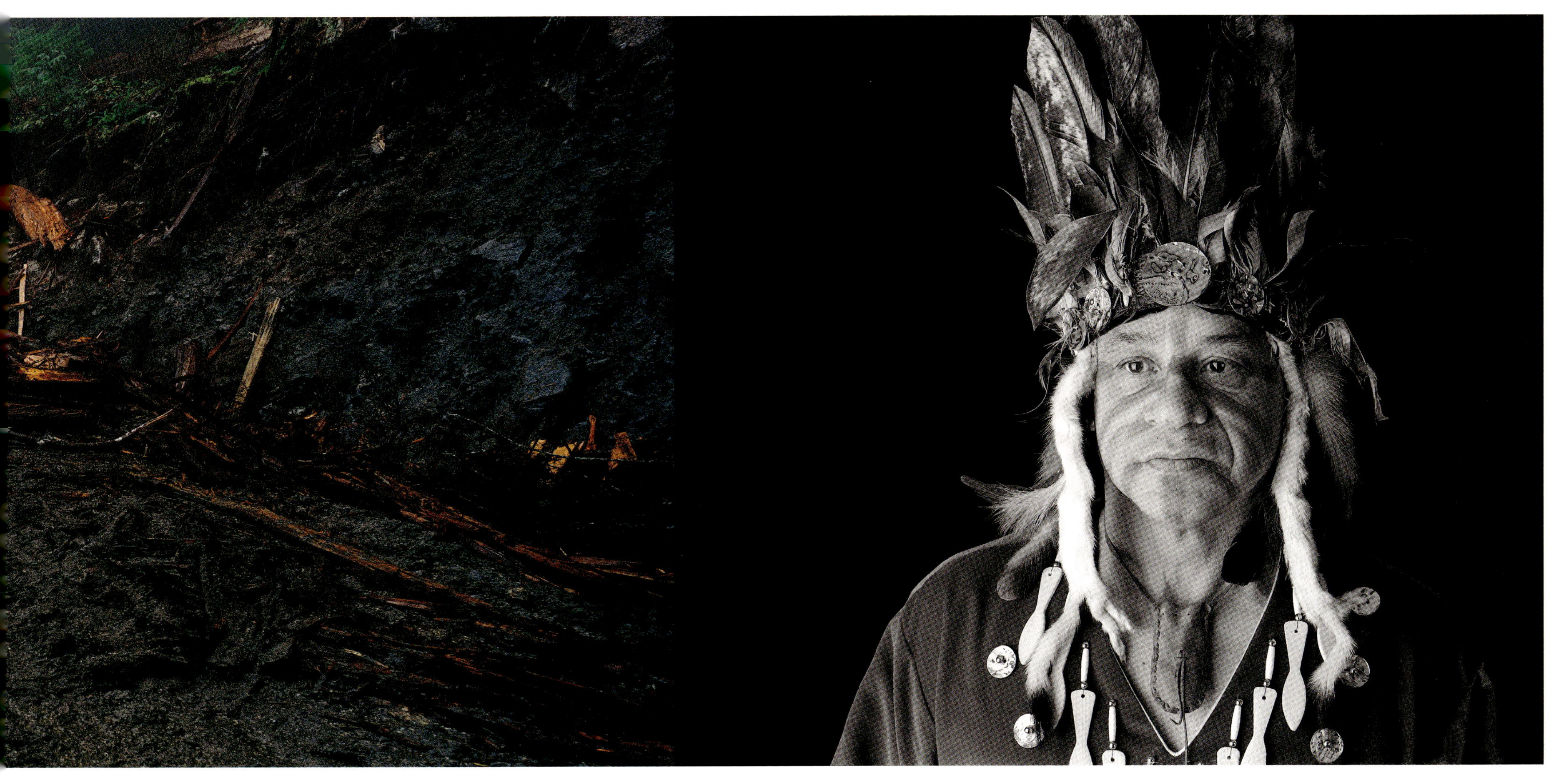

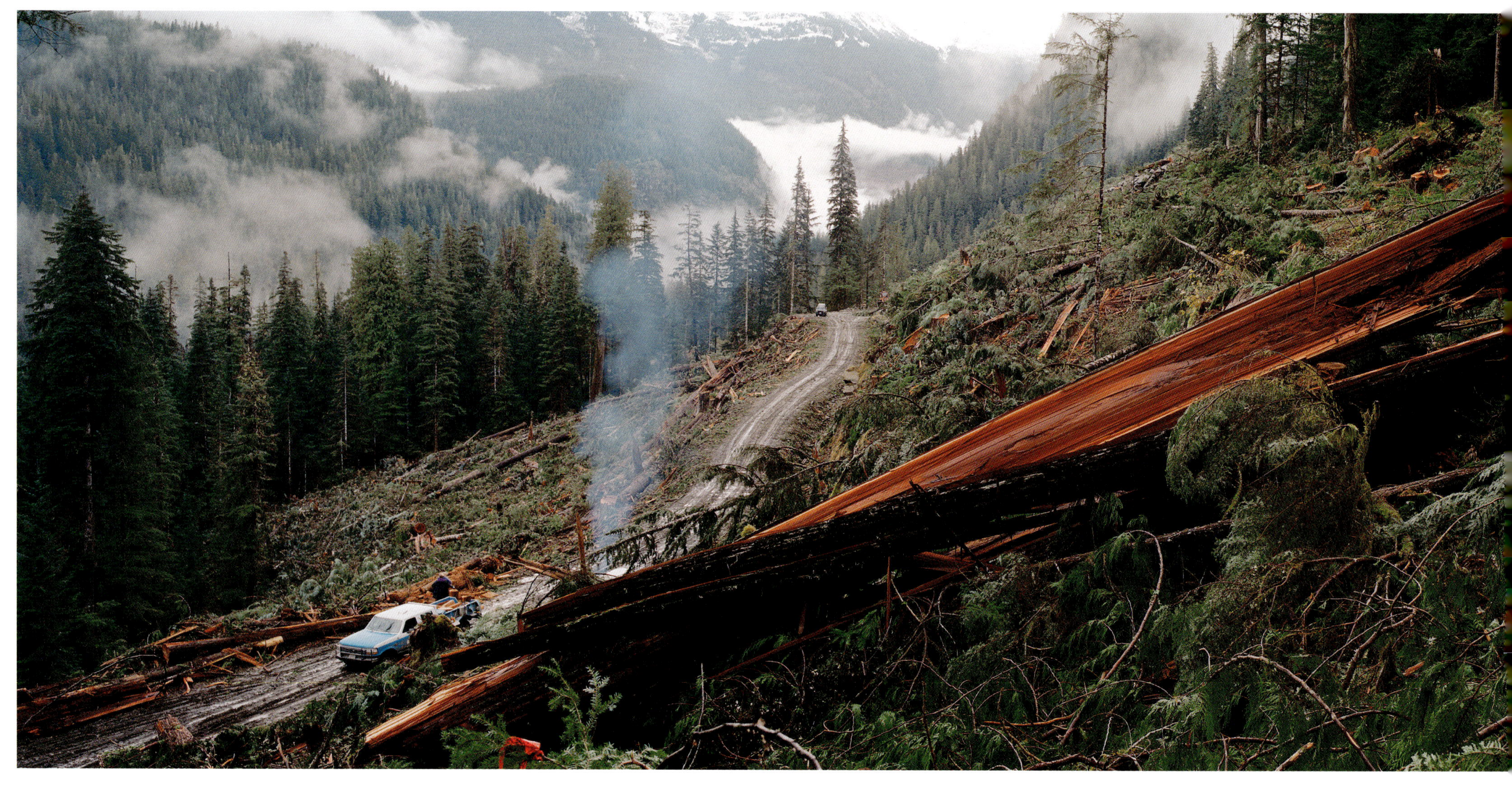

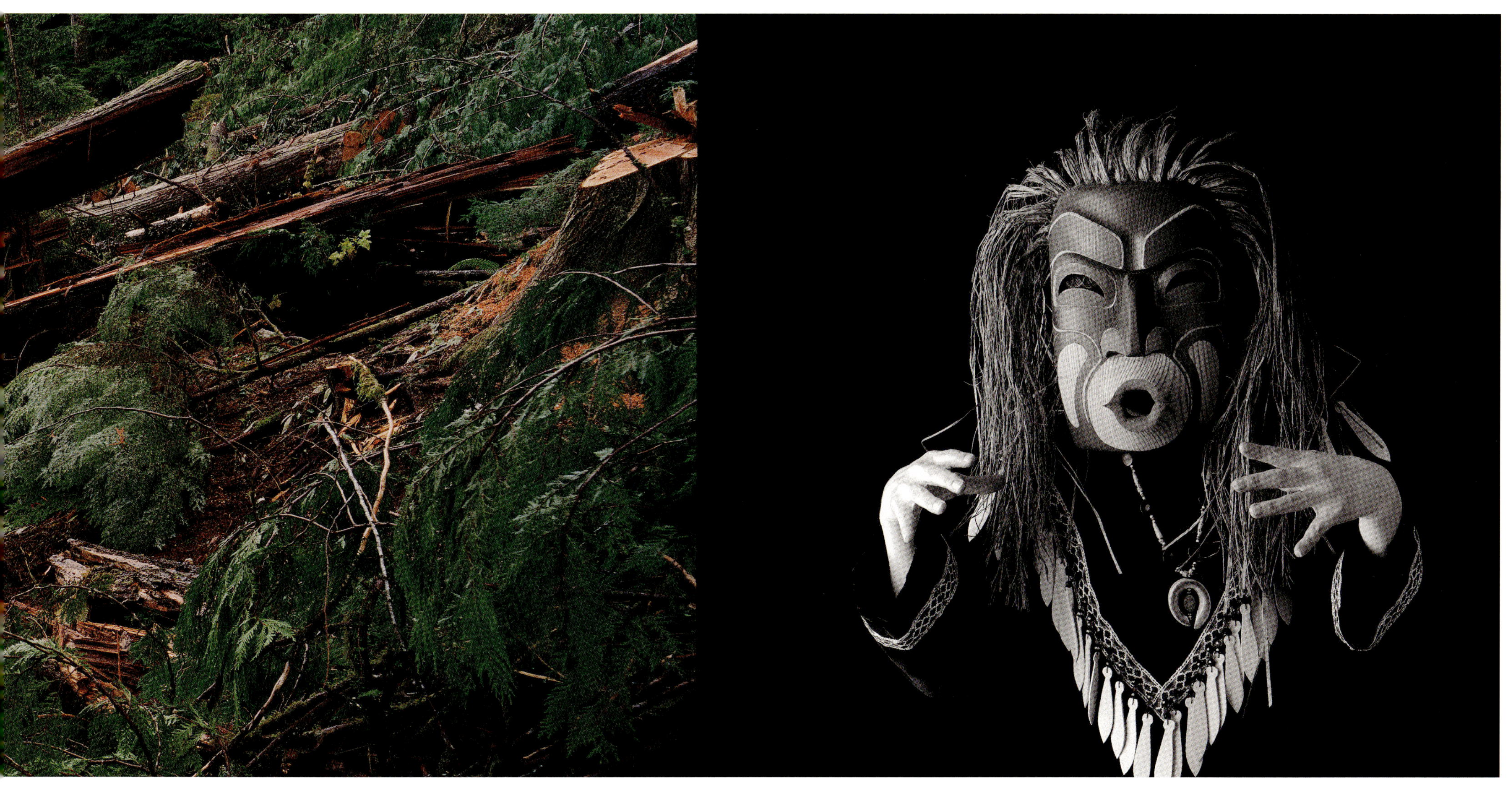

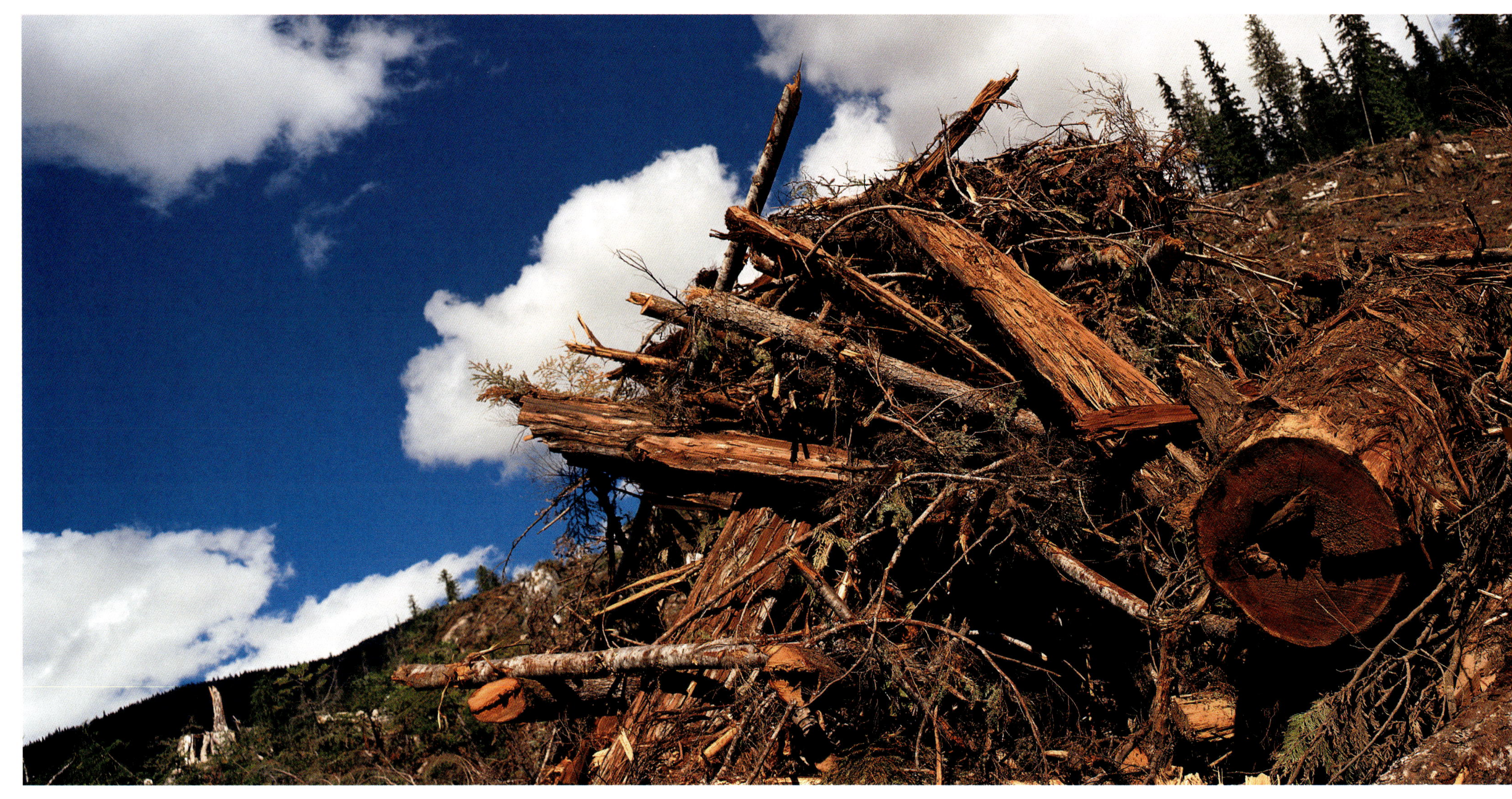

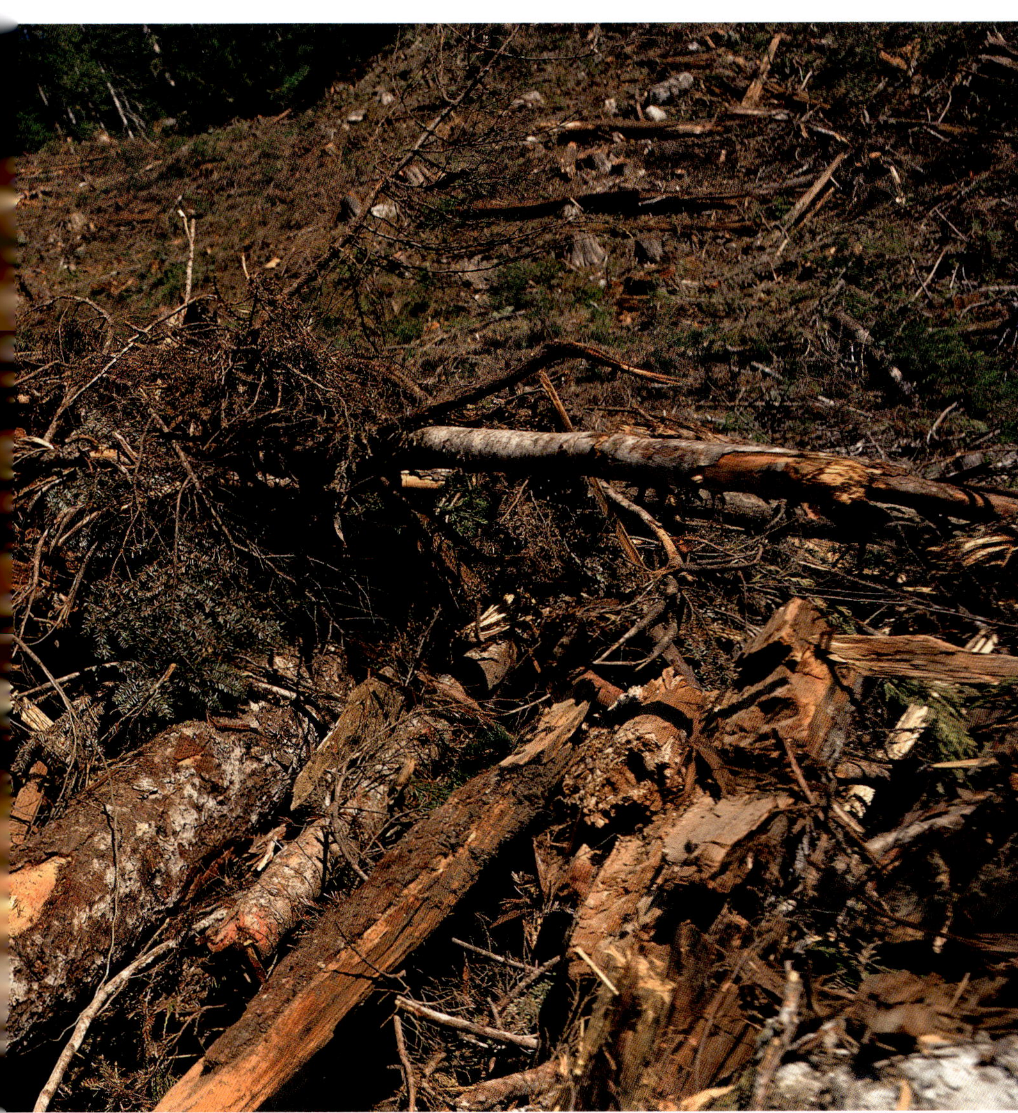

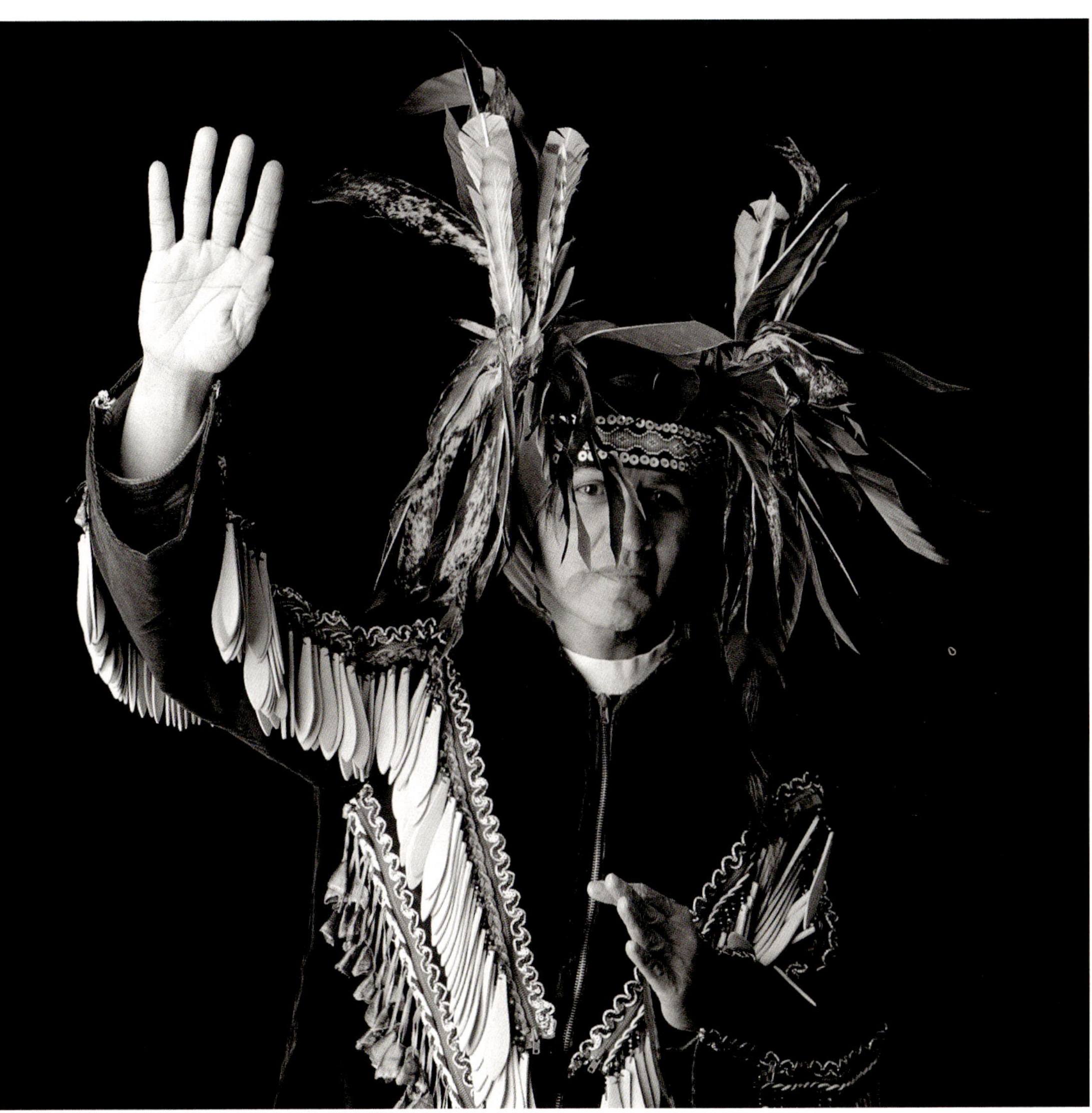

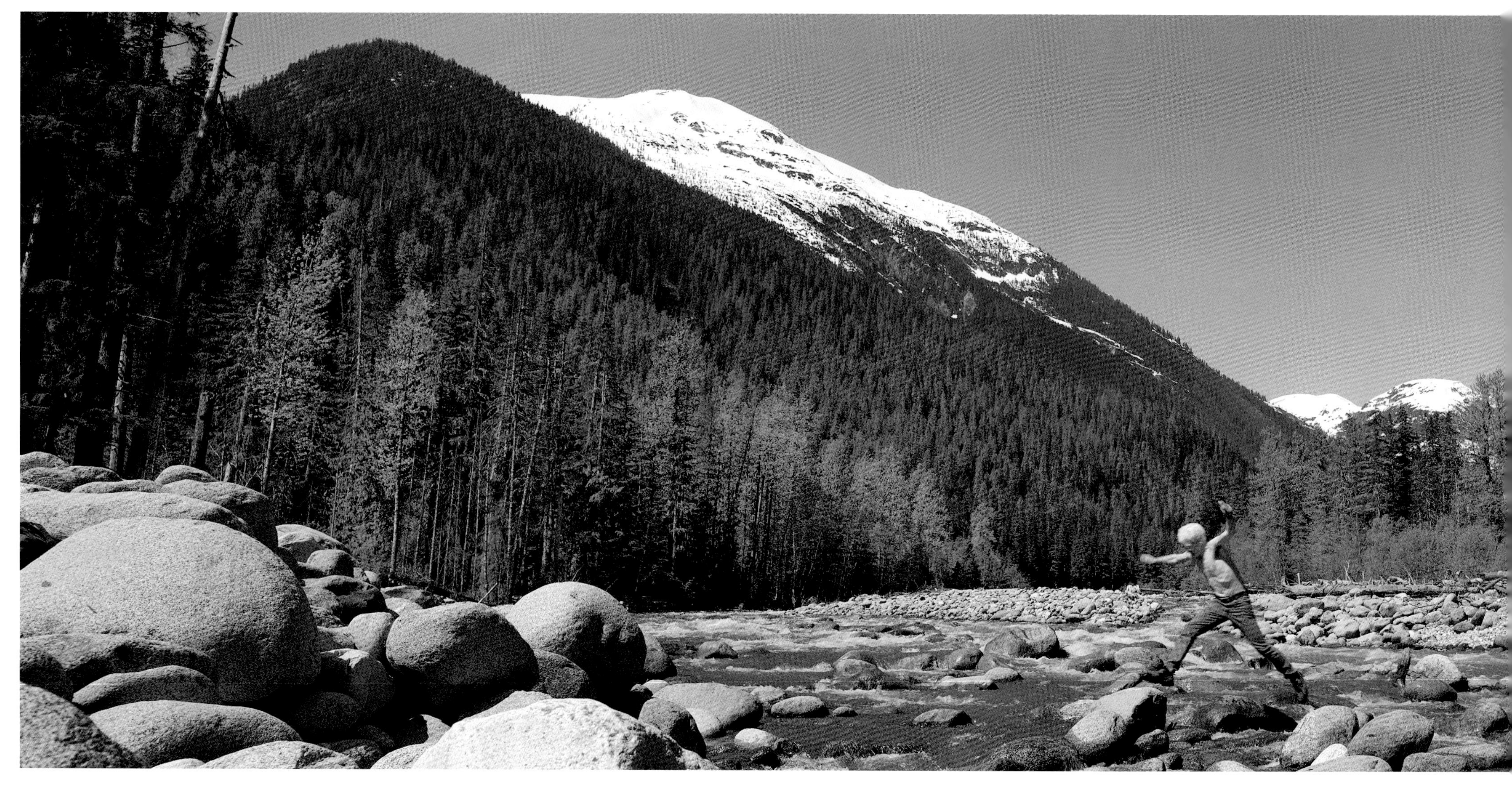

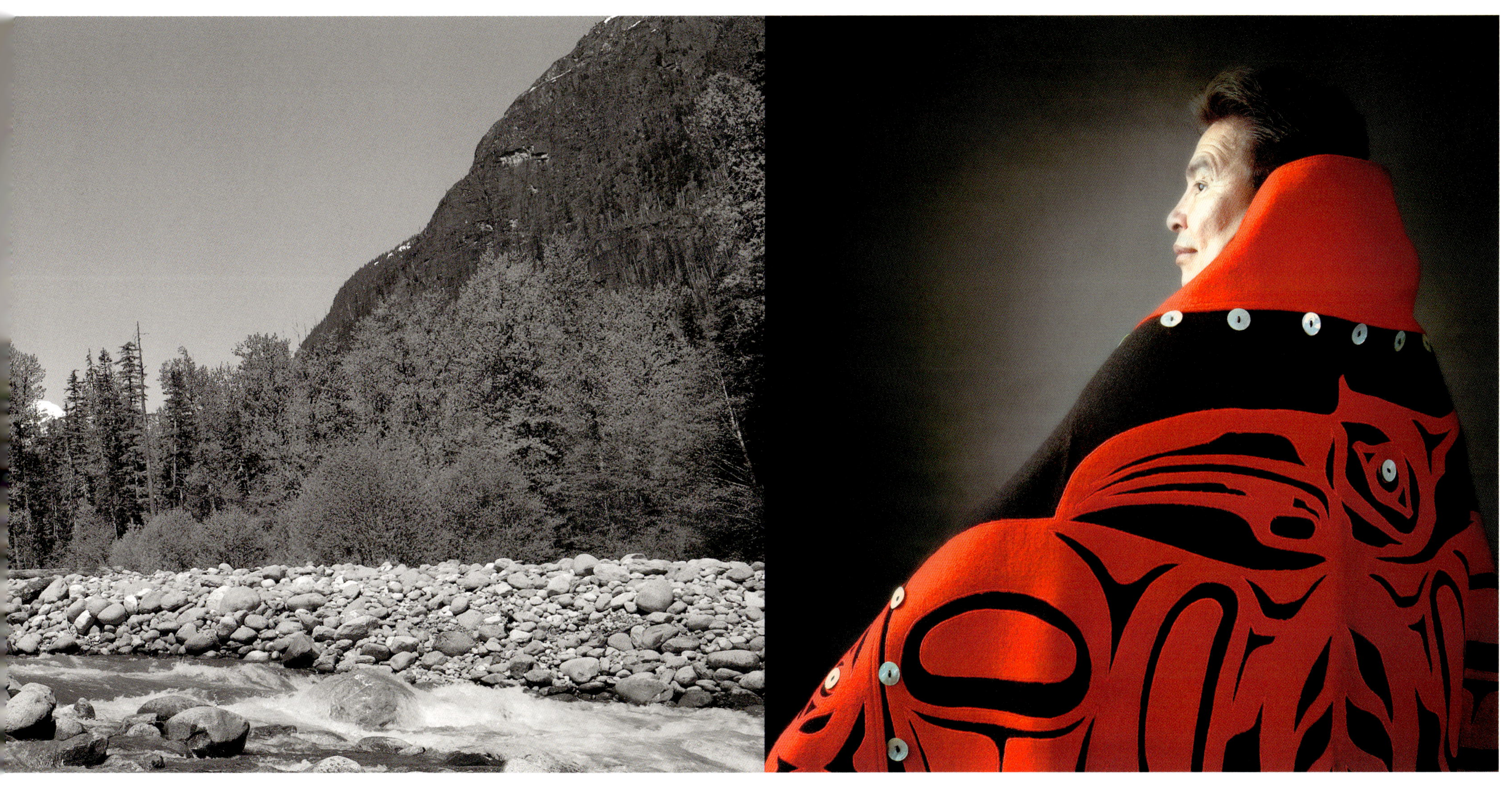

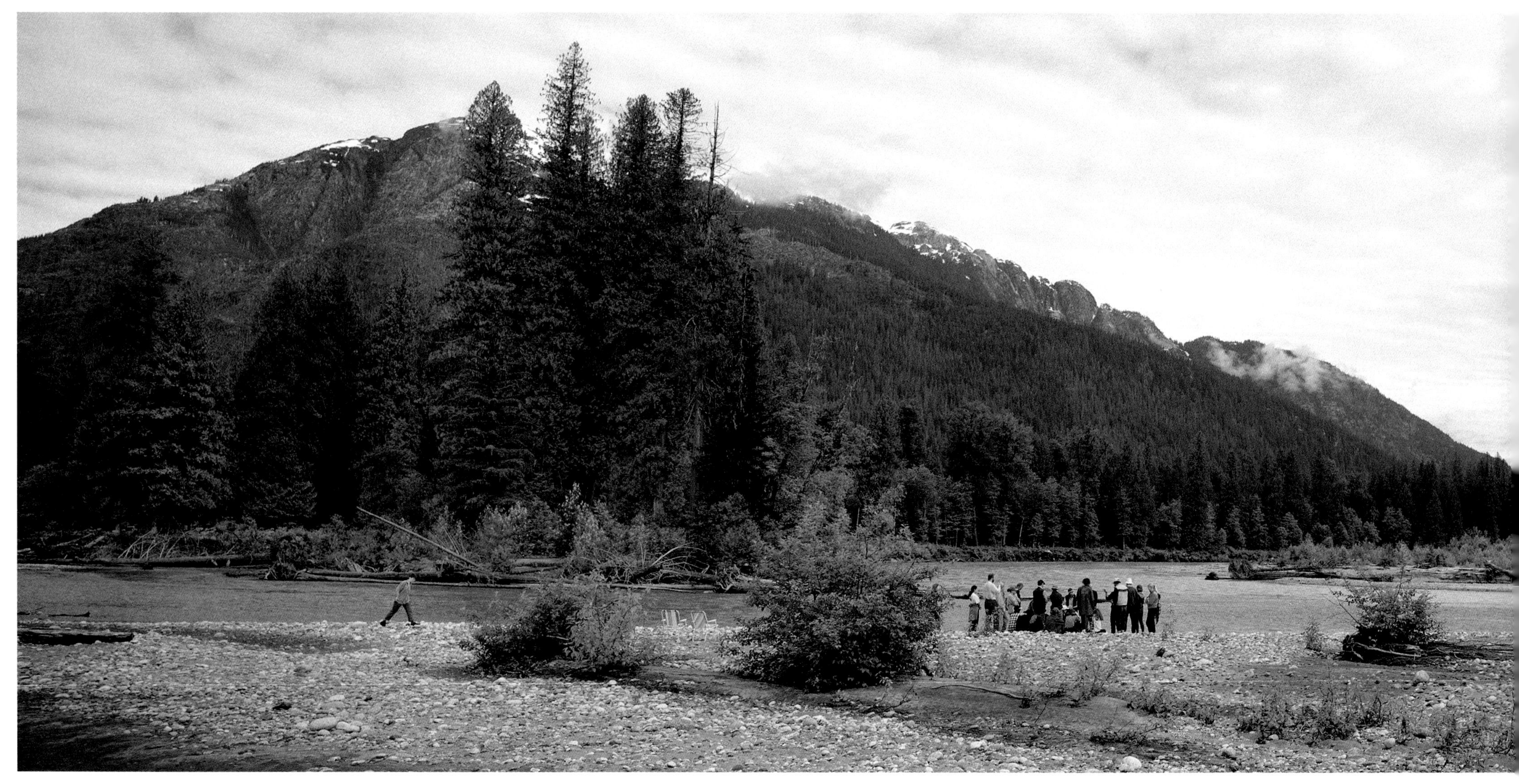

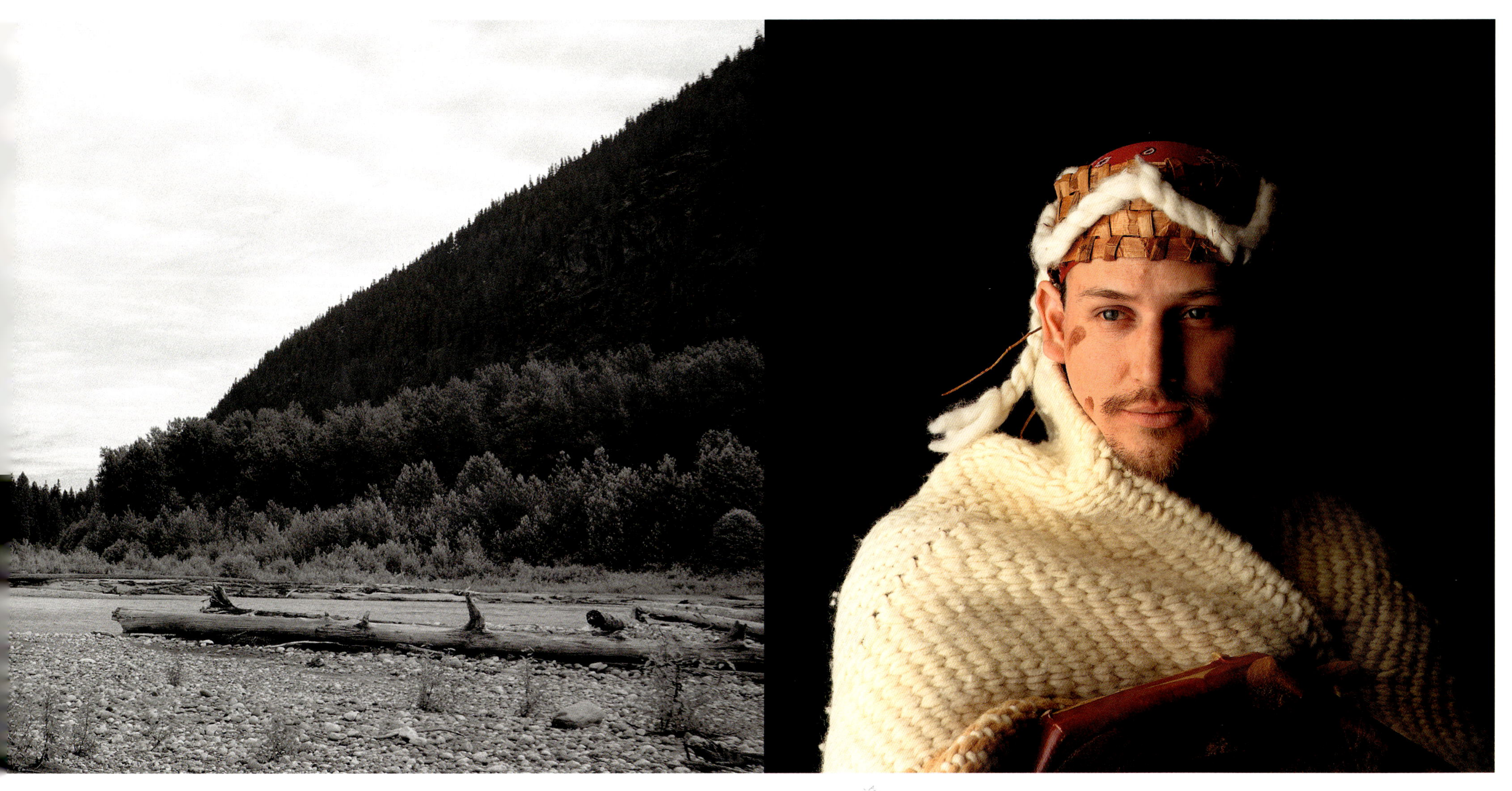

When the Witness project came, it made my heart wake up. To be able to take care of the spirit of the land, we have to take care of the spirit within so that we can venture and bring it out to the world. To care for the feelings, care for the spirit: spirit of the trees; spirit of the animal; spirit of the water; spirit of the unknown creatures in our forest.

EUGENE HARRY/HAYKWÍLEM

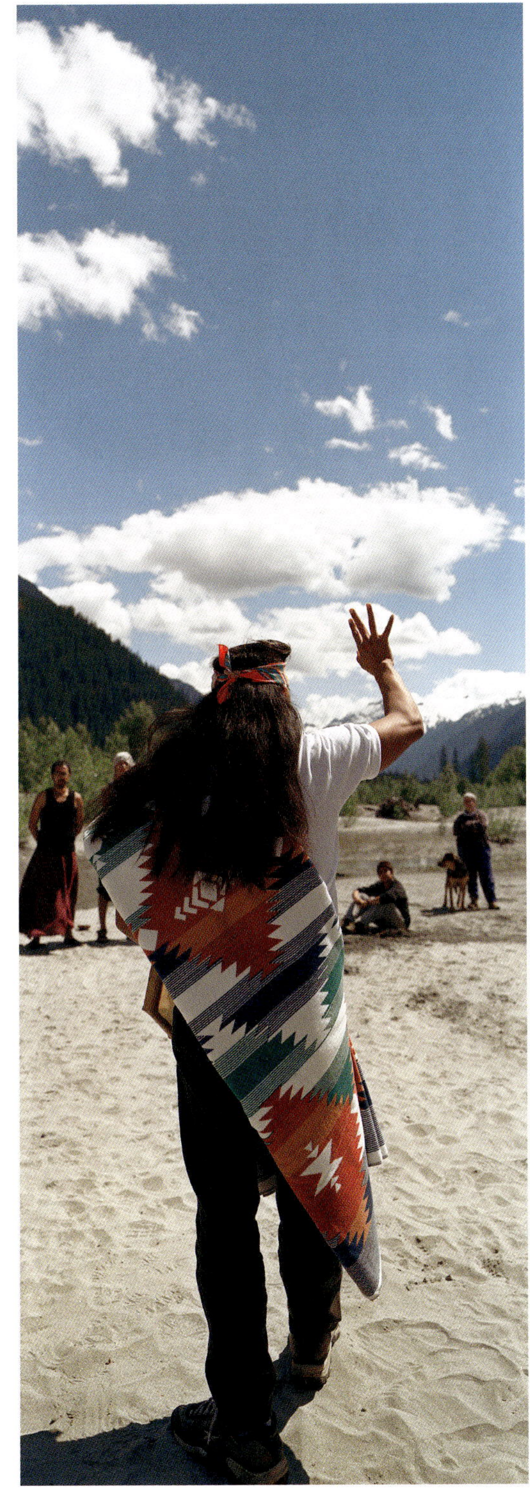
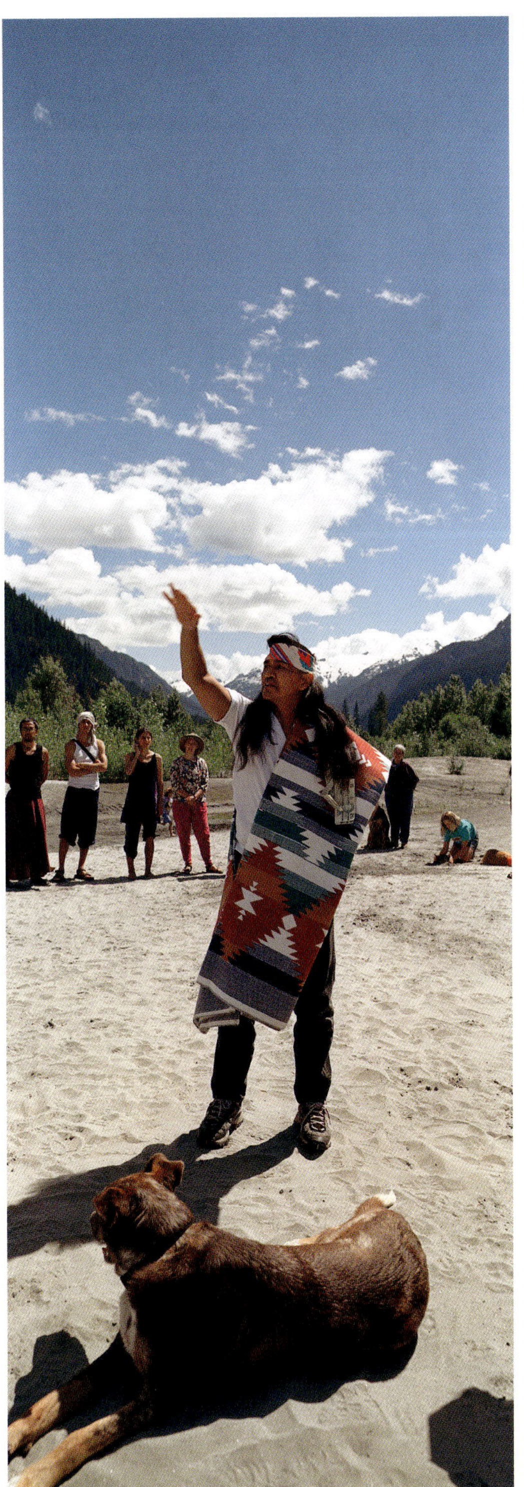
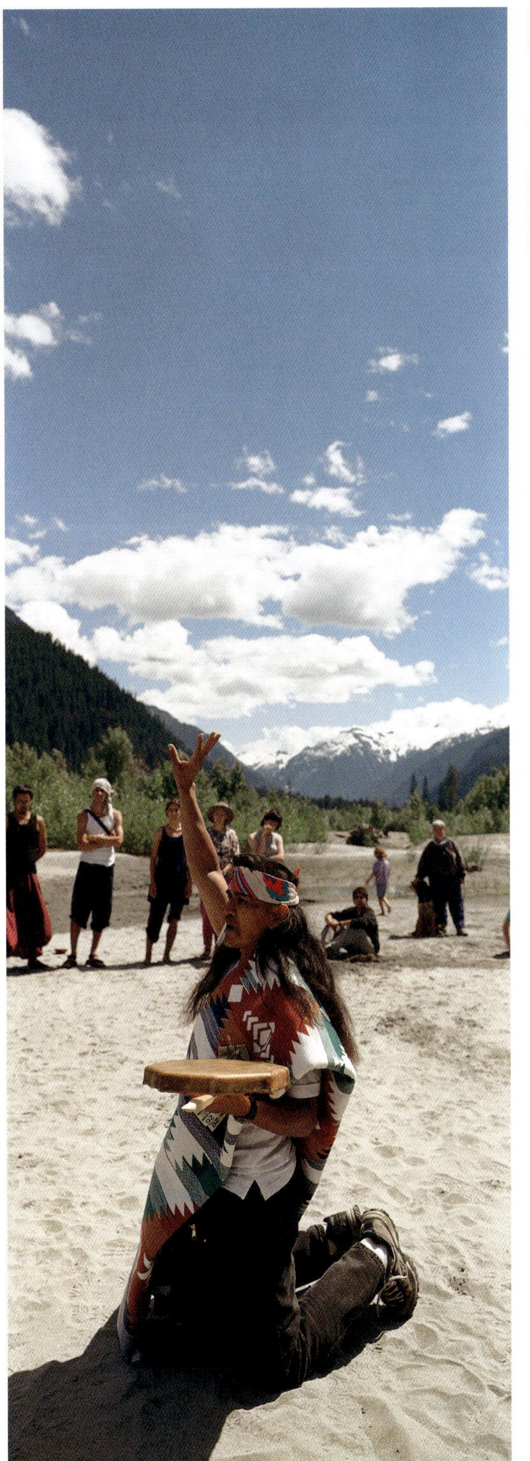
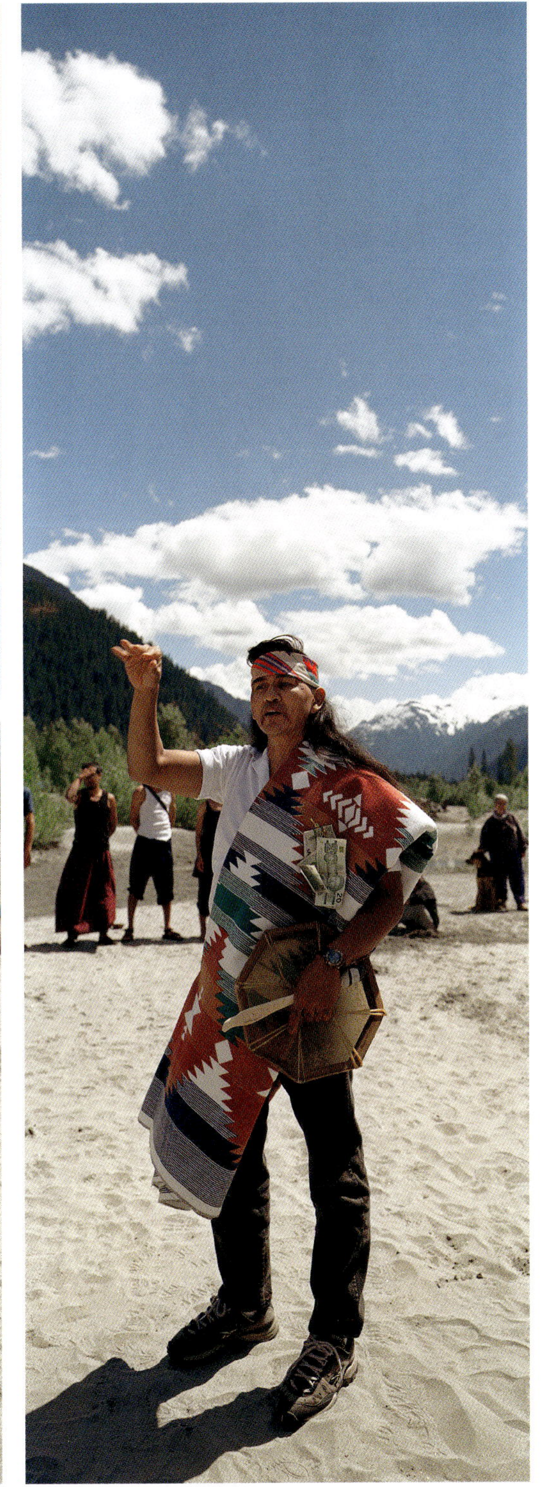

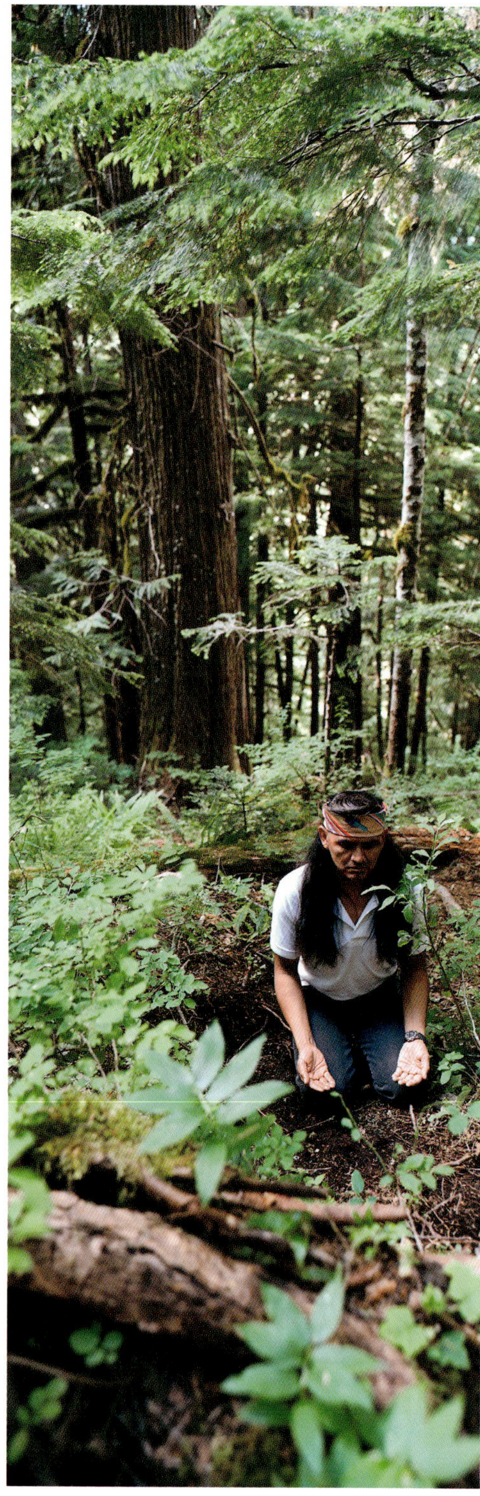

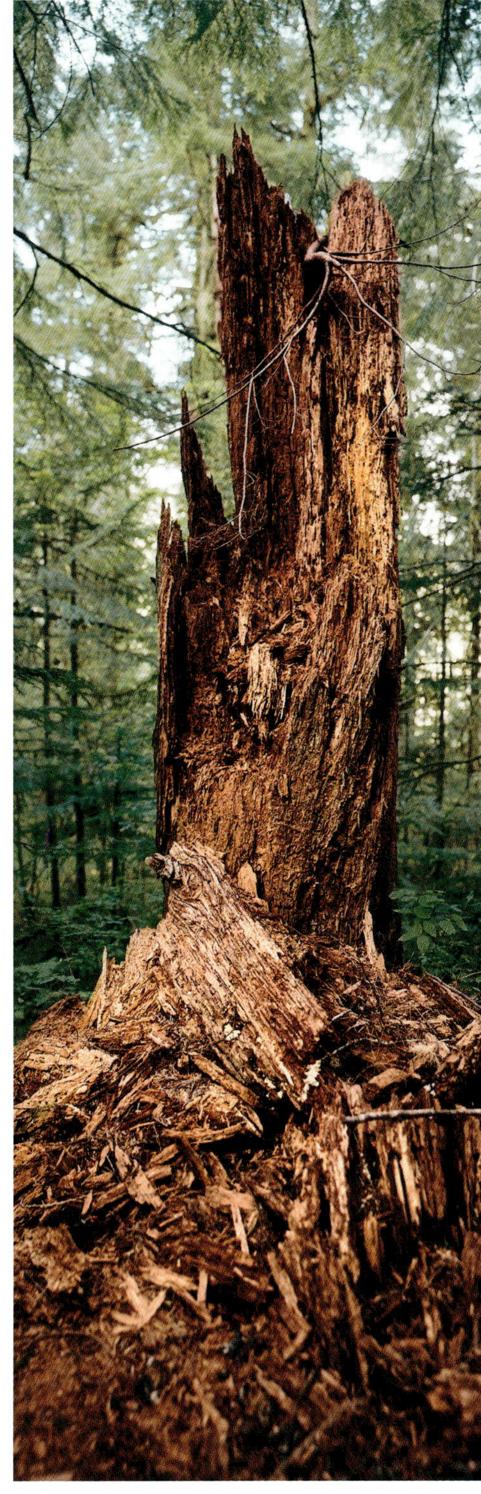

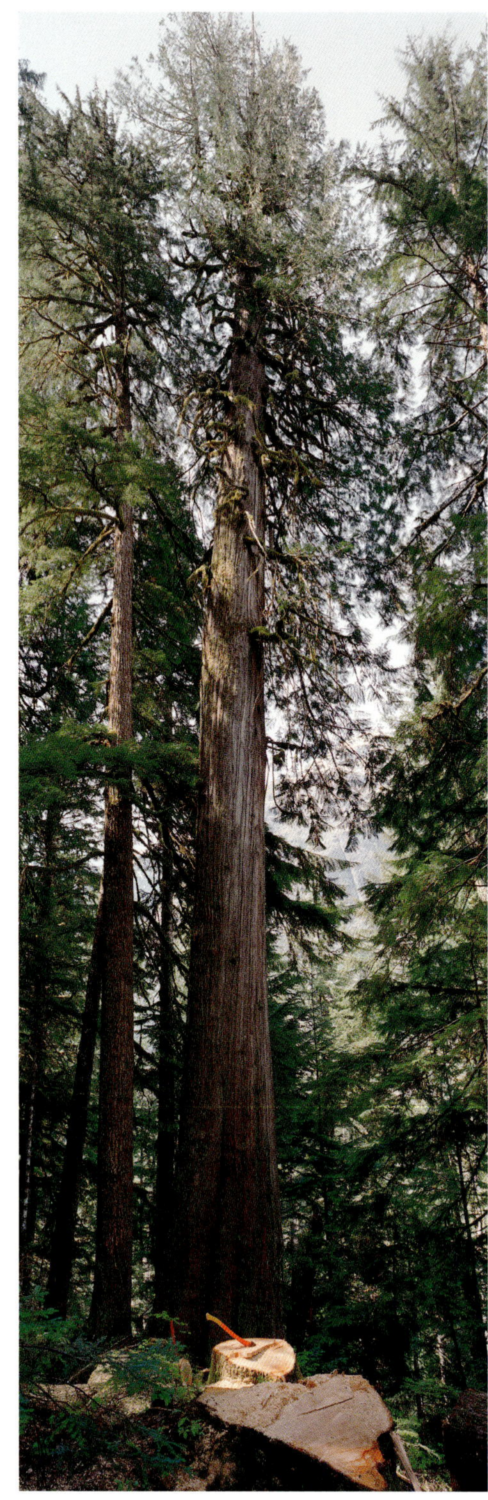

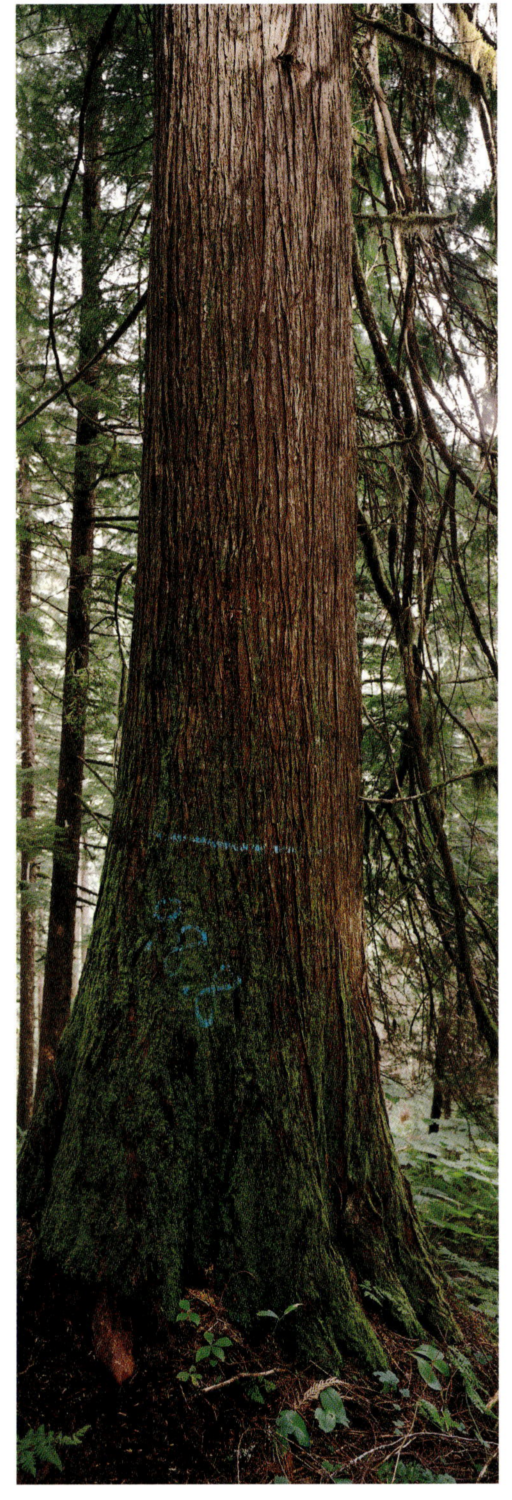

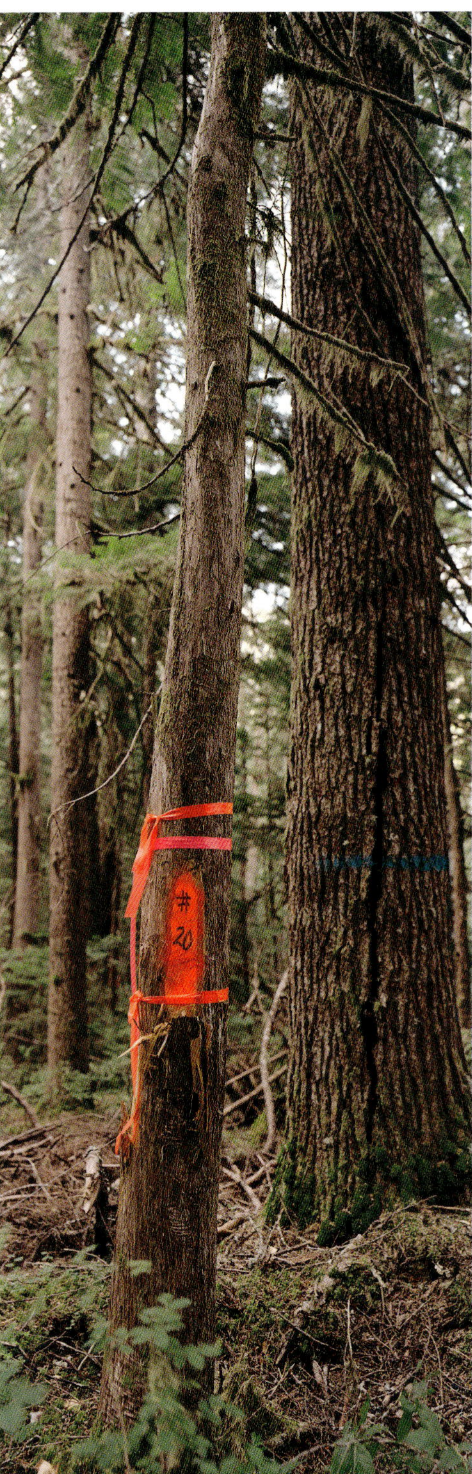
#20

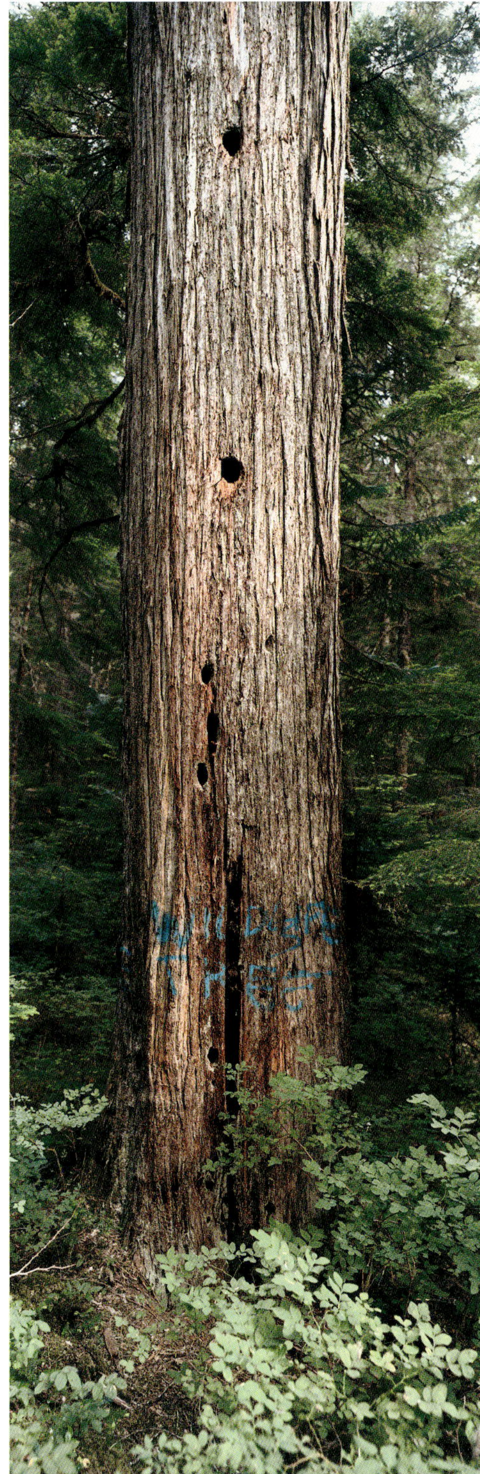

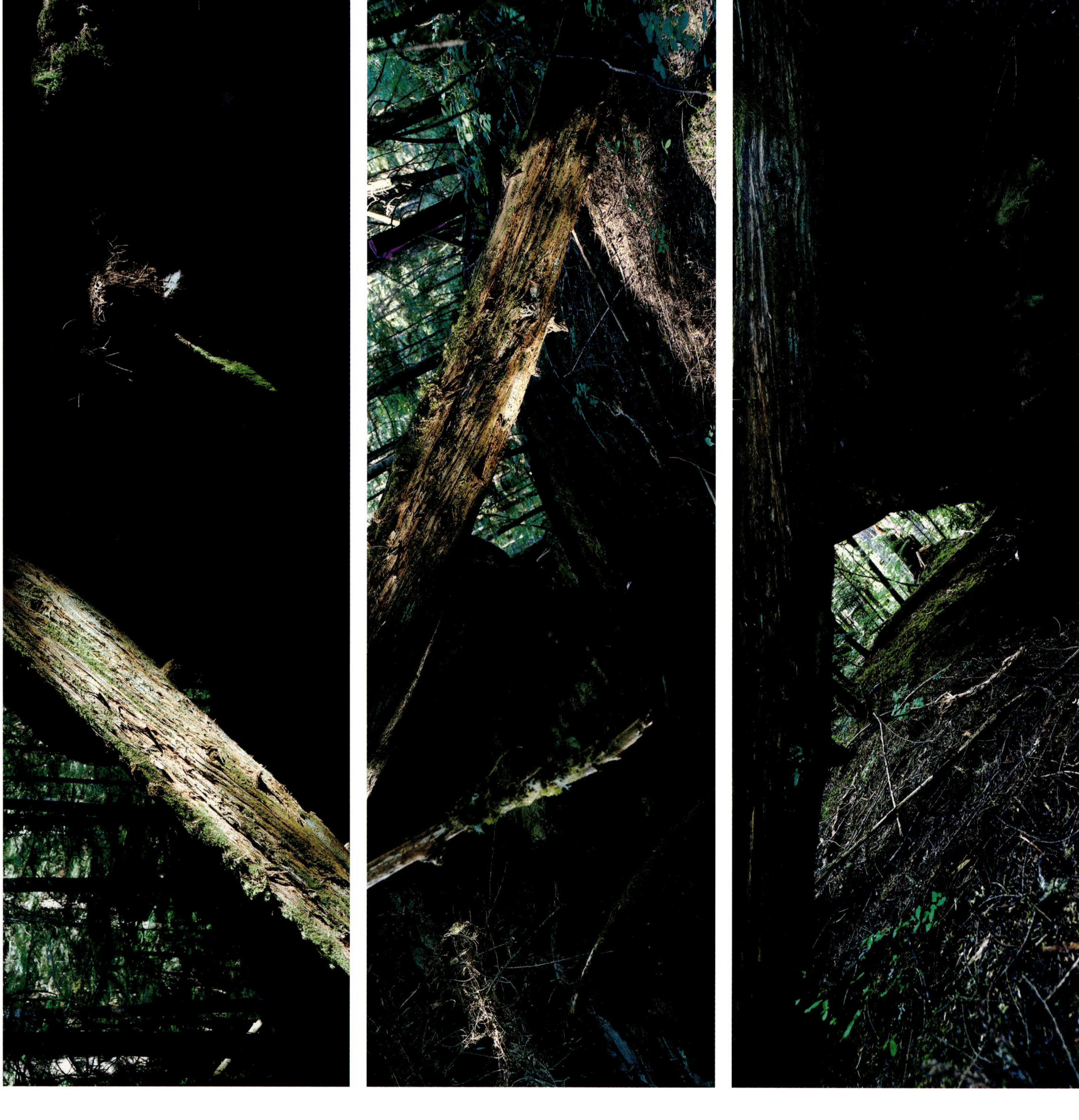

The tree falls in the forest in silent homage to death, to the great silence of natural law; everything being in the course of being constructed and in the course of being destroyed.
Succumbing finally to the great silence within the silence because silence is the reality and the motive of creation.
Because natural death is silent.
Like a tree silently standing witness to its own death.
Inopportune or untimely demise is never quiet or done in silence.
The percussive crack of a gun.
The explosion of a bomb.
The anger of a chainsaw, then silence.

EXCERPT FROM A POEM BY JAMES NICHOLAS, ROCK CREE WRITER AND ACTOR

DOUBLE PORTRAITS

1999–2013

We would like to explain the culture of the Squamish people to anybody in the world, to have them walk away and use some terms of Squamish, whether it be *Huy chexw a* or *Utsám̓,* but they learn at least one word, and they recognize that there is a language, there is a culture and there is a group of people that are attached to the land. The land was never barren, the land was never set free, the land was never unclaimed.

CHIEF BILL WILLIAMS/TELÁLSEMK̲IN SIY̓ÁM̓

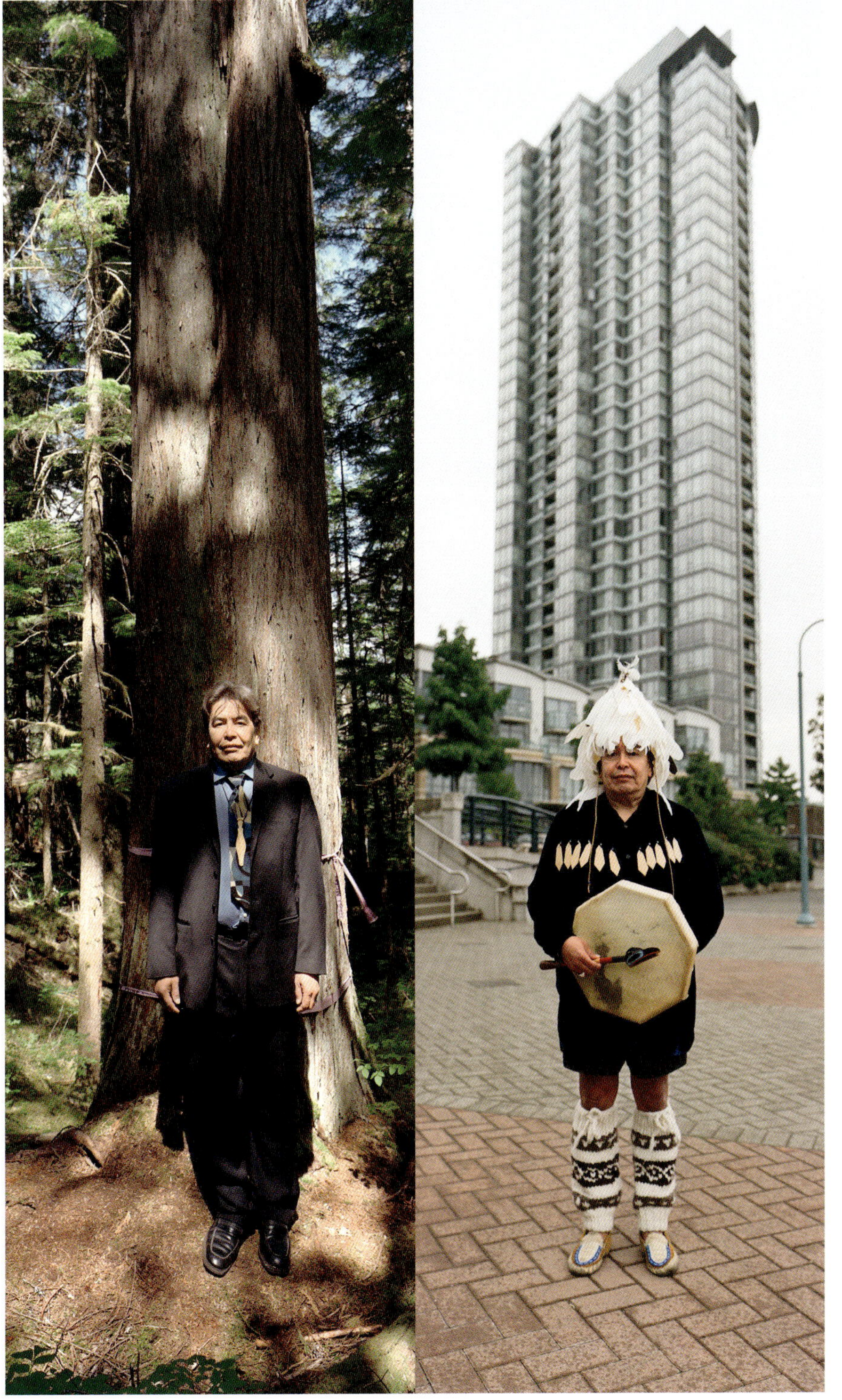

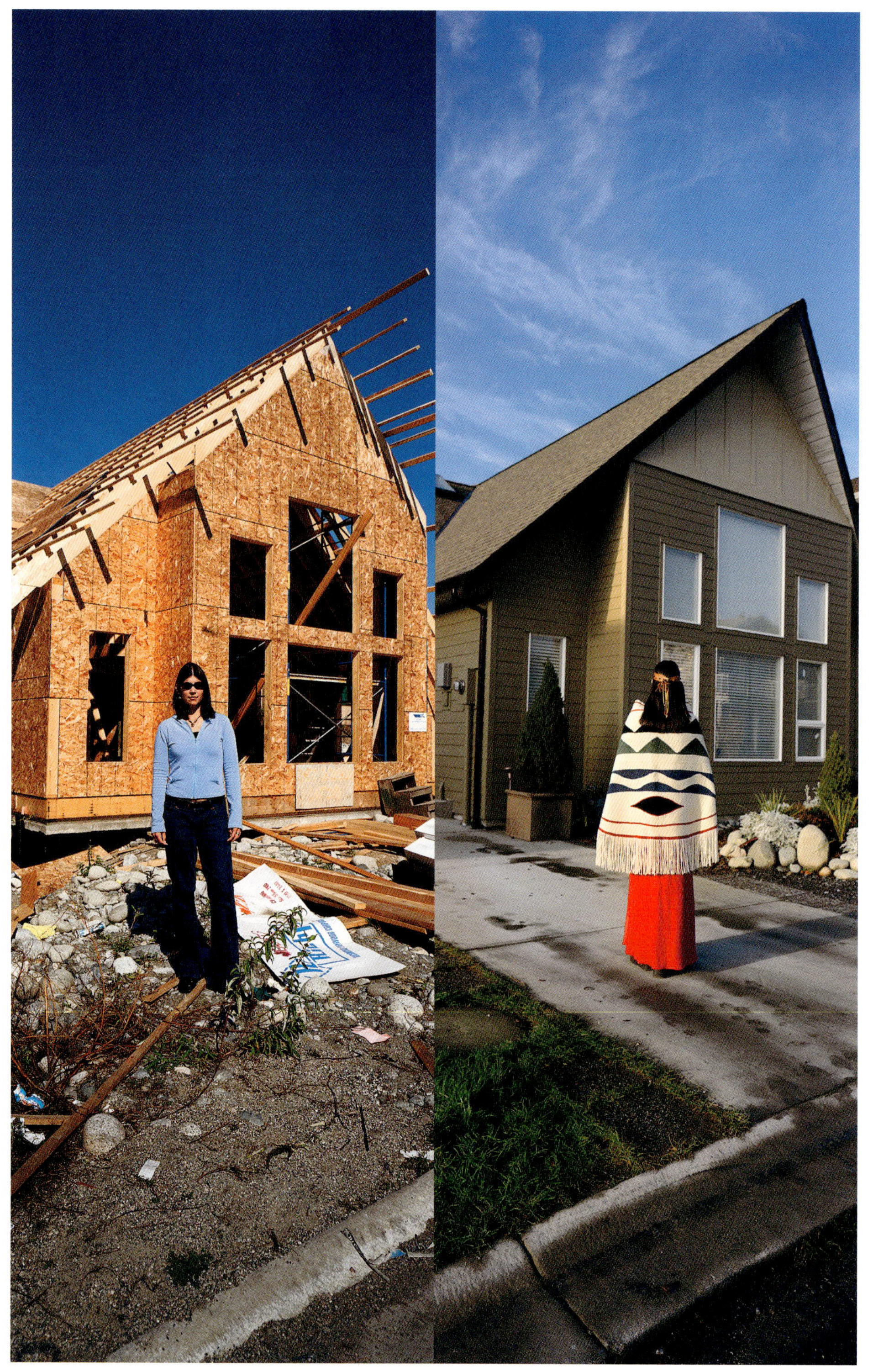

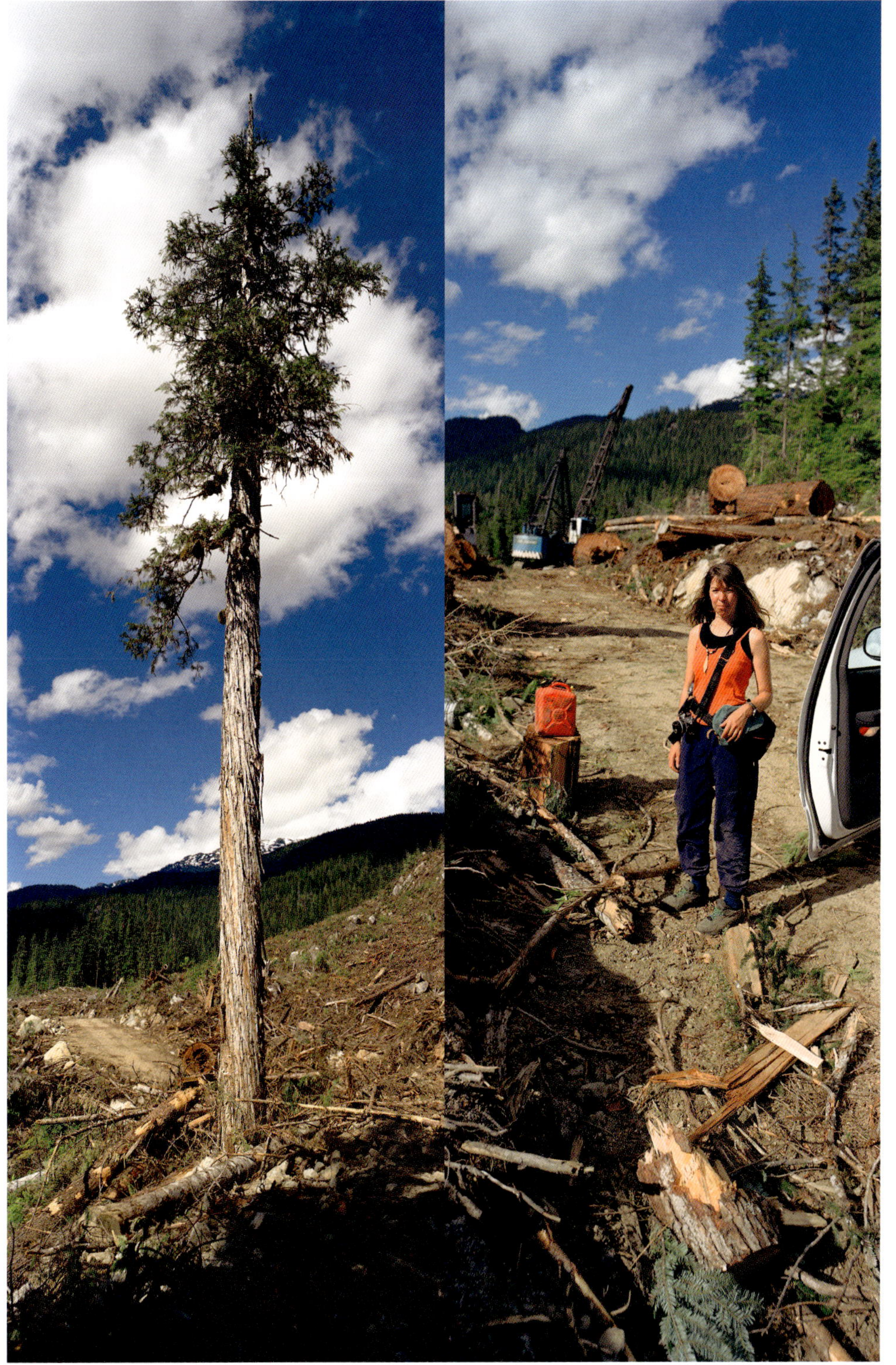

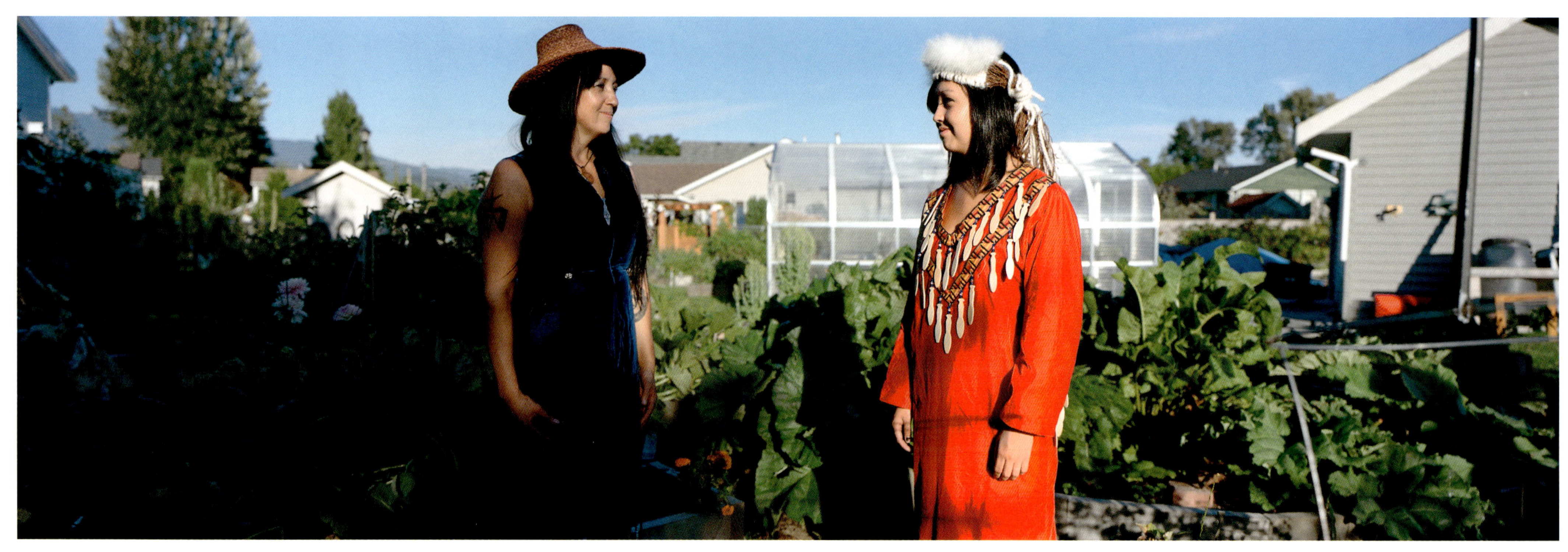

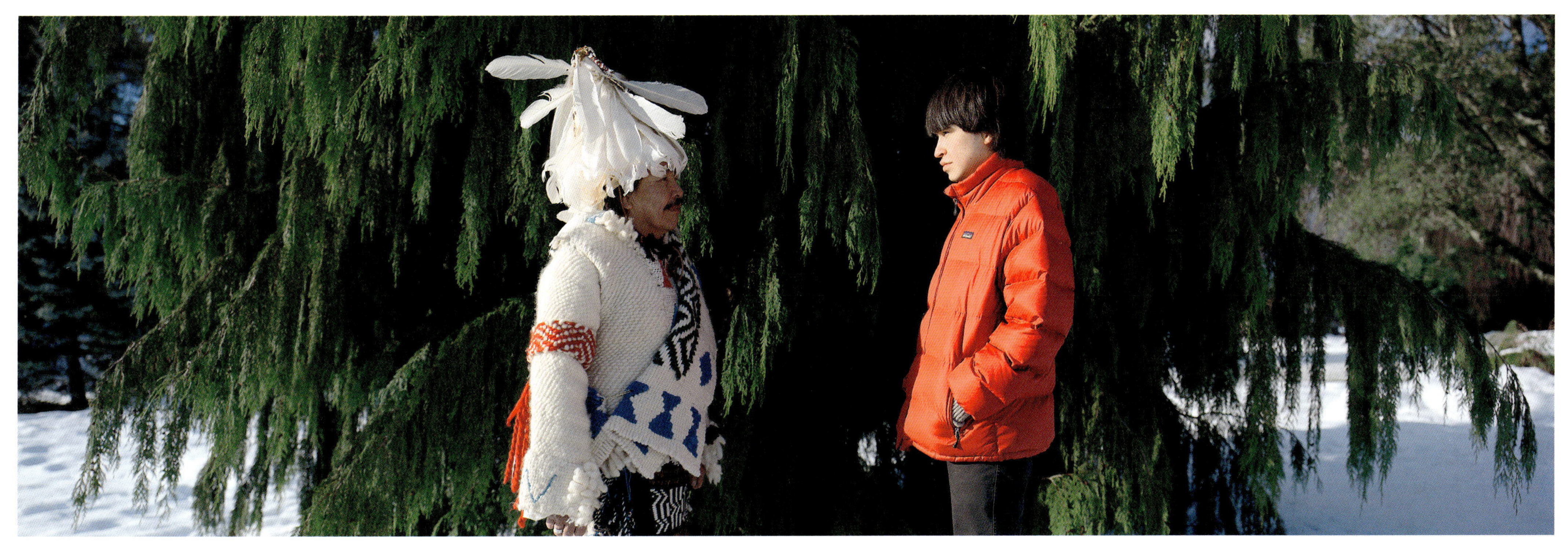

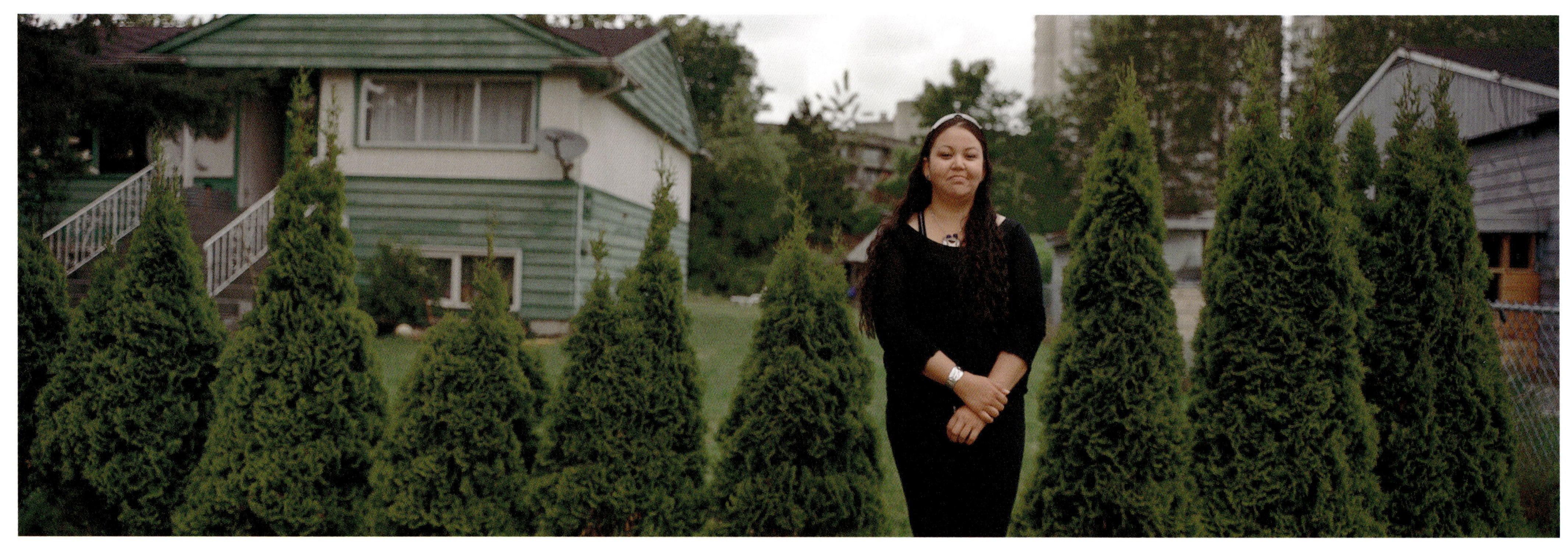

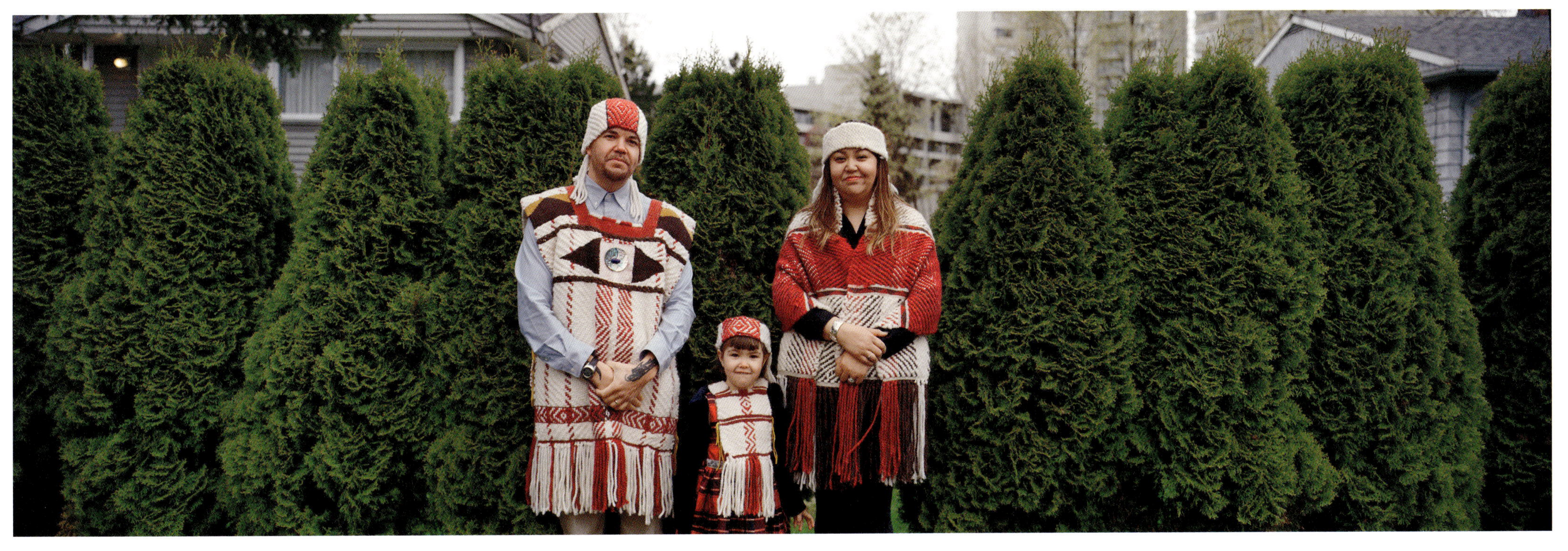

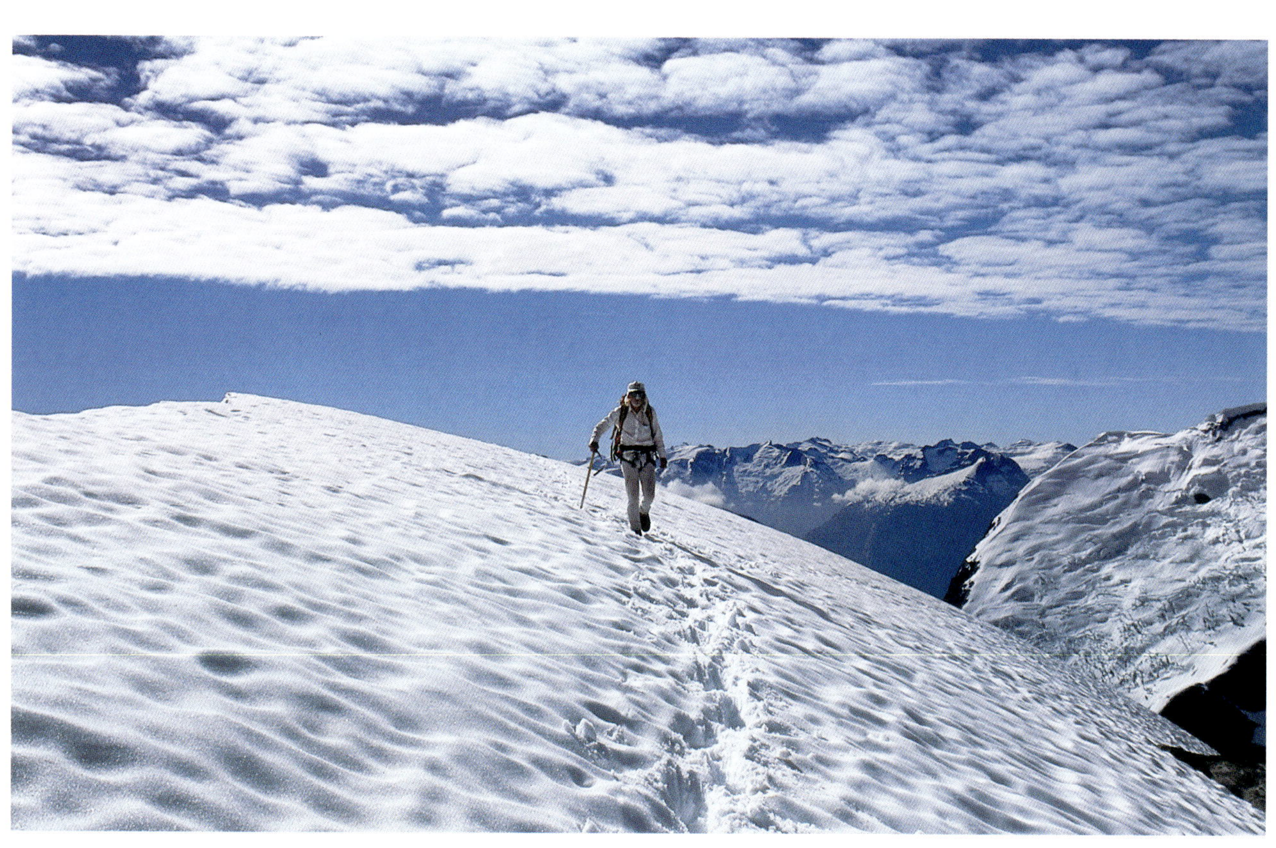

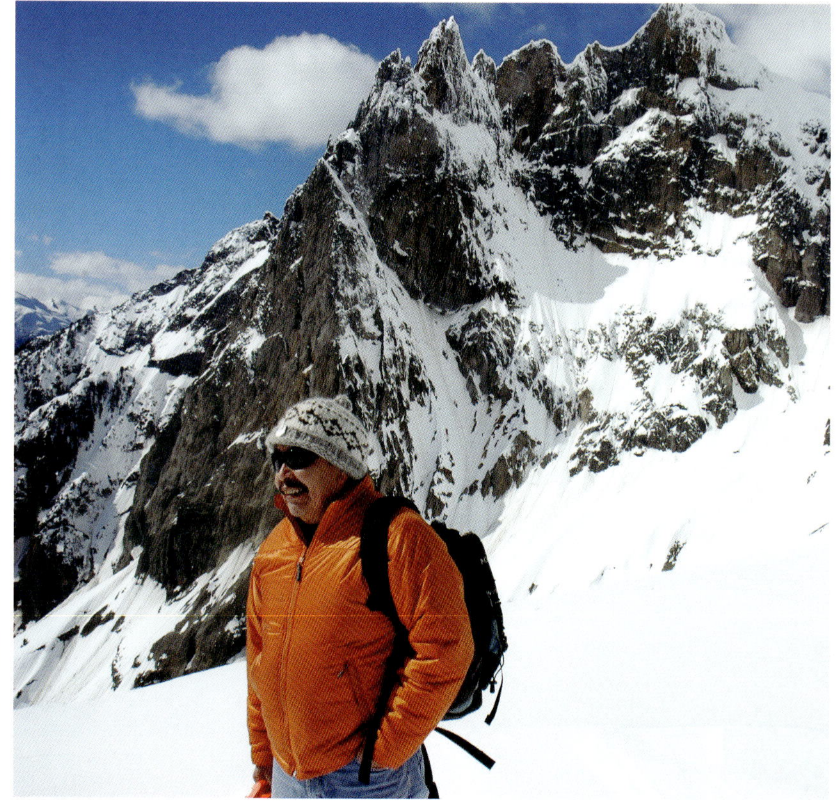

THREE

facing left: **John Clarke**, photo by Shel Neufeld

facing right: **Chief Bill Williams**, photo by Nancy Bleck, 2007

WATCHING OVER

As Nancy was taking photographic journeys, John was preparing to take Chief Bill on a trek across his own territory, to places he had not yet been. In European terms, John had done over six hundred "first ascents" of the peaks in B.C., more than any human alive. But he himself acknowledged that the real first ascents would have been made by indigenous peoples, on their own land, with no need to "discover" or conquer any peaks.

When the Witness Project began, John knew the moment had arrived to change his wandering ways. For the first time in thirty-three years he did not take off on a six-month journey in the mountains. Instead, he hung out on the sandbar at Sims Creek and took whoever was interested out on shorter hikes. He didn't do it grudgingly, far from it. He simply recognized when he met Nancy and Chief Bill that a new journey was starting.

John brought a contagious joy wherever he walked. Everyone felt it. Drew Leathem credits John with being one of the reasons he was drawn to the project in the first place: he was literally like an energy source. Drew describes a journey to Princess Louisa Inlet that John took a group of Witness volunteers on as the "funniest trip he'd ever been on." Aaron, too, remembers him as a funny, funny man: "The first time I went up to Witness, two people stood out: Nancy and John. There was a big group of people there, and I saw this crazy white hair sticking up out of the crowd. And I saw John, and I saw how careful he was with people; he was really looking after everyone. And he was a very loving man: he loved the world and he loved the people who lived here and he loved to engage with people. He loved to share jokes, and he loved to do something important."

For John, the magic of exploring new territories did not lie in seeing calendar-style vistas, but in looking around and realizing everything in the landscape is just as "if Christopher Columbus had never arrived." He resisted the "colonizer's legacy" by leaving no traces. The zero-impact version of hiking means no fires, and all garbage carried home. However, it's the trappings of progress that make it all possible, including light weatherproof gear, camp stoves and Gore-Tex. Said John, "It's a humbling experience to realize you need all this equipment to survive in the bush. You will never be more pitifully looked at than when you are being looked at by a wolf. It's almost as if they are saying

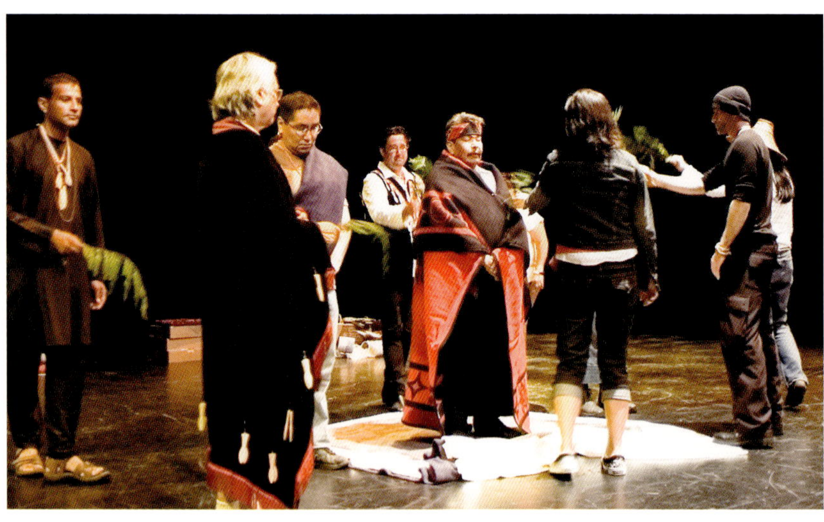

Honouring Chief Bill Williams,
photo by Guy Warrington, 2007

'What is that stuff? What's happened to you! You used to be out here with us, running around out under the stars.'"

Shortly after they met, Chief Bill asked John to guide him on a five-day hike across the glaciers from Princess Louisa Inlet back to the sandbar in time for one of the Witness weekends. From 7,200 feet above sea level, they could see from the northwest corner of Squamish Nation territory into Sims Valley and the Elaho. Chief Bill recalls that it felt so good to see his own territory in such a way, to walk on a similar path and see the same sights that his great-grandfather, who grew up in a traditional village within that area, would have seen as he hiked, hunted and fished there. The view from the peak across the territory is pristine and untouched, not like the view to the south where the land has been developed. And the Witness Project took ten thousand people onto that land on a journey to both nature and culture.

NAMING

Even before the Witness Project began, Chief Bill had noticed that this northern part of their traditional land had a few names the Squamish Nation had never given it. Like the province's name for the area Sims Creek was part of: Tree Farm Licence (TFL) 38. Like the name Randy Stoltmann had proposed for the area he'd precisely mapped out for the provincial government to consider as a "Protected Area Strategy" encompassing four major watershed rainforest valleys—Sims Creek, the Clendenning, the Elaho and the Upper Lillooet (then intact and unlogged): Stanley Smith Wilderness. Like the Western Canada Wilderness Committee's name for that same area: Randy Stoltmann Wilderness Area. This flurry of naming is why Chief Bill had headed up to the area that day in September 1996.

At that time, none of the wilderness or environmental organizations was considering the First Nations' own history and claim on the land they were busy naming. None of them was aware that Chief Bill, his father and his father before him were all "watchmen" over this part of the northern territory. He had centuries of history with that place. Nancy laughs about it now: "By naming, we claim." As settler culture had stamped its names all over the map, a bit of renaming and reclaiming was about to begin.

The Squamish Nation has a traditional ceremony when names are given within the community. Names are passed down to the Squamish people through their ancestors, and acknowledgement of these names is done in a sacred way through naming ceremonies. Witnesses are called when the "work" is taking place. Nancy explains, "Giving a name is way of acknowledging the work you've already done, but it's also a way of saying we don't want you to stop there, that this is a beginning of a new path, and with this comes a new purpose. They give you this incredible form of honour and you actually change to become the best person you can be; you do your best to carry that name and that purpose in the best way you know how." When a name is given that is not ancestral it is called *ninám̓in*, which is more like a nickname. It doesn't happen often, but there are times when non-indigenous people are given Squamish names. During the Witness Project several people were given *ninám̓in* names, beginning with John Clarke.

On January 18, 1998, the Roundhouse Witness art exhibition closed with a ceremony to name John Clarke *X̱wux̱wsél'ḵn* (Mountain Goat). It was the perfect name for him: in honour of his knowledge and respect for the land and also because, as Chief Ian Campbell/*X̱álek̲/Sek̲yú siyám̓* said, with his white hair, shirt and long johns, and the way he hopped around on the mountains, he was just like a mountain goat. (When John died of cancer in 2003, his funeral was held at the Squamish Nation Recreation Centre, with a Squamish Nation–style ceremony. It was attended by hundreds of people, and it was the first time such a funeral was held, on reserve, for a non–First Nations person with no family ties to the Nation. By being named, John had been claimed. He was family, now and forever.)

Nancy received her name *Slánay̓ Sp'áḵw'us* (Woman Eagle) in 2001. It was given in recognition of her gift of vision, since eagles can see from far away and also have excellent sight up close. She acknowledges that receiving a name in a traditional way from such a strong and ancient culture is also "a new way of seeing your own self, and your own potential begins to happen. Each time that would happen it was a furthering of an opening up, of being embraced by the enormous generosity of this incredible community. It is the highest form of honour one can receive. It's also a deep responsibility."

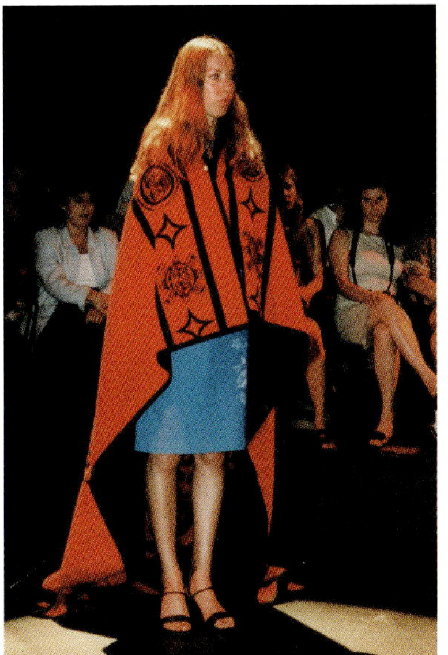

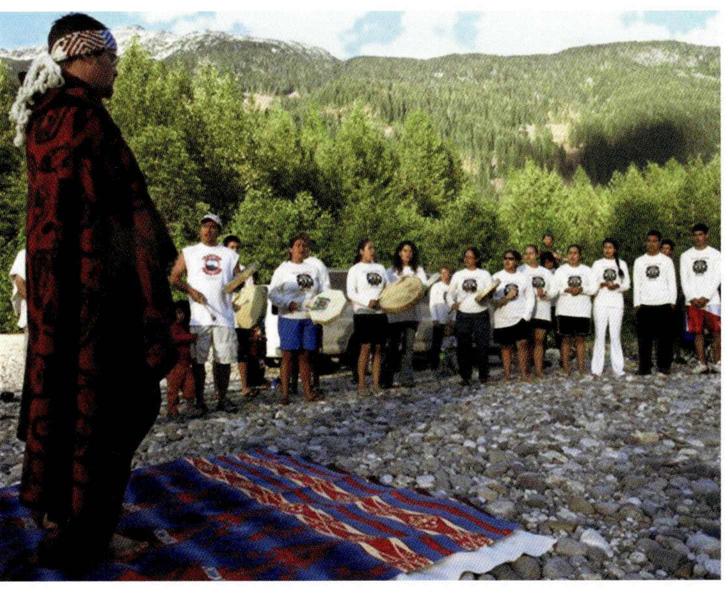

left: **Naming ceremony for Nancy Bleck,** photo by Daniel Collins, 2001

right: **Naming ceremony for Drew Leathem,** photo by Martyn Williams, 2005

(In 2006, Drew was the third person to be given a name, *Tsewátseltn*, which means resourceful person. About his name, Drew said: "I've never received such a prestigious award before. I look at it that way—as an award, as an achievement but also a warning that I need to continue to carry it, to walk with it in a proper and good way for the rest of my journey. I'll carry the name proudly for the rest of my life.")

By 2001, tensions among environmentalists, forest workers, artists, community activists and the Squamish Nation had been escalating, and people were on edge.

Logging threats were at a pivotal point, and more violence in the woods was feared.

The Squamish Nation had taken over naming this area in their territory, and around 2001 it added Utsám̓, which is the Squamish word for calling witnesses, to the Witness Project and it became known as the Utsám̓ Witness project. It was the time to take some more direct action.

VERIFYING/TK̲WÁYANI7M

The situation in 2001 was desperate. The area defined by Interfor as "cut-block 72-4" was scheduled for logging that spring. Interfor had said it was planning a public consultation process, but one employee had questioned whether there had been a "significant interest in the area." This comment was made despite the demonstrated interest by the more than five thousand people who had participated in the camping weekends and other Witness events to that point.

During the project, those designated as witnesses were accepting a responsibility to remember and, if called upon in future, to speak their memories. In 2001, witnesses were called upon to do just that. In so doing, Witness transformed a cut-block into a sacred space, and it did it by invoking a poetic licence that pre-empted Interfor's own sham of a public consultation process and replaced it with Squamish Nation protocol.

April 28, 2001, 12 PM. Location: Northern Squamish Nation Traditional Territory. Sims Creek, mile 56, cut-block 72-4. Hereditary Chief Bill Williams/*telálsemk̲in siýám̓* invited all those who had ever participated in Witness to attend a sacred ceremony known as *tk̲wáyani7m* (t-k-WHY-a-nay7-um), dating from more than ten thousand years in Squamish Nation history. He invited the media too. As the press release stated, "For the first time in B.C., Native and non-Native people will gather in this traditional Coast Salish ceremony to speak to what is happening in the remaining ancient rainforests in Sims Creek."

On the edge of a clear-cut, Byron Joseph/*Tsewk̲wílem* loudly spoke these words: "Interfor, you have awoken a bear!" Bears, awoken from their long winter's nap may not be plump and glossy, but they are still very large and definitely cranky. After Byron's powerful opening words, dozens more spoke, bearing witness to how they felt about the land, and about this place. More than four hundred people, including the media, attended this unprecedented event. It was clear that Utsám̓ Witness had transformed from an art project and camping weekends to a protocol-setting movement. And now it would prove to be unstoppable.

Nothing like this had ever happened before.

By opening up the witness ceremony to people outside his Nation, Chief Bill had taken a risk, and now the risk really paid off. As he puts it, "Utsám̓ Witness showed Squamish Nation people they had a right to return to sacred places." It drew back members of the Nation who knew the ceremonies and knew the locations to hold them but they were afraid to go because lumber company ownership meant they felt ostracized in their own land. It drew in urban indigenous youth, many of whom had not

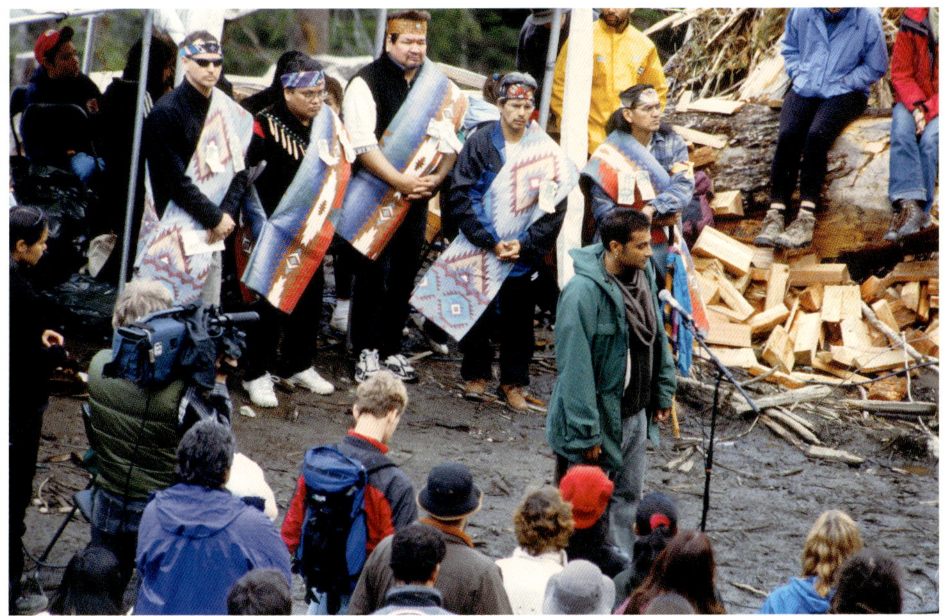

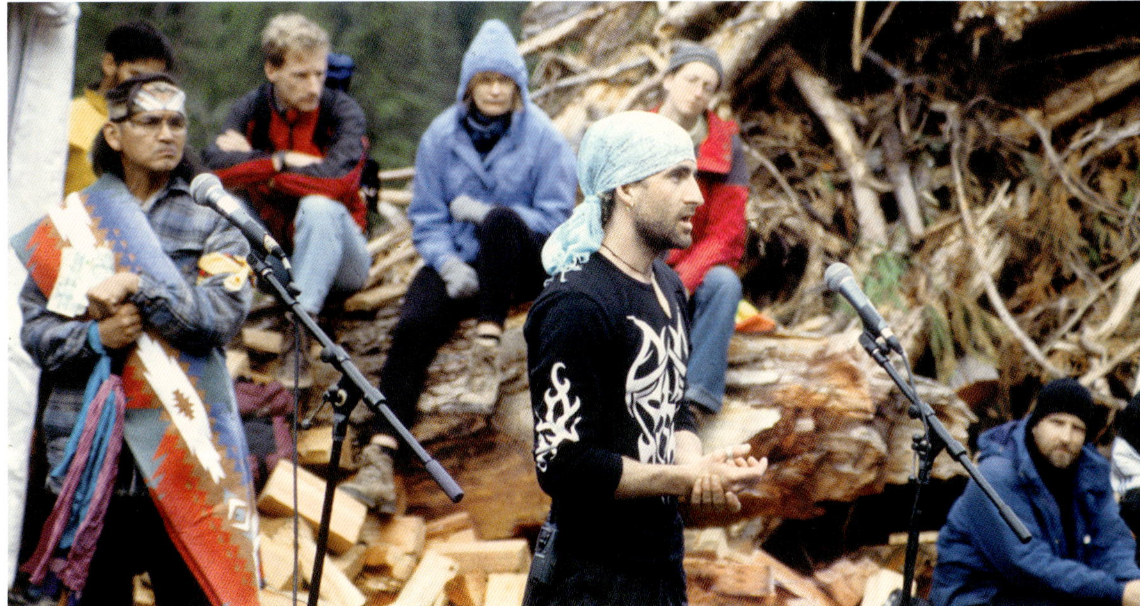

left: **Verification ceremony, Amir Ali Alibhai,** photo by Shel Neufeld, 2001

right: **Verification ceremony, Gregory Byrne,** photo by Shel Neufeld, 2001

experienced the land and ceremony in this way before. Out of this project, the Aboriginal Youth Ambassador program was formed. It made the general public aware of Squamish peoples, their culture and the deep attachment they feel for the land. All of these things would have an impact on what came next: the *tk̲wáyani7m* ceremony was proof.

Chief Bill describes *tk̲wáyani7m*, which means verification, as a term that is used when somebody questions whether or not an event has taken place. He explains: "What set this off, in this instance, was a meeting. Nancy, John and myself were there on the 26th floor of the Bentall towers. Ric Slaco of Interfor, and one of the managers—one of the five Daves—was there. Interfor had hired five managers, and for some reason each of their first names was Dave, so I don't know which Dave we were talking to that day. But in any case this was April when we sat down with Ric Slaco to talk about the May, June, July Witness weekends."

"This Dave-the-manager said: 'I have never heard of Witness, what are you guys doing? I'm pretty sure it's something we don't want to have happen in the TFL.' In response to Dave, Nancy and I pointed out that we had already sat down with Ric Slaco and brought it to his attention: 200 cards from participants of Witness over the summer who signed a self-identified declaration saying they liked what they saw in terms of Witness, and whatever other comment that they wanted to make. We had gifted these cards with comments to Ric Slaco the previous August."

Chief Bill did not like being questioned by Dave about what he was doing in his own territory, so he called the witnesses back. There had never been a *tk̲wáyani7m* in his

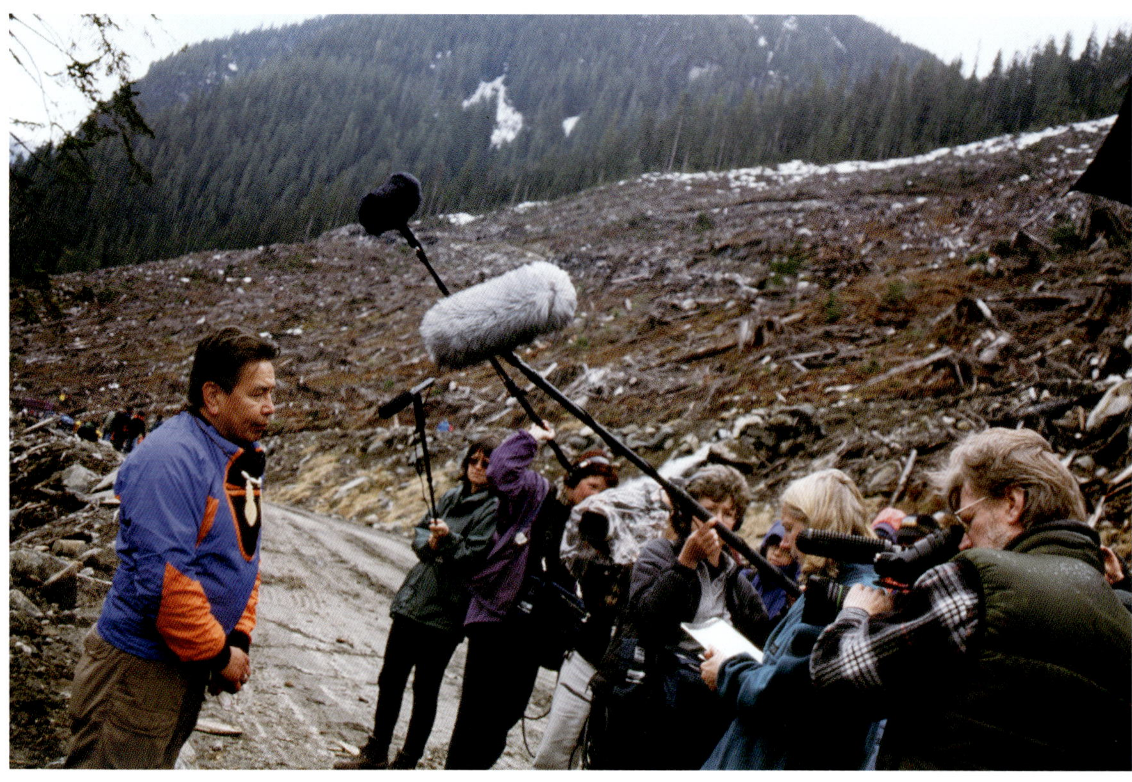

Chief Bill Williams in the media,
photo by Nancy Bleck, 2001

lifetime, and there had never been one involving non-indigenous public and the media. But there was going to be one now, and he made sure Ric Slaco would be there.

In order to do the verification ceremony, Chief Bill had to find out what the protocol for calling back the witnesses would be: "I had to go back and contact at least ten different Speakers that I had hired, and then each of those ten different Speakers had to contact each of the people that he had called as witnesses for that event. We had the privilege and honour to work with WC² at that time, and they in fact helped us a lot, because they sent out notices to their people, organized buses, and we sent out notices through local newspapers, and asked people who were witnesses to please show up at the *tk̲wáyani7m*. At the event we had the ten speakers, recognized and re-blanketed, and we had people step forward and talk about the Witness Project."

In his letter to the past participants he wrote:

> You will recall that with each Witness ceremony, participants were reminded that they might one day be called to verify what they did, and saw, in the course of their Witness experience. I am now calling on you to do exactly that. The time has come when all witnesses, participants and people that the project has touched are being called back to make their voices heard as witnesses for our sacred wilderness.

The culture of the environmental groups in B.C. had shifted. For the first time in the area of Sims Creek, the Western Canada Wilderness Committee was working with the Squamish Nation to protect their traditional territory—and WCWC had long ago stopped referring to it as the Randy Stoltmann Wilderness Area.

Chief Ian Campbell remembers, "Those areas were very interesting during that day because the situation pitted environmentalists and forestry companies against each other. Some of the last remaining stands of B.C. forest, with 1,200-year-old Douglas-firs and massive red cedars, and for us, we've always known those places, they resonate, they hum with power and beauty. It was very important for us to protect these areas." He added, "We're not just against development; we've always been forestry conservationists and environmentalists, we've always utilized the natural resources."

Interfor VP and management executive Ric Slaco attended *tk̲wáyani7m* by invitation of Chief Bill Williams, and was shown on national TV thanking Chief Bill for including him. By so doing, he was acknowledging the ceremony as being public process. He became a public witness to the fact that the Squamish Nation and all the Witness participants had demonstrated that people did, in fact, care about the trees of "cut-block 72-4."

And so it was that in 2001 the province of British Columbia and the forest industry's bluff was called. Not long after that verification ceremony, logging in the area was stayed. The Squamish Nation had set a new precedent that had so much power, Interfor had no authority to stop it.

NEXW-ÁYANTSUT, PLACE OF TRANSFORMATION

Before, during and after the decade of Witness, stories were also unfolding anew for the Squamish Nation, with their own history taking on a contemporary context.

This place where Witness was happening had a history of stories and spirit that would never completely belong to the settler nations, no matter how sympathetic or how curious. To really experience the spirit of the place takes a certain kind of time.

All this naming that had been floating around caused Chief Bill to seek the traditional name of the area around Sims Creek that was part of TFL 38. He went to the elders, and Chief Ian's grandfather Lawrence Baker/*X̱álek̲-t/S̱ek̲yú-t siyám̓* told him, "This place is called Nexw-áyantsut (Nook-EYE-en-tsote)." As Chief Ian tells it, "The entrance to Nexw-áyantsut, Sims Creek, is where the Witness Project gathered people from all walks of life, from all denominations. People were welcome to come, to bear witness to the thousands of years of history of the Squamish connection to the land and to the relationship with the spirit realm and to all of creation."

When Chief Bill first met John and Nancy, he had known the story of Nexw-áyantsut, but none of them knew that the place they were camping was literally on the threshold of such an important story. Chief Bill says, "Nexw-áyantsut is a very powerful word that is very rarely used. It means a transformation or a place of transformation. The story that we have about its history is probably before the time of when the animals turned their back to us as human beings." The story speaks to the deep connection to the land and to the animals, through the very ancient story of a young man, a young woman and a family of mountain goats.

Nexw-áyantsut is a very significant location in Squamish Nation mythology, and when Lawrence Baker revealed the name, Chief Bill responded: "The place where the man transforms from a human to an animal spirit?" Although there was evidence at every turn of just how much the Utsám̓ Witness project was transformational for people, for places, no one had been thinking consciously about the wild spirit myth that lives in this very location. Yet Chief Ian and Chief Bill had given John the *ninám̓in* name of the animal spirit—*X̱wux̱wsél'kn*, meaning mountain goat—whose story lived there before, during and after the Utsám̓ Witness project.

Chief Bill had found even more reason to make sure that this area did not remain TFL 38. This place had a spiritual and cultural significance with a history as old as the trees. If you are so lucky as to have *telálsemḵin siy̓ám̓* tell you even part of the story of Nexw-áyantsut, you need some time. Maybe a lifetime.

But for the rainforests, lifetimes were running out. Imagine trying to conduct ceremonies while Sikorsky helicopters are taking a log out of the forest every minute, for days on end, which is exactly what was going on in areas not far from Sims Creek.

Although the project was so specific to the location in which it took place, it at the same time represented a universal struggle for Indigenous sovereignty and for the inherent integrity of the land. Before the Utsám̓ Witness project began, at the *nice place to be* exhibit of work by Emily Carr students in '95, James Nicholas had invoked the words of Thomas Banyacya of the Hopi Sovereign Nation—one of four "interpreters" selected to carry the message of Hopi prophecy to the world and, at that time, the last living spiritual leader of these ancient and sacred wisdoms:

> I have studied comparative religion and I think in your own nations and cultures you have knowledge of the consequences of living out of balance with nature and spirit.
>
> Nature, the First People and the spirit of our ancestors are giving you loud warnings. Today, December 10, 1992, you see increasing floods, more damaging hurricanes, hailstorms, climate changes and earthquakes as our prophecies said would come. Even animals and birds are warning us with strange change in their behavior such as the beaching of whales. Why do animals act like they know about Earth's problems and most humans act like they know nothing?

Later, both James and Nancy realized how prophetic these words were in light of Witness.

From deep within his own territory, and adding a new chapter to the stories that will be told to generations to come, Chief Bill Williams had decided it was time to inform the Province of British Columbia that this was sacred land. He was not negotiating this time, just serving notice that the Nation had its own plan for their land.

The Squamish Nation had started a *X̱ay Temíxw* (Sacred Land) Land Use Plan of its own, the first draft of which was unveiled for public consultation on the Nation's website in 2001. Over the next thirty days, the website was flooded with more than 75,000 visits.

Melanie Rivers explains, "Witness really got the ball rolling on a number of issues in our community, such as getting a Squamish Land Use Plan together. And that was born out of the relationships that were built at Witness and some of the experiences that happened there.

"Witness brought a number of Squamish people who lived in the city onto their traditional territory, and had brought people closer and more connected to their own land. People were asked in the Nation how they wanted our traditional territory to be used, for different purposes, such as for cultural purposes, spiritual purposes, medicines, as well as areas for logging. It's hard to go to a government and ask for what you want if you haven't defined what you want. The Squamish Land Use Plan did that for our community."

Drew Leatham recalls: "Witness was such a simple thing: taking city people camping. I was amazed and astounded though, over the time that I worked with it, how much it accomplished. We built a full-blown land and resource management plan for the Squamish Nation, partly by virtue that we had people visiting all aspects and areas of the traditional territory as a regular part of the Witness Project." Drew's work with the youth of the Squamish Nation had made him an obvious fit to work on the land use plan when it began in 2001, and he was part of the community engagement team that interviewed more than sixty members of the Nation about their views on how their traditional territory should be used.

Chief Ian Campbell identified the project as "an important dynamic that solidified a lot of those processes, because there was a debate, in public, in the media, with propaganda from forestry companies and government, and we said that we're not going to side with anybody: we're going to take our Squamish lens of the world and we're going to do this in our way. I'm very proud but I can't take ownership for that; it's taken generations of effort to get to that point. So I feel like a relay runner: I simply just take the baton from my predecessors and do the best that I can while I still have those responsibilities, ultimately to bestow that onto our future generations so it is that legacy that we are continuing to lead, and of course Utsám̓ is an integral part of that."

Although some battles (like the forest above the sandbar at Sims Creek) were lost, the true beauty of it all is that Witness won the war. Not by fighting, but through sharing stories, through ceremony. By the end of the project, more than ten thousand people had a chance to see, and have their say. No one was hurt. No one was arrested.

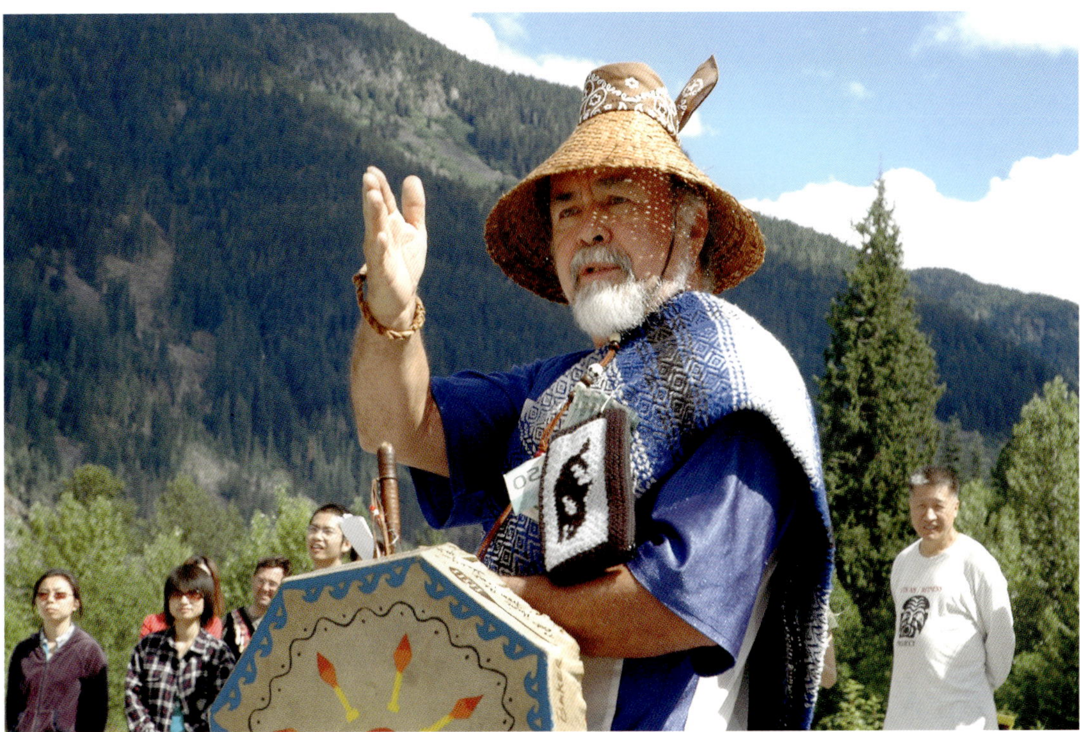

Speaker, S7áplek̲, Bob Baker,
photo by Nancy Bleck, 2006

DREAMING FORWARD

2006

For a million years or more, we humans lived outside, under the sun and stars, our lives guided by the seasons, the weather and the tides. For all this time we were a community of plants and animals, where day-to-day living, landscape and spirituality were intertwined. The Witness camping weekends reconnect us, however briefly, with that world. When we drink from the cold mountain streams, or sit around the fire at night, we are coming home to that place from which we all evolved.

JOHN CLARKE / X̱WEX̱WSÉLḴN, CONSERVATIONIST AND MOUNTAINEER

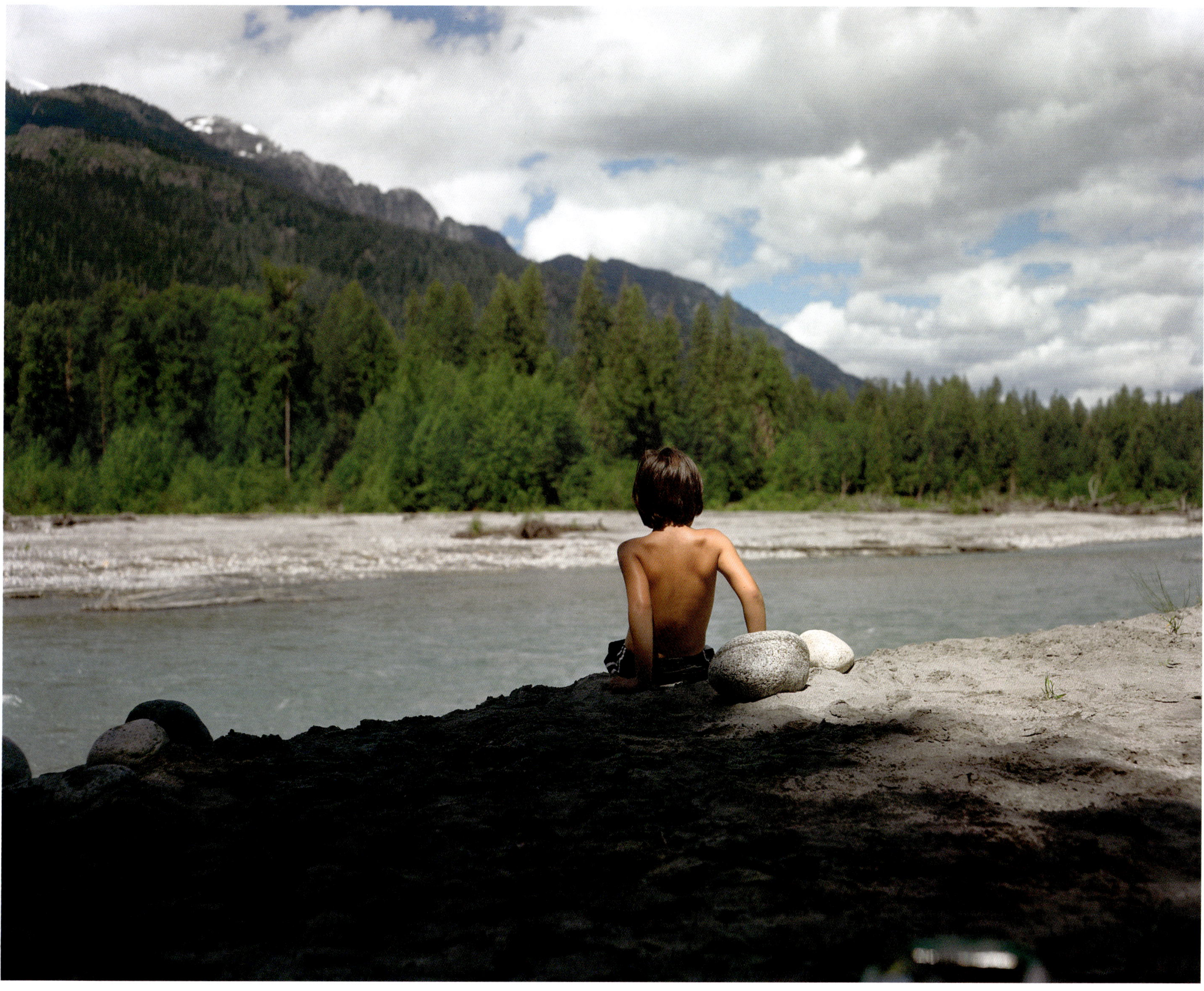

I think that working together between cultures, more than any other single activity, learning from another culture, sharing world views, sharing perspectives on climate, on sustainability, on the environment, is one of the single most important ways that we will not only get our own ideas but receive the inspiration necessary to make change.

DREW LEATHEM / TSEWÁTSELTN

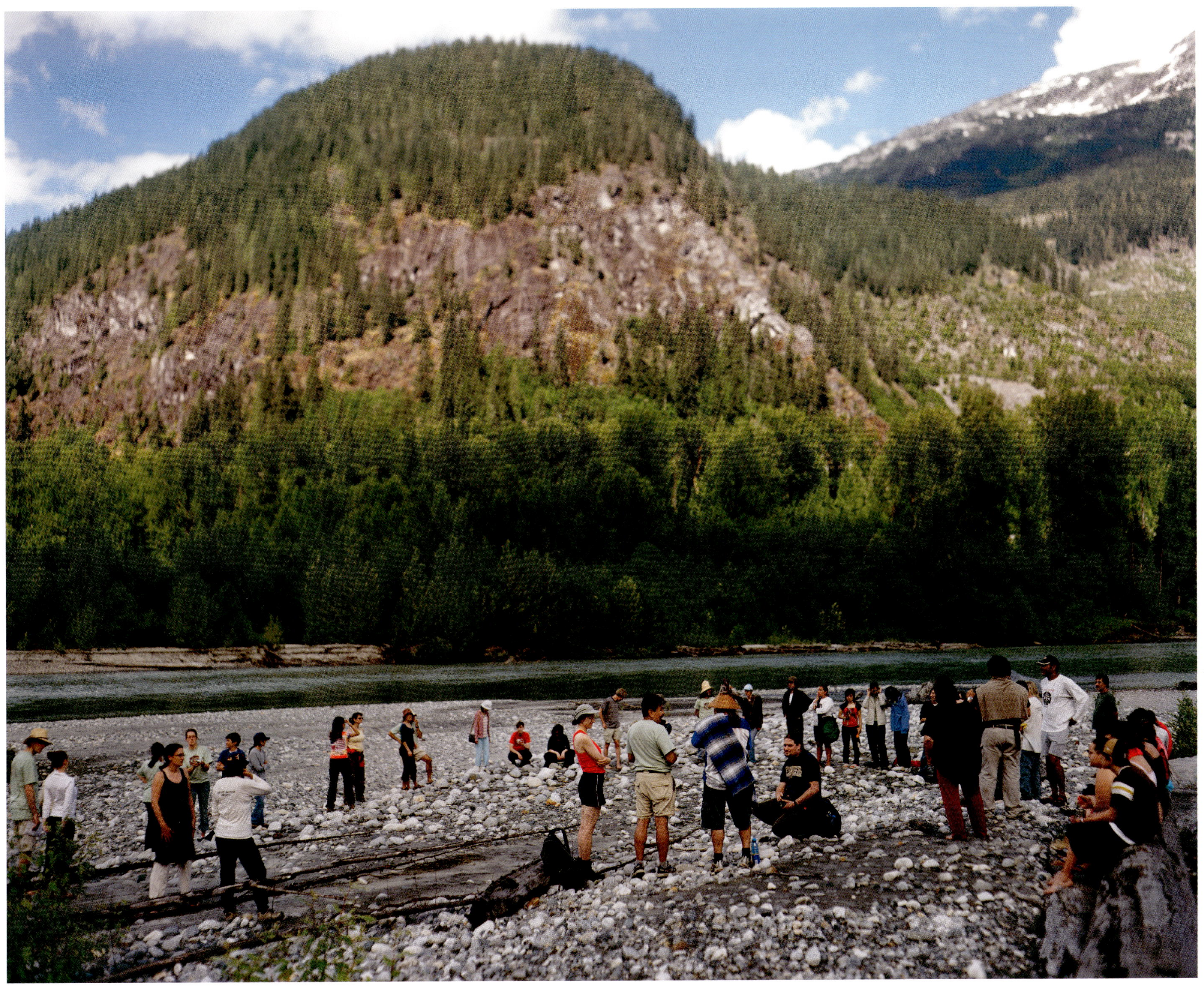

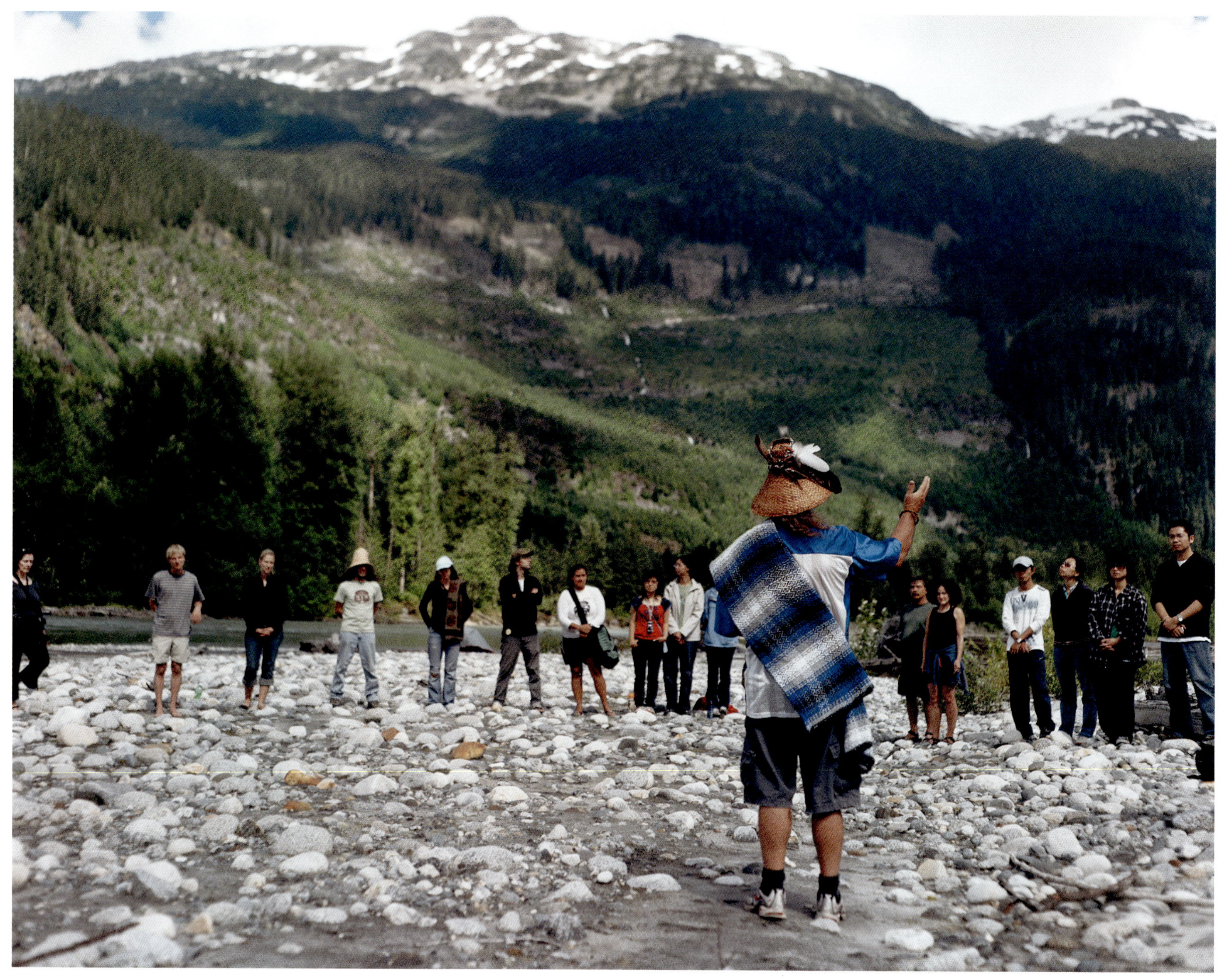

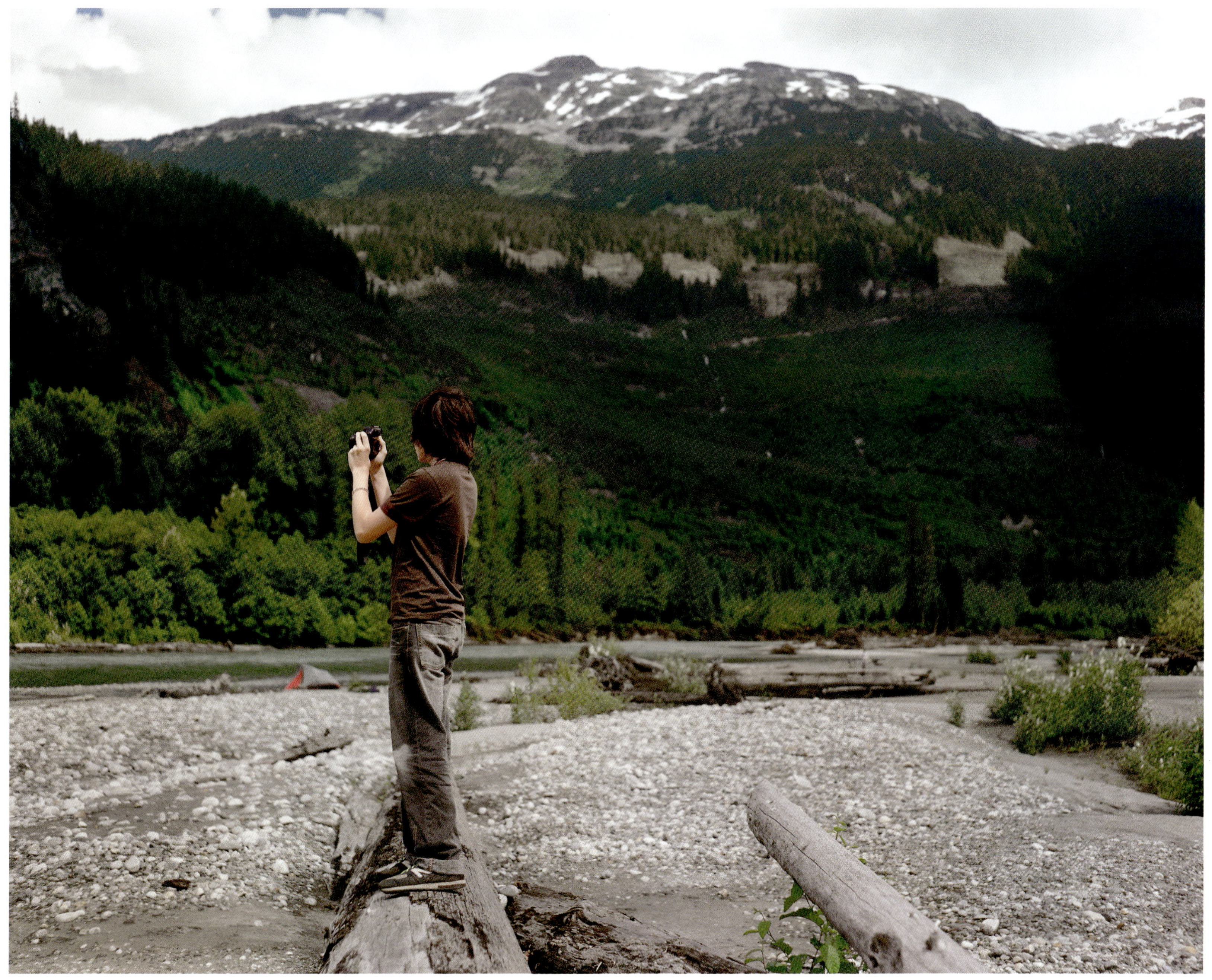

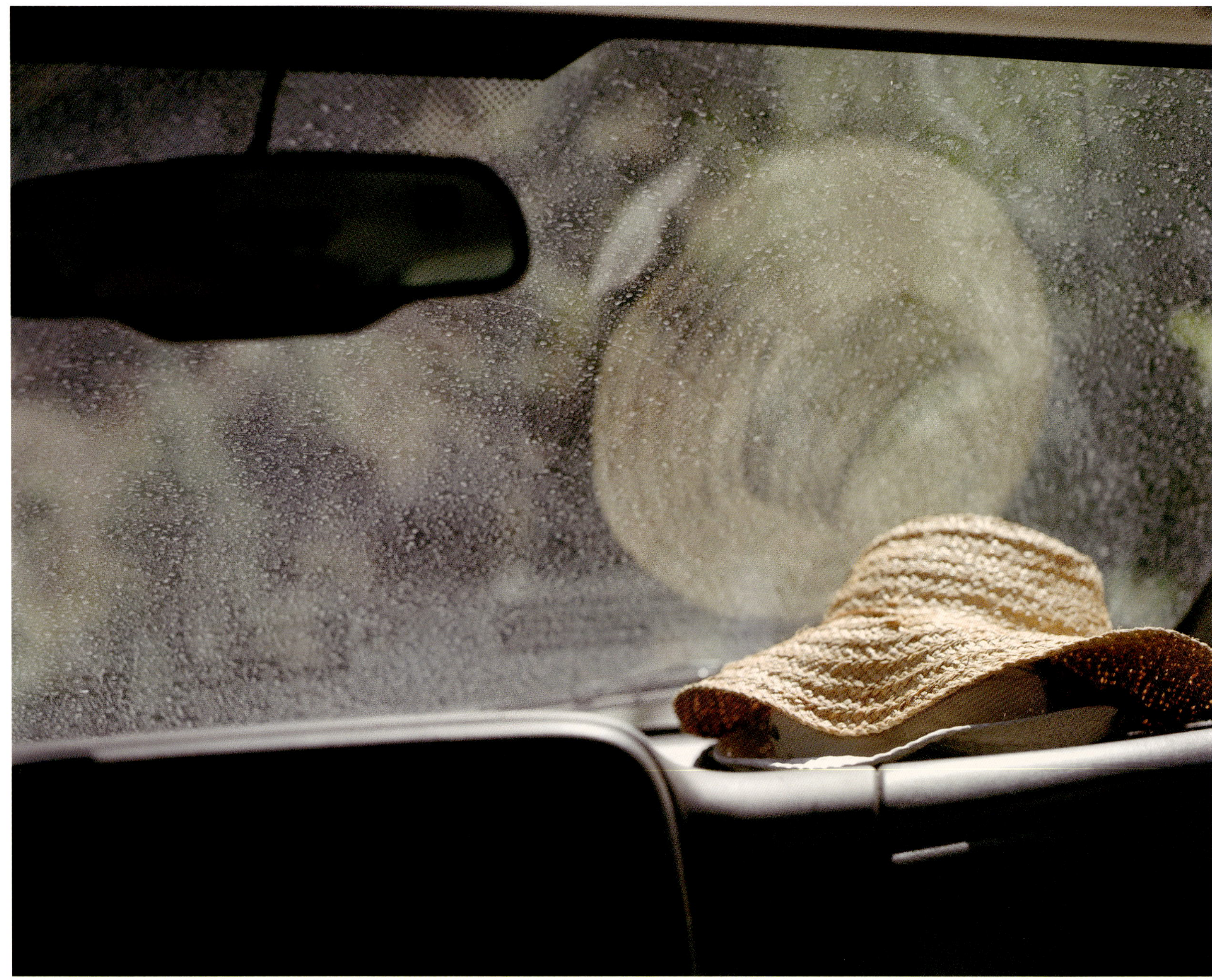

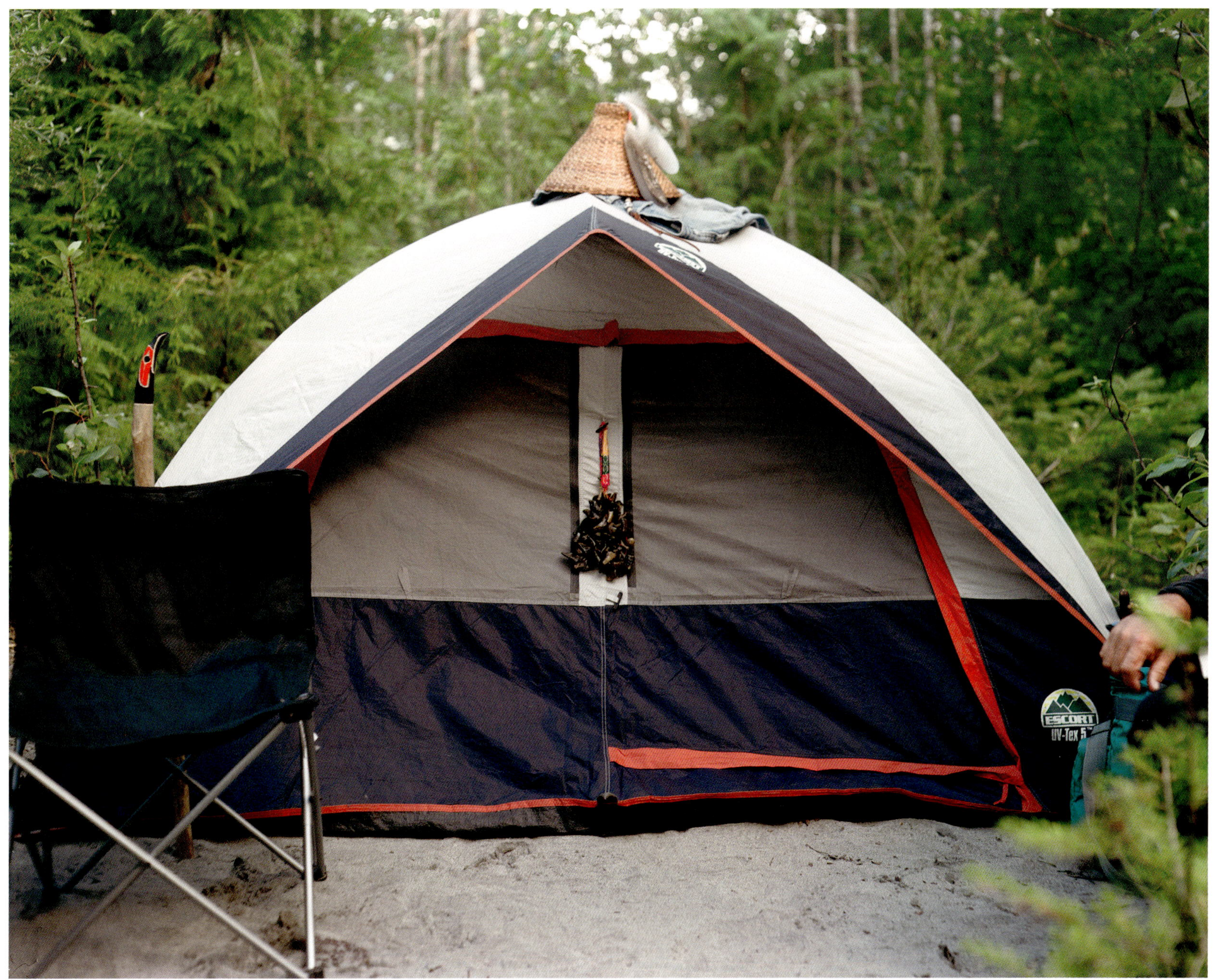
ESCORT
UV-Tex 5

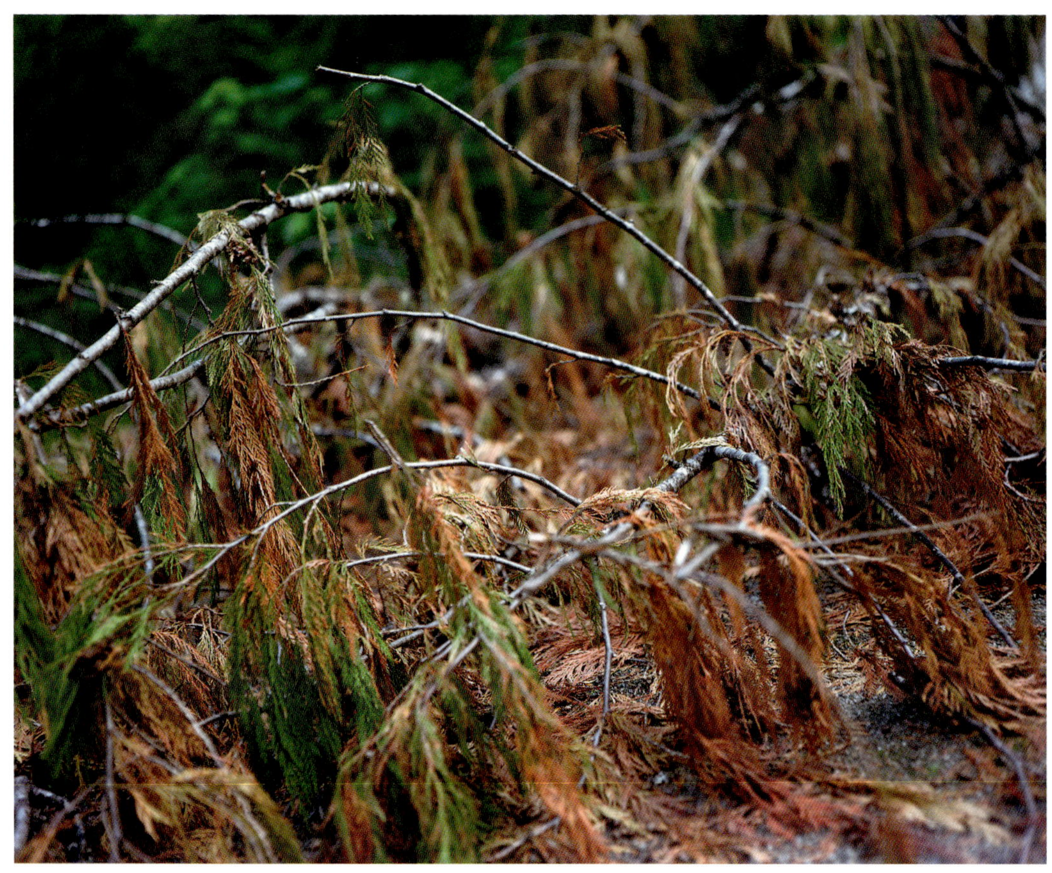

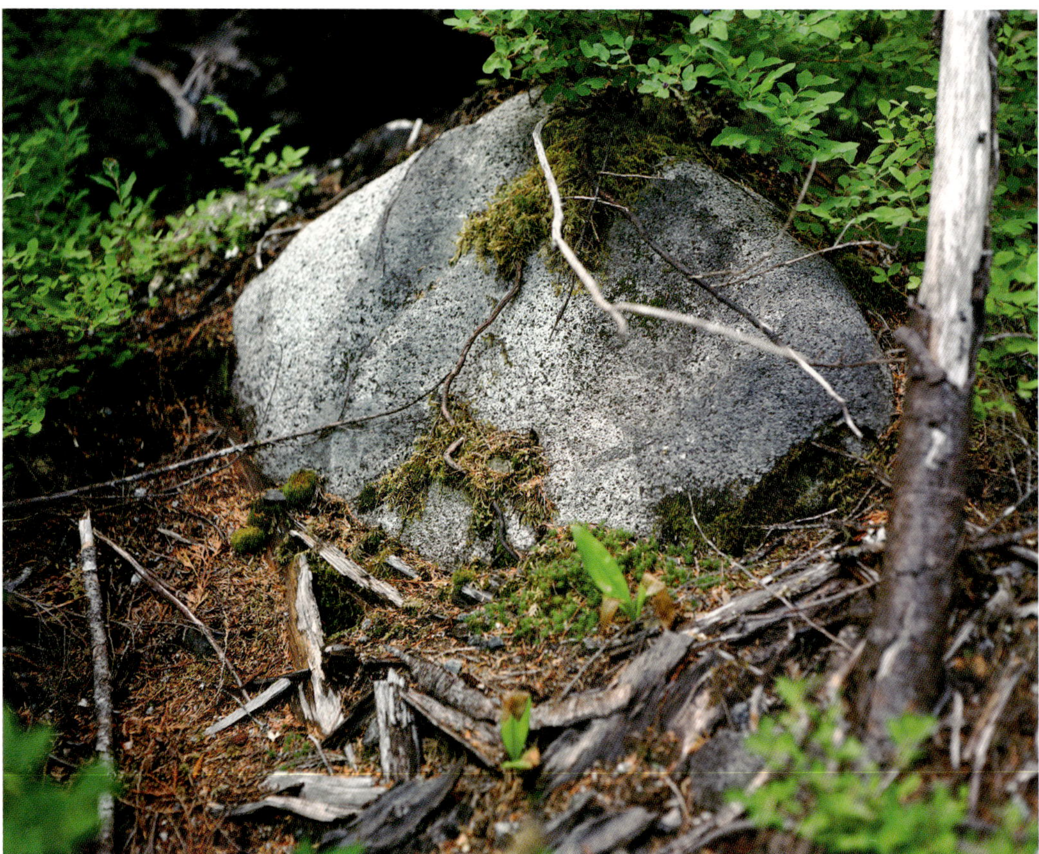

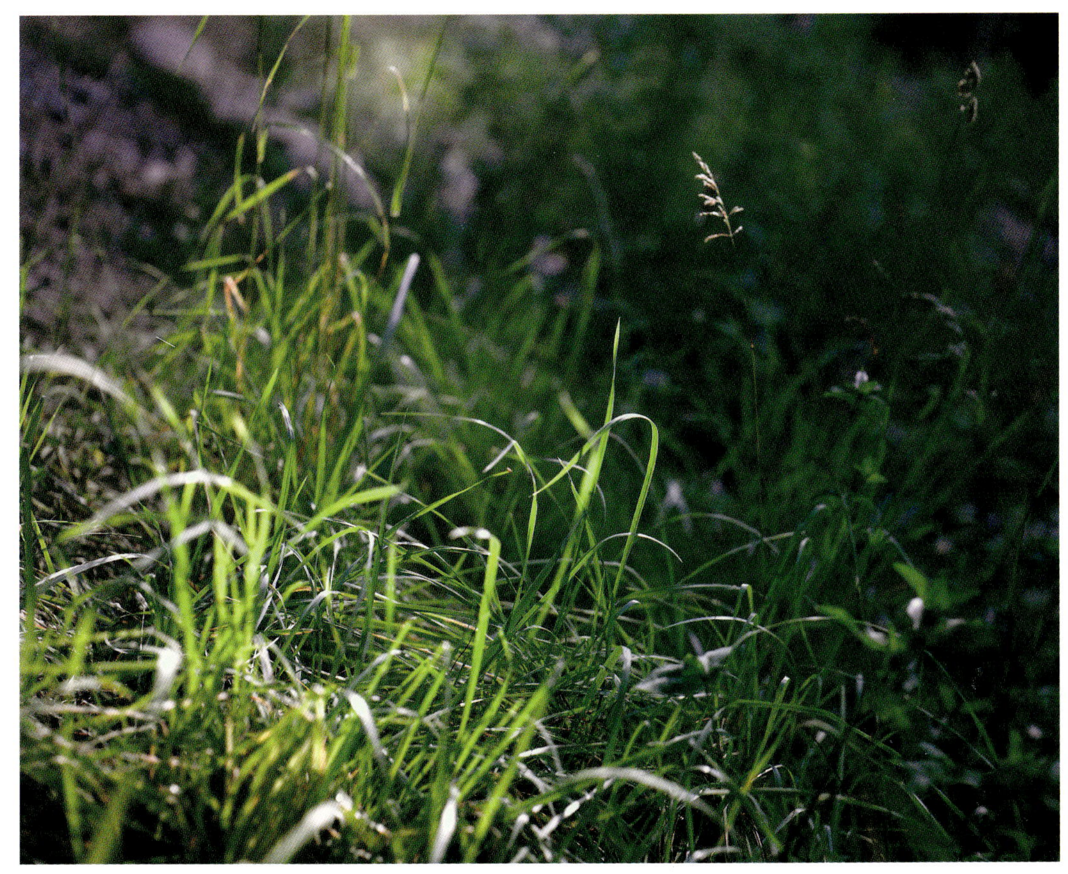

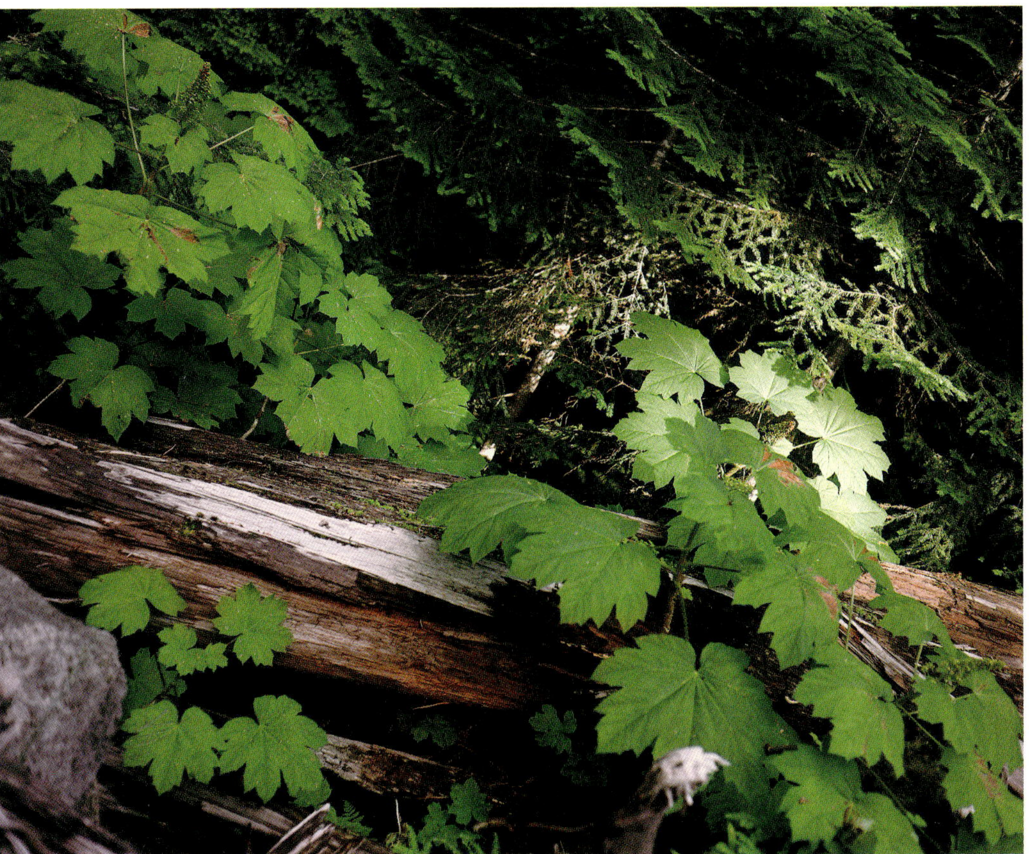

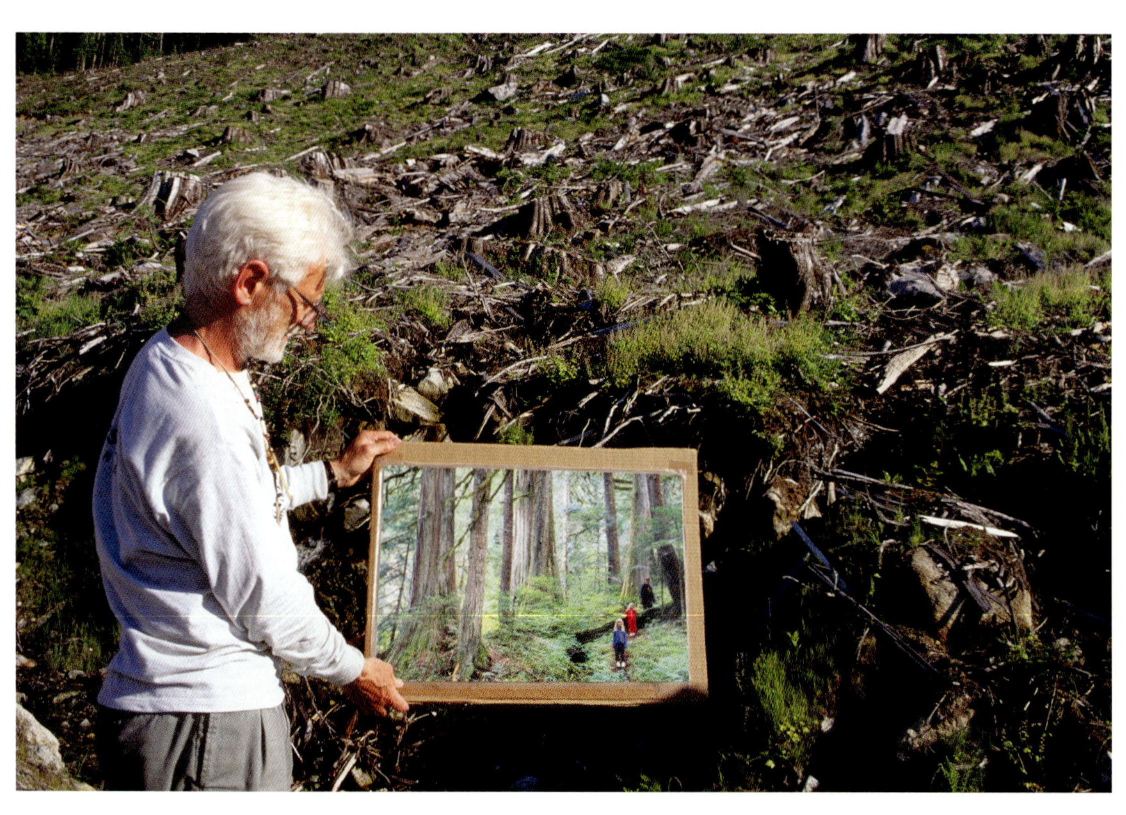

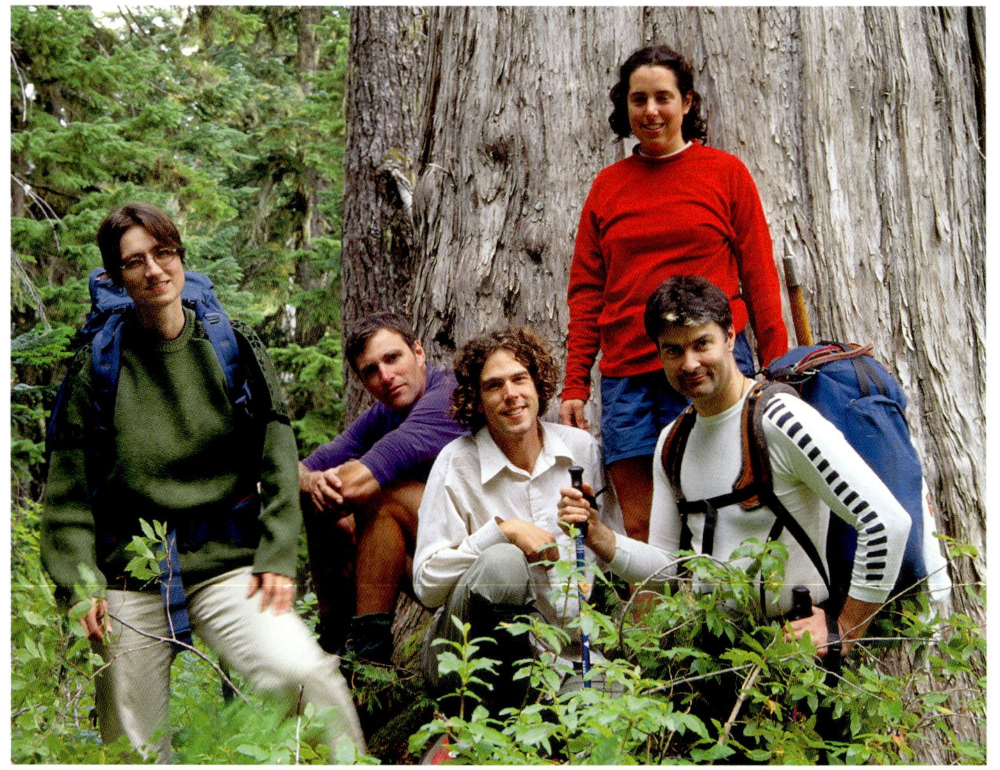

FOUR

MAPPING CHANGE

In 2005, Chief Bill Williams/*telálsemk̲in siỷám̓* signed an agreement with the provincial government to set aside the Wild Spirit Places, *Kwa kwayx welh-aynexws*, which includes Sims Creek and Nexw-áyantsut as a protected area under the Squamish Nation's *X̲ay Temíxw* (Sacred Land) Land Use Plan. That plan looks forward not the typical corporate five years, but five hundred, ensuring that old-growth cedar would have time to mature, and grow big enough to carve ocean-growing canoes.

Chief Ian Campbell/*X̲álek̲/Sek̲yú siỷám̓* said shortly afterward: "As a negotiator, I am very pleased that we were able to produce the *X̲ay Temíxw*, our Squamish (Sacred Land) Land Use plan, and in our land use planning we designated *Kwa kwayx welh-aynexws*, Wild Spirit Places. This was something that we said at the table with the province: we're not asking permission, we are asserting that these areas are sacred. And these were the last un-roaded, non-industrial valleys in our territory, and they comprise about 50,000 hectares, which is about 8% of the Squamish traditional territory—Sims Creek, Nexw-áyantsut, being one of them."

As of March 29, 2010, the summit that had been known as Sun Peak was officially named Mount John Clarke by the provincial government. This was the result of the vision and efforts of John's mountaineering friends Lisa Baile, John Baldwin and Glenn Woodsworth. Drew Leathem points out that a lot of climbers name peaks after themselves, but despite his many "first ascents," not John. Drew adds: "John Clarke would be very embarrassed that his name is now on a map, but he would be secretly really happy. I can't see him admitting to it publicly, but I think knowing that a peak stands with his name on it, he would see that as one of the biggest honours that any human being can achieve."

If you were to hike up the glaciated summit that is Mount John Clarke, as part of the Loquilts–Bug Lake traverse between Princess Louisa Inlet and Sims Creek, you would overlook the Sims Valley where Utsám̓ Witness took place, within the area that was known, and is now again known as Nexw-áyantsut, Place of Transformation.

If you were to pull out a map—these places, these names would both be there. These areas will remain set

facing left: **John Clarke**, photo by Shel Neufeld, 1999

facing right: **Sabine**, **Dwayne**, **Shel**, **Christy**, **Scott**, photo by Shel Neufeld

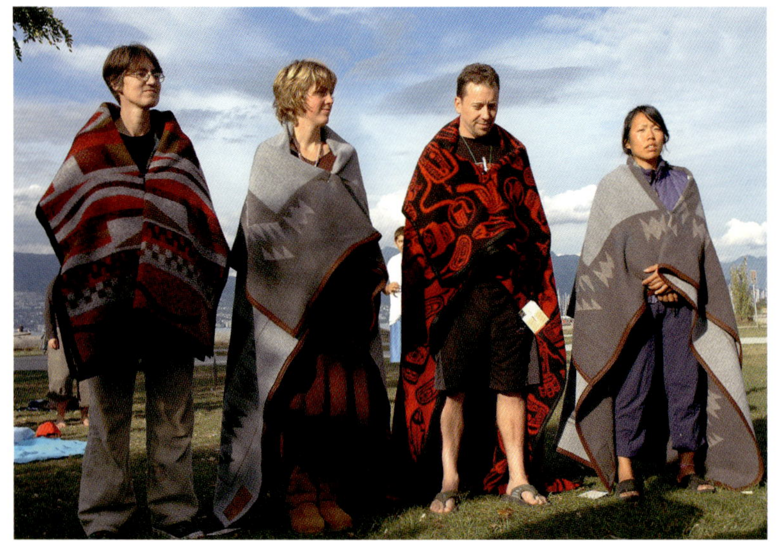

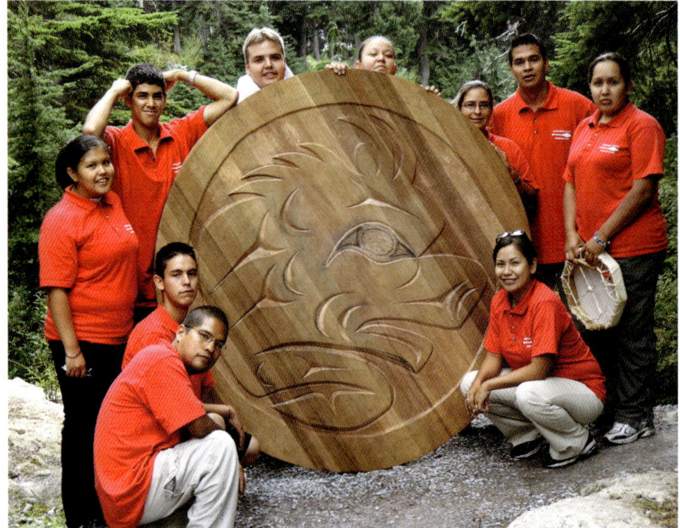

left: **Honouring volunteers Sabine, Sarah, Mark and Janey,** photo by Nancy Bleck, 2005

right: **Cultural Youth Ambassadors,** photo by Drew Leathem, 2005

aside for spiritual and cultural use. Untouched, forever and a day, never to be logged. Always to be respected.

LEGACY

Utsám̓ Witness formally ended as a project in 2007 after ten years because, once the area was formally protected and restored to its traditional name of Nexw-áyantsut, the work that began in Sims Creek was done.

When Utsám̓ Witness started, there was no clear course of action, only a desire to *do something*. However, the only sure outcome back then was that if nothing was attempted, the area would have been logged out. That was Interfor's plan.

But a different plan prevailed. It is important to recognize that tension is part of the medium of collaboration, that out of what really did begin as a desperate attempt to save a forest turned into a series of solutions that were at first unimaginable in their specifics. There was only one common ground in the beginning: the idea that if people experienced the land and accepted the "invitation to witness," the inevitability of the area being entirely clear cut could be turned around. There were no guarantees this approach would work.

However, the outcomes of Utsám̓ Witness were actual and many. Not only did the project preserve the area from logging and assert Squamish Nation sovereignty over its use, it also altered the map of British Columbia to include the Squamish traditional name Nexw-áyantsut and the new name Mount John Clarke. And it provided an example of activism that was more peaceful and inclusive and avoided direct confrontation.

Utsám̓ Witness opened up possibilities across modes, cultures and generations. The solutions crafted were economic, political, personal, artistic, social, tangible and, finally, unstoppable. So if there is any ultimate lesson to take away from Witness, it's that we have to try: we have to pick up the work and run with it. As Aaron Nelson-Moody puts it, the table needs to be carefully set. Then if the right group of people sits down, the work will be done in a good way. It takes protocol, it takes care and it takes time.

Obviously not every one of the ten thousand participants was as deeply tuned in to all the aspects of the project. But every one of them, in however small a way, accepted the invitation to witness, and with this window into Squamish Nation culture came the responsibility to share their concerns. This dialogue was open and, as Nancy said, could go both ways: anyone who attended a camping weekend had the ear of a Chief, for at least a while.

Similarly, not every member of the Squamish Nation was part of the project, but its impact did ripple through their community and many other communities. To put this in perspective, the Squamish Nation at the time the project began had a population of about three thousand people, mainly in urban areas of the Lower Mainland. So to have their culture shared and their concerns amplified by the Utsám̓ Witness community was powerful.

Aaron thinks one of the biggest lasting legacies was what the children observed. He explains, "It's called 'master learning.' You could see the little kids watching us, oblivious to our formality, but they'd be looking at the adults and what we were modelling. When a child sees something done many times, and when it is done, and the attitude it is done with, one day they just do it themselves."

Chief Bill now talks about how many of the people of hisNation, and especially the young people, feel comfortable going out on their own land. It has to be remembered that before the Witness project, this was not the case; in fact, many of the Nation's youth had never been out of the city. Chief Bill's youngest son, Marc, was only seven when he first attended a Witness weekend. At the time he didn't realize Utsám̓ Witness was having such a "life-changing effect on so many people." He says, "I just thought of it as going camping with my dad."

In some ways, Utsám̓ Witness created both a kind of "land literacy" and a sense of pride and purpose for many Squamish Nation youth. For example, when he was fourteen, Marc picked up a camera and started to explore the idea of witnessing the world through that lens. Others developed their confidence through Chief Bill's strategy to get youth onto the land through Witness.

Specifically, in 2000, the "E Team" was born from Drew Leathem's request to do more for the Nation. He and Chief Bill set up the Utsám̓ Witness Society to flow through funding and were able to access provincial money for eight youth to form an Environmental Youth Team. In the beginning they helped with logistics, including setting up and taking down the campsites during Witness weekends, and taking away the temporary toilets. But during the week they explored the territory, learning more about what their ancestors would have done to survive on the land. In addition, their exposure to

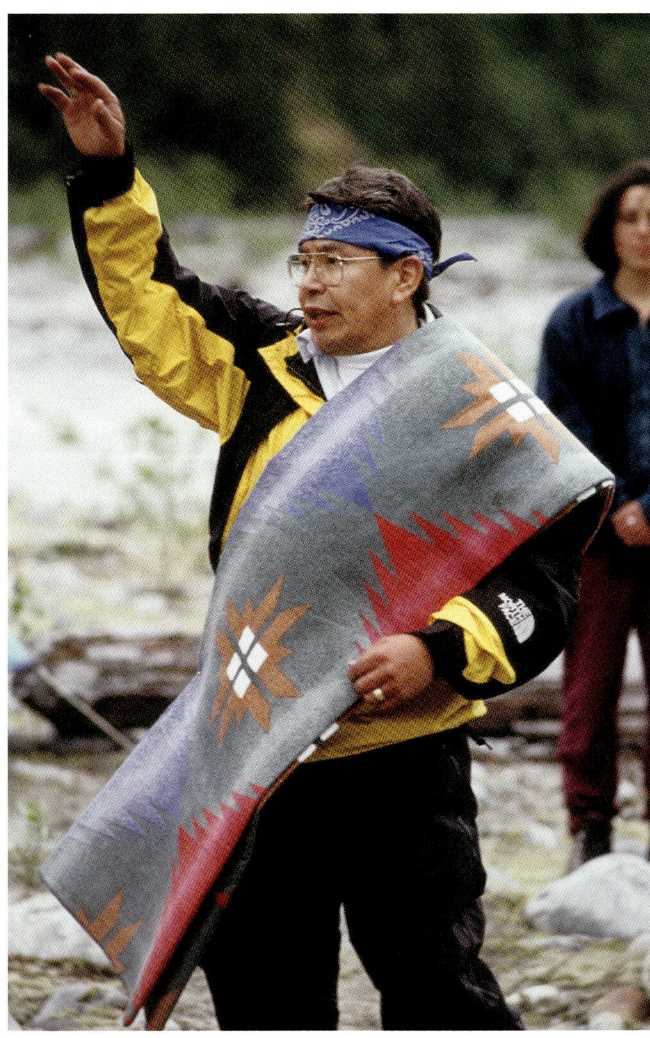

Chief Bill Williams, photo by Jeremy Williams, 1999

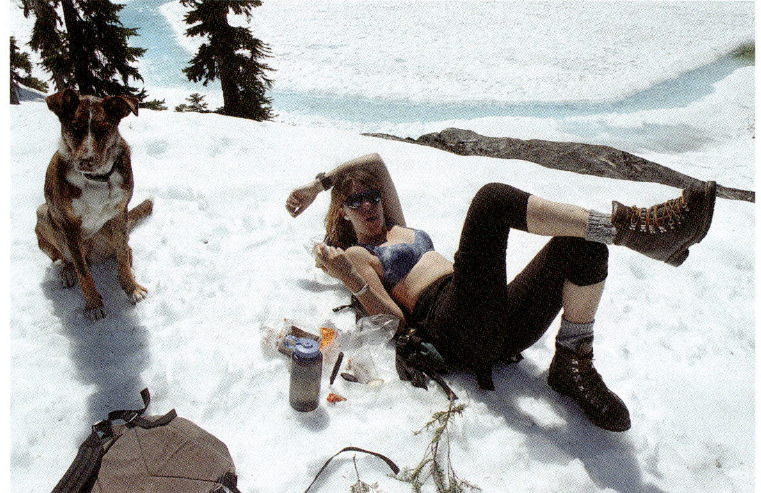

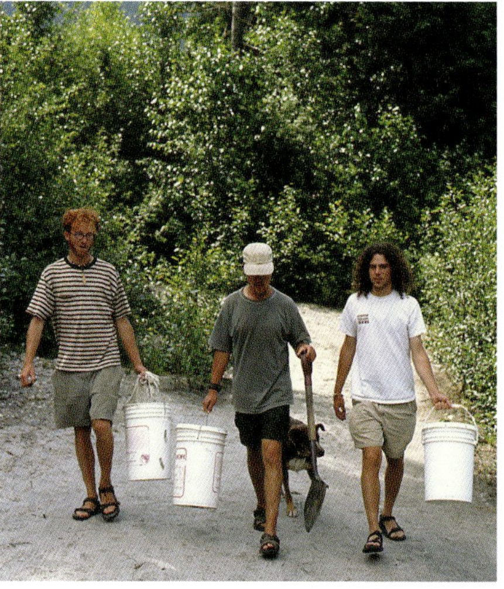

left: **Nancy Bleck**, photo by Heather Royal-Brant, 1998

right: **Nigel, Drew, Shel,** photo by Nancy Bleck, 1998

the cross-cultural aspect of Utsám̓ Witness gave them an understanding of how they could be ambassadors of their own culture to the public. It was like going to school to learn both traditional and contemporary ways to reflect their culture.

The E Team changed its name first to the Guardians to reflect a greater sense of responsibility over the territory and finally to the Aboriginal Youth Ambassadors, a project that lasted past the official end of Utsám̓ Witness. This program found a permanent home in the newly formed Squamish Lil'wat Cultural Centre.

Drew explains that the Nation developed a protocol to create the centre in 2001, then the society that owns and runs it was formed in 2002. It was completed and opened in 2008. He continues, "I started working on the project in 2004, coordinating youth teams responsible for community engagement and involvement. My role escalated to being an assistant to the project manager responsible for what was called 'cultural experience'—including exhibitions and marketing." Eventually Drew was promoted to the role of general manager. He set up a permanent model to train B.C. First Nations youth as cultural ambassadors who can work at high-profile tourism sites and bridge the indigenous and settler worlds.

Drew continued his studies while working with the Squamish Nation, earning a certificate in community economic development and an MBA. He has since established a consulting business and continues to work with the Squamish Nation and other First Nations groups.

Similarly, many of the Utsám̓ Witness participants and volunteers went on to continue working on projects that had a connection to Witness. Drew's friend Shel Neufeld took up environmental photography during the project and has turned this hobby into a business called Wildart, through which he exhibits and sells his photos.

For some, the effects of the project were even more personal. Both Aaron Nelson-Moody and Melanie Rivers speak of the influence Utsám̓ Witness has had on their personal lives and careers. The same year Witness ended, Melanie became program manager of Chee Mamuk. In 2013, she completed her master's in public health. And in 2005, Aaron and Melanie were married, just after Aaron completed his third Cedar Woman carving—based on Melanie—and it was raised in Tricouni Meadows. The raising of the figure illustrates the lovely hybrid of tradition and technology that became a sub-theme of the project. As he was organizing that the carving be lifted in by helicopter and placed atop a rock, Splash kept requesting that a few more items to be added to the payload. As they were finalizing the plan, the pilot finally asked, joking, "Anything else you need?" to which Aaron replied that a coffee would be nice. The helicopter arrived, laden with the carving, Splash's tools—and an insulated carton of coffee!

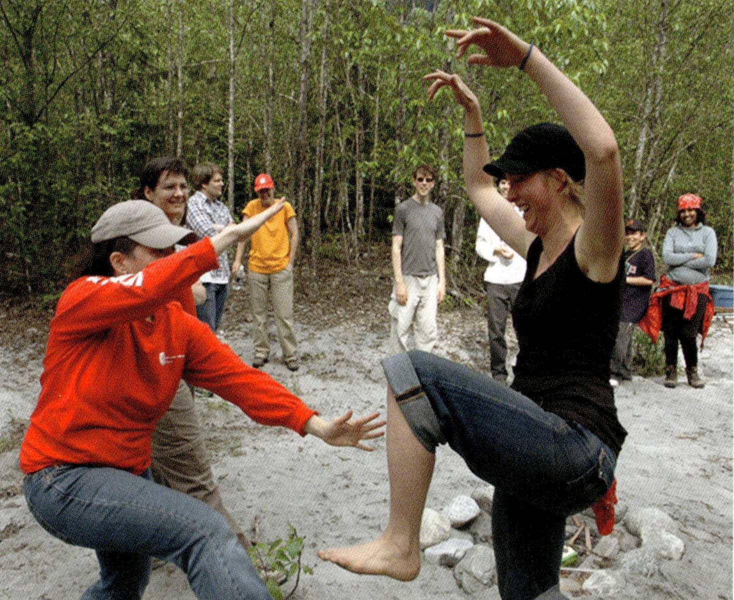

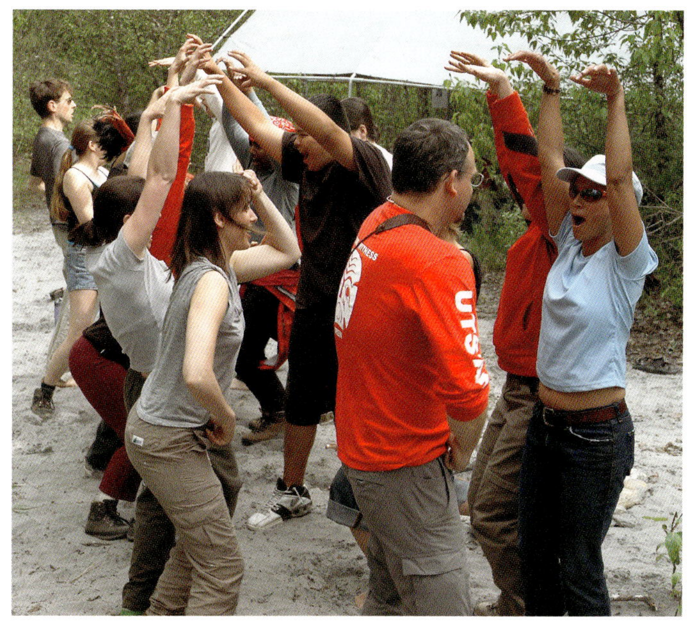

left: **Sarah Belanger and volunteers,** photo by Nancy Bleck, 2005

right: **Volunteer training weekend,** photo by Nancy Bleck, 2005

John's influence lives on through a book about his life, *John Clarke: Explorer of the Coast Range,* written by his Wilderness Education Project (WildED) co-founder Lisa Baile and published by Harbour Publishing in 2012. Perhaps more importantly, when John came down from the mountains during Utsám̓ Witness, he married Annette Lehnacker in 2002 and they had a son. Although Nicholas was only a year old when John died, thanks to his father's work, he will have the chance to hike in his footsteps in the Sims Valley. John once said: "One day we will undo the trail," and in a sense that is happening now. Without the need to take people into the valley to protect it, the land is being returned to a more traditional use. In the woods around Sims Creek, the Squamish youth are visiting the sacred sites and enacting the traditional puberty rites and ceremonies, which is a first for this generation.

The forging of paper trails, however, is never-ending, and the *X̱ay Temíxw* (Sacred Land) Land Use Plan is very much a document in progress. In many ways, mapping new claims, outside of the need to take the public into the woods, is the work that Chief Bill carries on in his role as lead negotiator for the Squamish Nation. In 2007 he presented Phase One: Naming and Recognition of Land in Squamish Territory by Squamish Nation, which included a map of the boundary of the territory. This was accepted by the province, as was Phase Two, which specifically names and maps several spiritual and cultural sites within the area, in 2011. Once again, the Squamish Nation was one step ahead of the government: Phase Two asserted the significance of the land for the Squamish Nation a year before the federal government ruling on the Williams case, which requires Aboriginal groups to prove the site-specific location of significant areas. Phase Three, which began in 2012, will map more sacred sites, and as Chief Bill notes, there will be many more phases to come.

Nancy had a son, Sasha, with her partner, Ivailo, in the final years of Utsám̓ Witness. The family spent a year in the Netherlands while Nancy completed her master's in fine arts, in which her artwork and writing about Witness figured prominently and in which she involved international collaborators, such as her advisor, Dr. Rosi Braidotti. Back in Canada, Nancy resumed her work with Utsám̓ Witness and began teaching at Emily Carr University of Art and Design and exhibiting and presenting her work internationally. In 2007, she received the YWCA Women of Distinction Award in the category of arts, culture and design for her work with Witness, and she continues to exhibit and create new art based on the project. In 2012, she and Ivailo were married in a witness ceremony, surrounded by many members of the Witness community.

Ivailo and Sasha at Peaches Falls, photo by Nancy Bleck, 2006

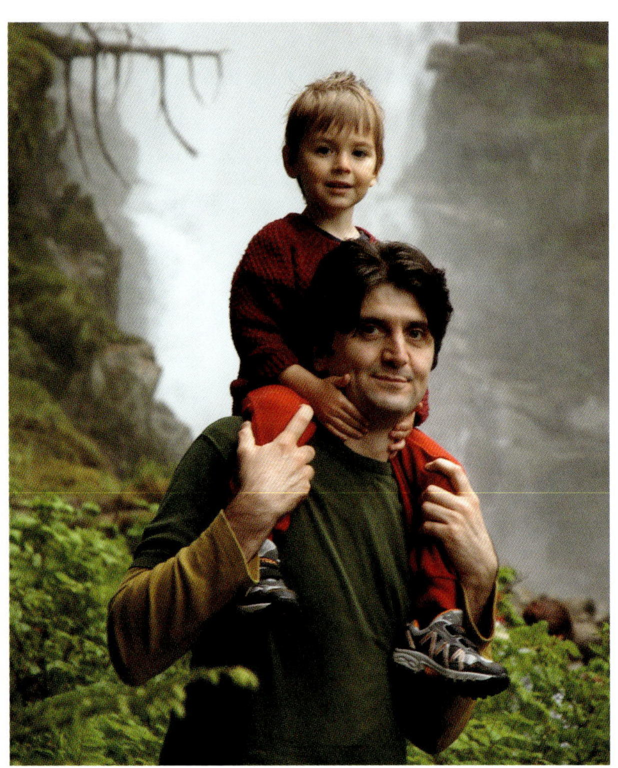

Beyond the immediate area, and through the diverse connections of many of the project's participants, Witness's transformative power has inspired others nationally and internationally. Celia Brauer and her husband, Michael, knew John Clarke from the mountaineering community and were drawn to participate in Witness. "I saw it immediately as a brilliant combination of strong and necessary forces for change that put the earth front and centre," says Celia. "The strength of the Witness Project and other interactions with local historians and First Nations was key for me in the creation of the False Creek Watershed Society and the Salmon Celebration." While leading a workshop in Quebec, she explained to a woman from New York what a watershed is, proof to Celia that "the influence of Witness travels far!"

More than one international group made the pilgrimage to the sandbar at Sims Creek. One in particular was Peace It Together, which, with the help of Abir Saadi and James Griffiths, brought together youth from Israel, Palestine and Vancouver to participate in a Witness weekend, using creativity and wilderness experiences to engage youth to tackle conflict resolution and international concerns. Recently, Peace It Together co-founder Reena Lazar has talked about working with indigenous and non-indigenous youth in Canada: "We want to test our model in other 'conflicts,' and we realize that Canada has this historical issue that is rarely talked about or addressed."

Another project to increase understanding and strengthen relations among indigenous, recent immigrant and older settler communities is the Vancouver Dialogues Project convened by the City of Vancouver. Zool Suleman, author of the publication that resulted from its first phase, recalls the Utsám̓ Witness project was often cited as an inspiration during the dialogue circles that were an integral part of that project.

As community-engaged practice, Witness set the bar for arts projects with measurable outcomes. When Devora Neumark, an interdisciplinary artist, researcher and writer, first heard about the project from Amir at a conference many years ago, she was immediately impressed by its significance. She's quick to say that Witness is not a model, in that it cannot be repeated to get the same results. But it is fertile ground to find those points that could seed other dialogues, other projects, other work. She says, "Witness was never just a project about contestation, it was a project of vision, and the way it holds the tension between the two facets is worthy of much more study."

Joe Foy of the Wilderness Committee points out that Witness was not the first time that First Nations in B.C. had successfully engaged with environmentalists and the public around land issues. He recalls being part of protest events back in the '80s in the Stein Valley north of Pemberton, including the Stein Valley Music Festival that was part of the Save the Stein campaign to prevent logging by B.C. Forest Products. Finally, on November 22, 1995, the area was preserved as Stein Valley Nlaka'pamux Heritage Park and is jointly administered by the Lytton First Nation and BC Parks.

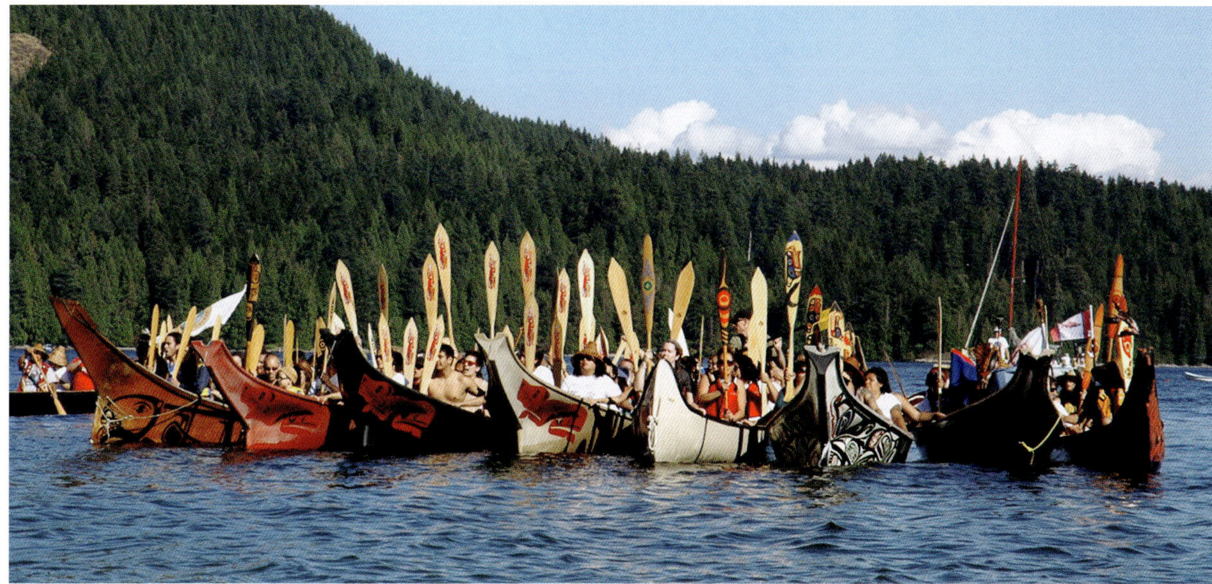

Canoe gathering at Cates Park, photo by Nancy Bleck, 2012

What was unique about Utsám̓ Witness, for Joe, is how it stayed personal. The sustained face-to-face aspect of it was transformative on an individual basis, and was therefore strong enough to provide a complex solution. It wasn't merely a strategy; it became a family, and the struggle was appropriately familial and intergenerational. Chief Bill would add that the fact that it was rooted in ceremony, in protocol, contributed to its resilience.

The greatest legacy of all is that the land the Utsám̓ Witness project sought to protect is being allowed to remain untouched by logging. It is a living place for ceremony to happen for many generations to come.

And the many stories that flow from the experiences of ten thousand participants have the power to give hope to other people with similar struggles.

Whose responsibility is it then to sound the alarm of the slow dying, to raise the voice of protest, to open the eyes and ears of the homo sapiens, sapiens, man, the doubly wise?
Of course it is the artist, the sage, the mystic, the child.
The artist because she is the one who can see through to the world of our ancestors, the veiled world obscured to the common and ordinary vision.
The artist because her mere ideas would awaken voices from other beings, and one call awaken another in dialogue.
The one whose superior work of art proceeds from a hidden and spiritual principle, which in fasting, detachment, forgetfulness of results and abandonment of all hope of profit discovers precisely the tree that is waiting to have her particular work carved from it.

EXCERPT FROM A POEM BY JAMES NICHOLAS, ROCK CREE WRITER AND ACTOR

EPILOGUE
BACK TO THE LAND

The significance of the Squamish Nation's *X̱ay Temíxw* (Sacred Land) Land Use Plan was unprecedented. What the Squamish Nation did was to opt out of the provincial dialogue, in essence to say it would not participate in land use planning as a mere stakeholder. The Squamish people asserted: "We are going to do our own plan. And we will present it to you." And they did. The province had also done a land use plan, but the Squamish Nation got there first. And the province had to respond to their plan, not the other way around.

Until that time, the province was forcing First Nations to prove their cultural and historical ties to the land through a "traditional use study," in which they were looking for point features, like the culturally modified trees Rudy Reimer/*Yemḵs* had discovered. That was why Chief Bill had sent Nancy to document the cedar trees—because it was a step towards postponing the logging. Those studies required mapping the specific significant locations, or point features, but typically once the point features were mapped, within the TFL, the forestry company could actually log up to three metres beside them.

This required "proof" of cultural relevance in order to protect tiny pockets of his own land just wasn't good enough for Chief Bill. This was the Squamish Nation's own territory, and it should have been enough to say: "This sacred area, as a whole, is untouchable." Which is what the Wild Spirit Places/*Kwa kwayx welh-aynexws* does. And Phase One of the land use plan maps the entire boundary. The Squamish Nation's plan changed the rules: it forced a shift in how B.C.'s provincial government is dealing with First Nations in relation to land use. And not only was it the first land use plan of its kind, but it inspired more Nations on the Central and North Coast to say, "We want to do our own land use plan and we want funding for it, and we know it happened for Squamish Nation."

Joe Foy said Utsám̓ Witness was a major part of achieving that success. He explains, "When Interfor and the province were ready for a resolution, Witness had demonstrated that they, literally, had a plan." He continues: "So when the Nation moved forward to take over the TFL, people had had time to find ways around it and be ready. Interfor gave up the TFL, but without a solution designed by a pool of knowledgeable people, it may have fizzled." The Squamish Nation had to be ready to pay for and take over the logging that was occurring in the TFL. And by this time, Interfor could no longer argue that this was just a bunch of

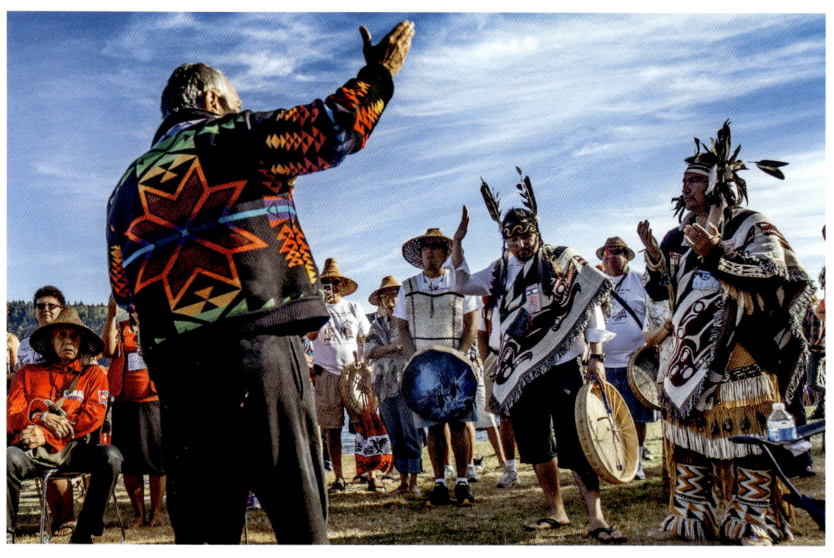

Tsleil-Waututh Nation and Squamish Nation sign Save the Fraser Declaration (Chief Ian Campbell on right), photo by Zack Embree, 2012

environmental activists; it was a Nation with a claim, a business plan and broad public support.

As this book goes to print, the Wilderness Committee continues its active opposition to the Kinder Morgan energy company's proposal to build a pipeline transporting oil to tankers waiting in the Burrard Inlet. And the impacts and risks of the Enbridge Northern Gateway Project, which would carry oil in two pipelines from Alberta to Kitimat, are still being internationally debated. As Joe Foy says: "Big Oil is toughening its grip on the province." Just as it did at Sims Creek, confrontation is escalating between the companies and the people, including many First Nations, who live on and watch over that land. Once again, the Squamish Nation is using ceremony and protocol to assert its sacred connection to these lands and waters.

The federal government's omnibus Bills C-38 and C-45 have re-ignited the spirit of these protests, including the Idle No More movement started by four First Nations women in Saskatoon as a "teach in," about the implication of these bills for treaties and resource extraction. Again what's at stake is First Nations' right to assert their sovereignty over unceded lands and the government's need to recognize and honour the treaties that uphold these Nations' fundamental rights. Like Witness, Idle No More has garnered the support of many "settler allies" and environmentalists, but also of indigenous peoples around the world. As Cease Wyss says, "ceremonial activism" has been awakened, and in an international context.

Nancy has observed that many of the photos of drumming, singing and circle dancing coming out in the mainstream media resemble some of the photos of Witness gatherings, though these protests and ceremonial round dances are not exactly the same as the public being invited into a witness ceremony, with the protocols that make it "law." They are evocative, however, and they are waking up supporters and allies globally. Melanie Rivers has also been seeing some parallels to Witness in how the leadership within the Idle No More movement has consistently called for non-violence. She feels there has been a tremendous sense of positive excitement and unity, which the mainstream media has actively tried to minimize. To succeed as a movement, Melanie feels "Idle No More needs the support of non–First Nations people."

One of the long-term effects of Witness was that it established true cross-cultural partnerships that created understanding about what these ceremonies are all about. Non-indigenous members of the Witness community are more likely to stand up as public "allies" of First Nations people, Melanie says, and are "not afraid to show their support and speak up about the injustices First Nations people are experiencing." Cease laughs when she observes that some people have felt threatened by the now-common sight of traditional drumming and singing. "The beating of the drum emulates our heartbeat; it's one thing all people have in common."

The question to ask is, Can we learn from the experience of the Utsám̓ Witness project to pre-empt the "official" public consultation process? In other words, to invite ceremony and enact much older protocols than the provincial and federal governments have up their sleeves?

It remains to be seen how the Nations who have land use plans relevant to the land in question will play out this card. The potential damage to traditional and spiritually significant sites if there was a major accident would be unfixable. What would happen to the waterways? Can we afford to find out if it's true that oil and water do not mix? The world Utsám̓ Witness emerged from is still watching, just as the Squamish Nation still watches over Nexw-áyantsut and the Wild Spirit Places/*Kwa kwayx welh-aynexws.*

In one of Nancy's panorama composite art pieces, Chief Bill Williams/*telálsemk̲in siy̓ám̓*, in button blanket regalia, of his mother's Raven clan, is a portrait on the right of the panorama photo. He watches over the now-famous creek bed with those big round river rocks. Leaping over them, shirtless and joyful, is John Clarke. The title of the piece is *Watchmen.*

In his own artwork and life practice, Marc Williams, Chief Bill's youngest son, is exploring what it means to inhabit the story of Nexw-áyantsut, what it could mean for him to take on the family tradition as a watchman over this land. Marc's photo series called Training Grounds, some black and white, some in colour, are taken with an eye to the contemporary, yet they are rooted in his own witnessing of his tradition. These photos were taken of a journey in Tricouni Meadows, the same spot where Aaron Nelson-Moody's Cedar Woman carving was placed years before. It is fitting that that carving tells the story of Witness; with Cedar Woman are a mountain goat, a raven and an eagle—John, Chief Bill and Nancy.

Aaron's fourth and final Cedar Woman carving was placed in the spring of 2013 at the Squamish Lil'wat Cultural Centre in Whistler. Above the crouching Cedar Woman is the powerful Thunderbird and its companion, the lightning snake that curves down to the roots where it forges the link between the spiritual and material worlds. By placing this carving in a location that is accessible to more people, Aaron hopes it will inspire them to explore tradition and imagine what might come next. All this art and work share a kinship within this territory of text.

Nancy's new work, too, continues to be born from the medium of Utsám̓. Just as her first Witness artwork contained text from the Squamish Nation *Assertion of Aboriginal Title*, her latest images are made up of water and words as she returns to some poetic images that were part of the work she was doing in the earliest days of Witness. Water is what we are all mostly made of, as is our planet. Water breaches all our human-made borders; it is the lifeblood of the land.

TRAINING GROUNDS 2012

PHOTOGRAPHS BY **M.V. WILLIAMS**

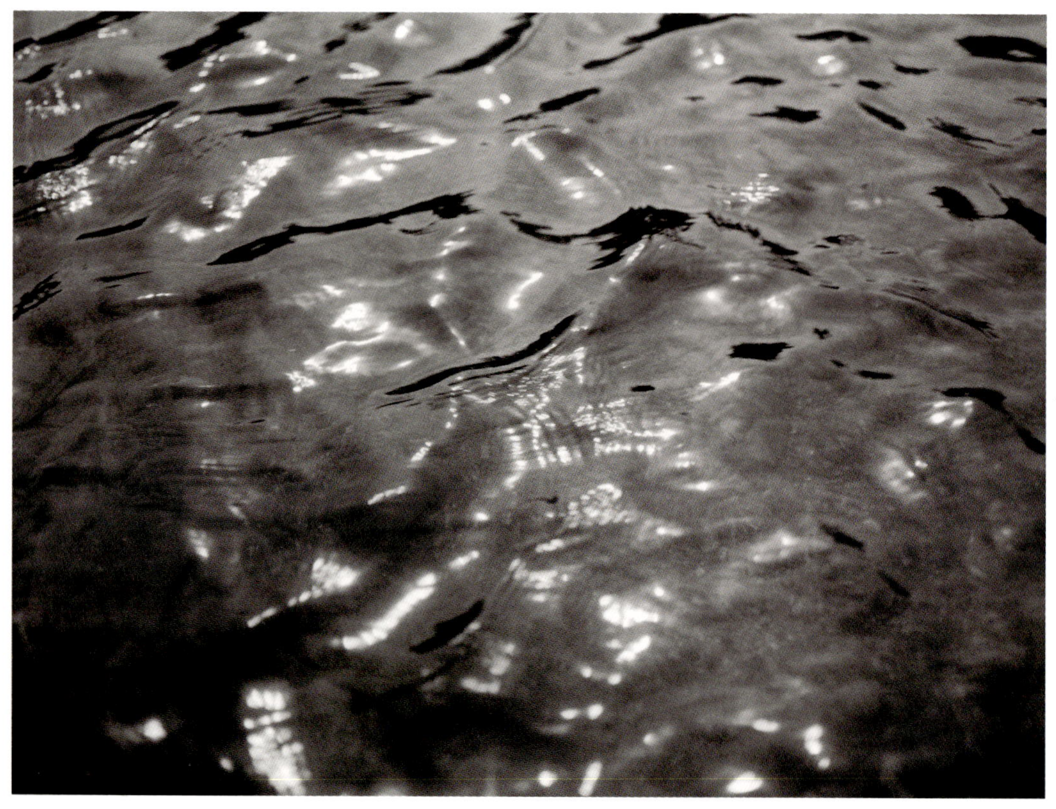

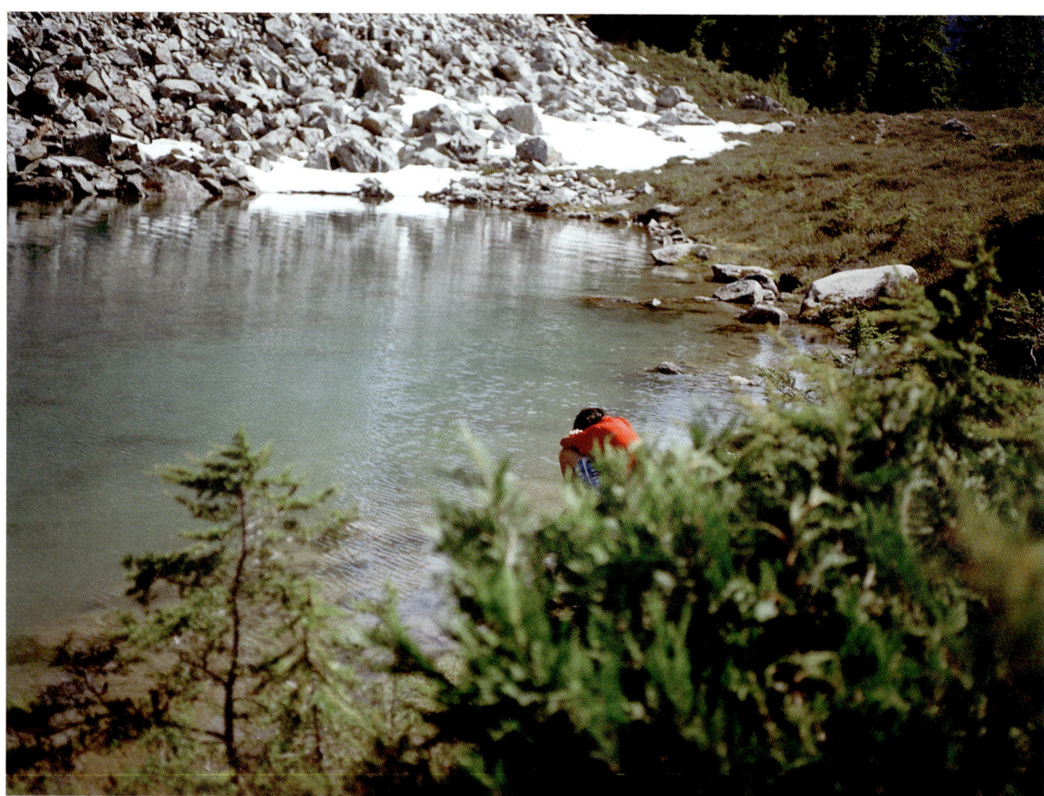

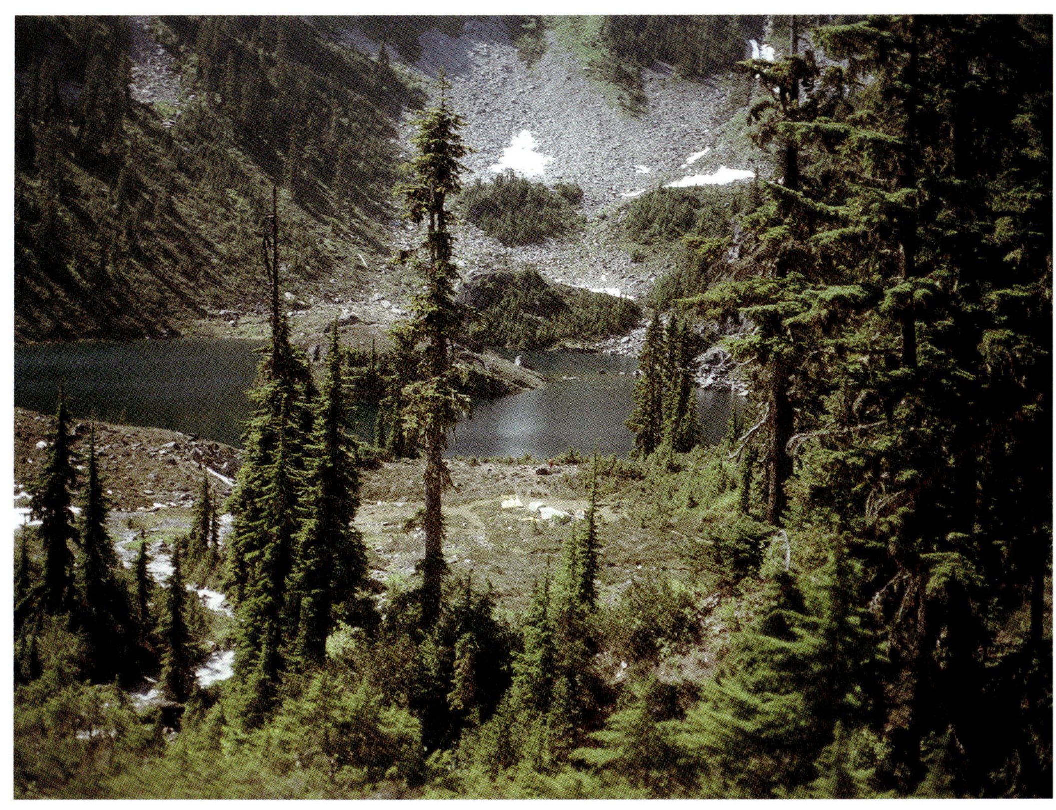

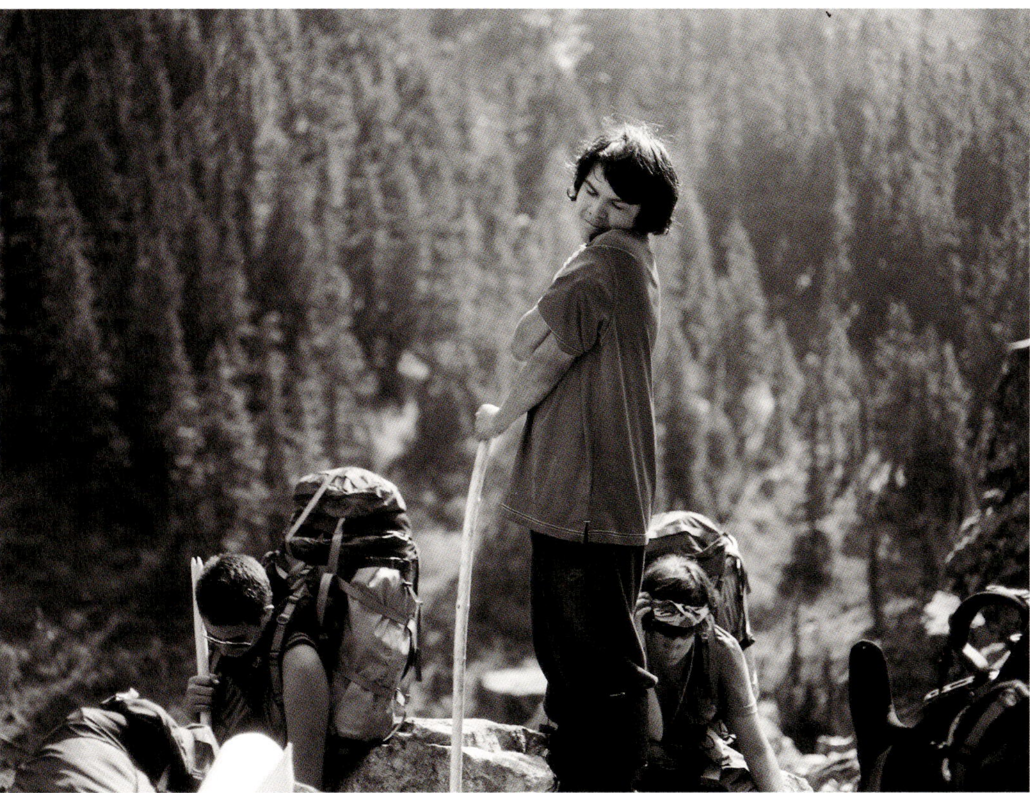

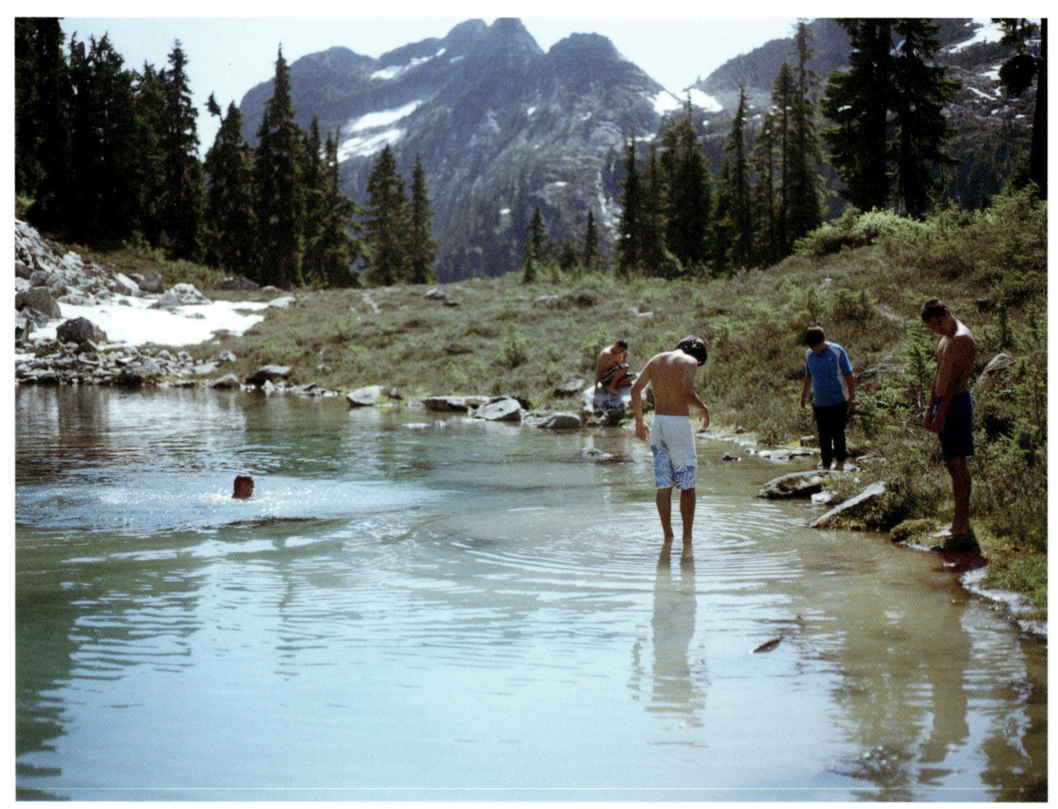

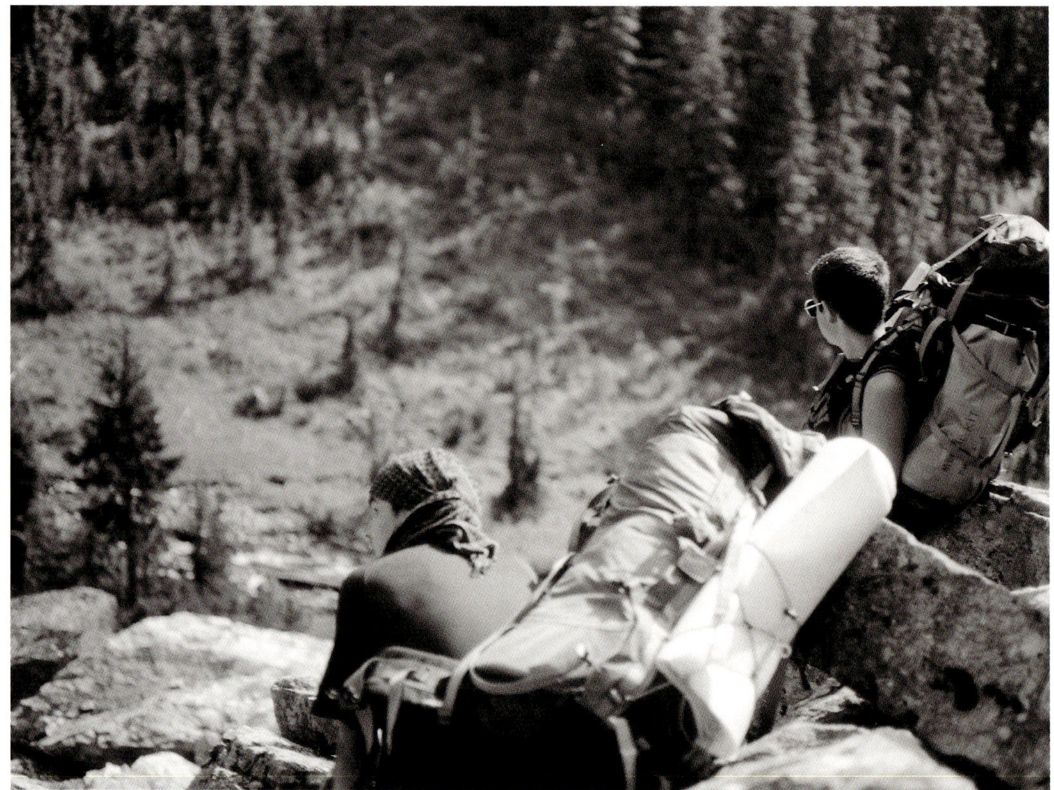

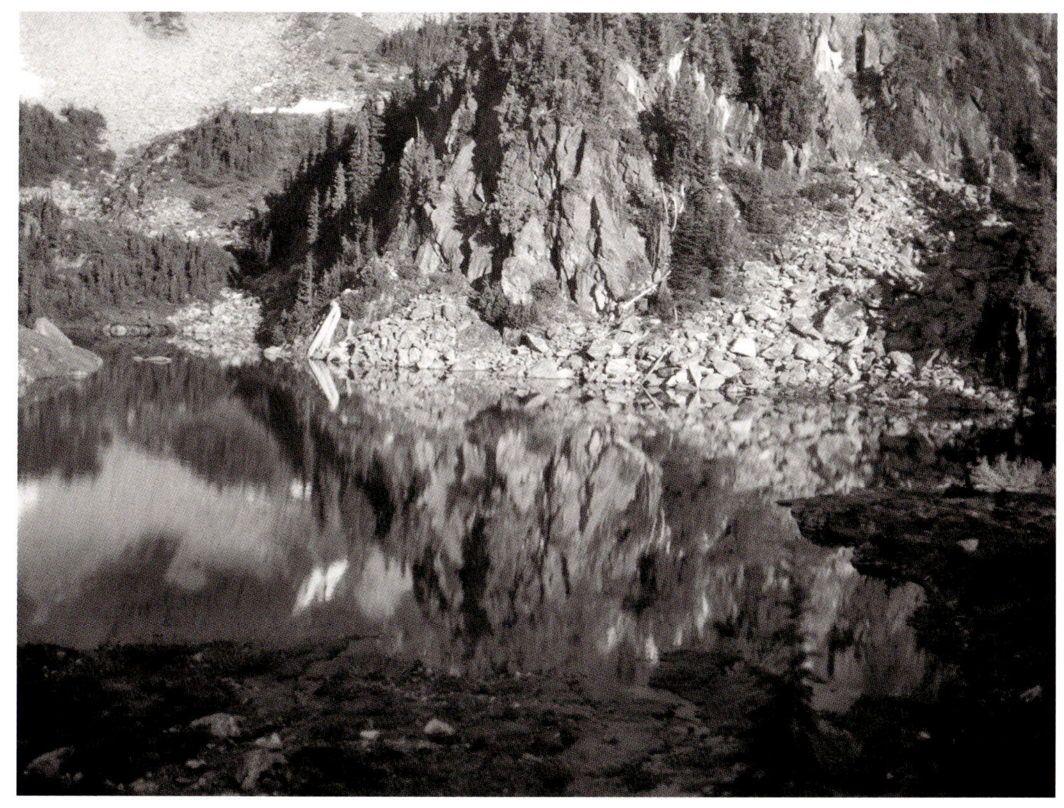

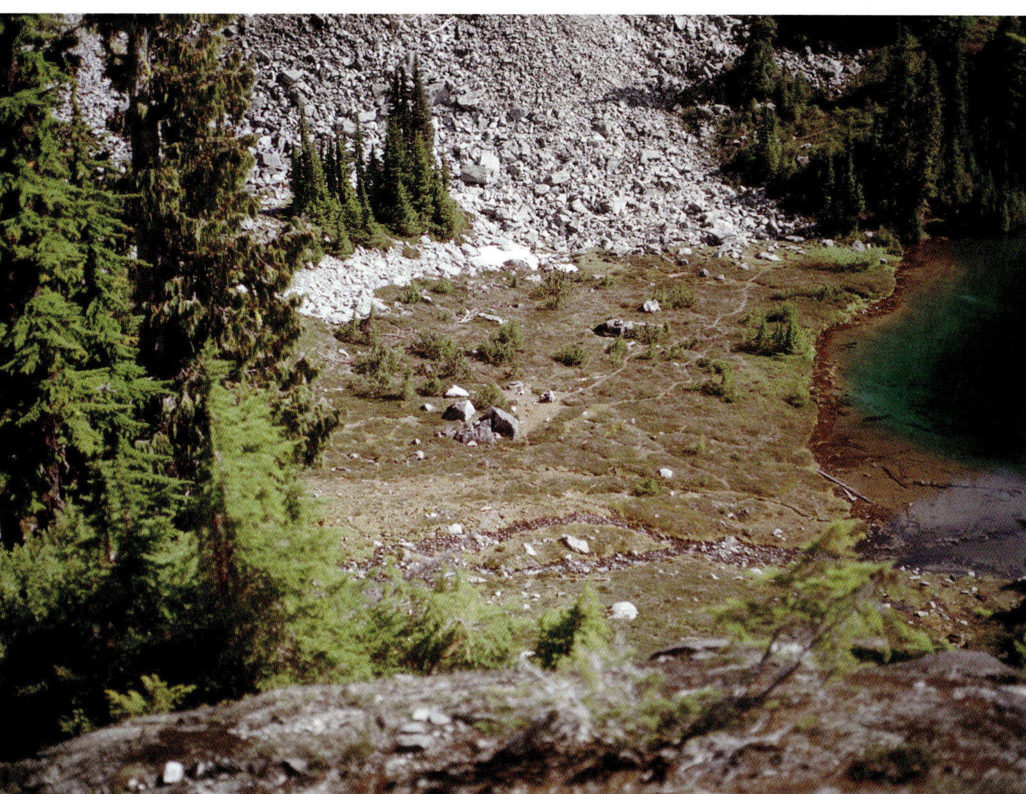

HOW LIKE WATER

2007–2013

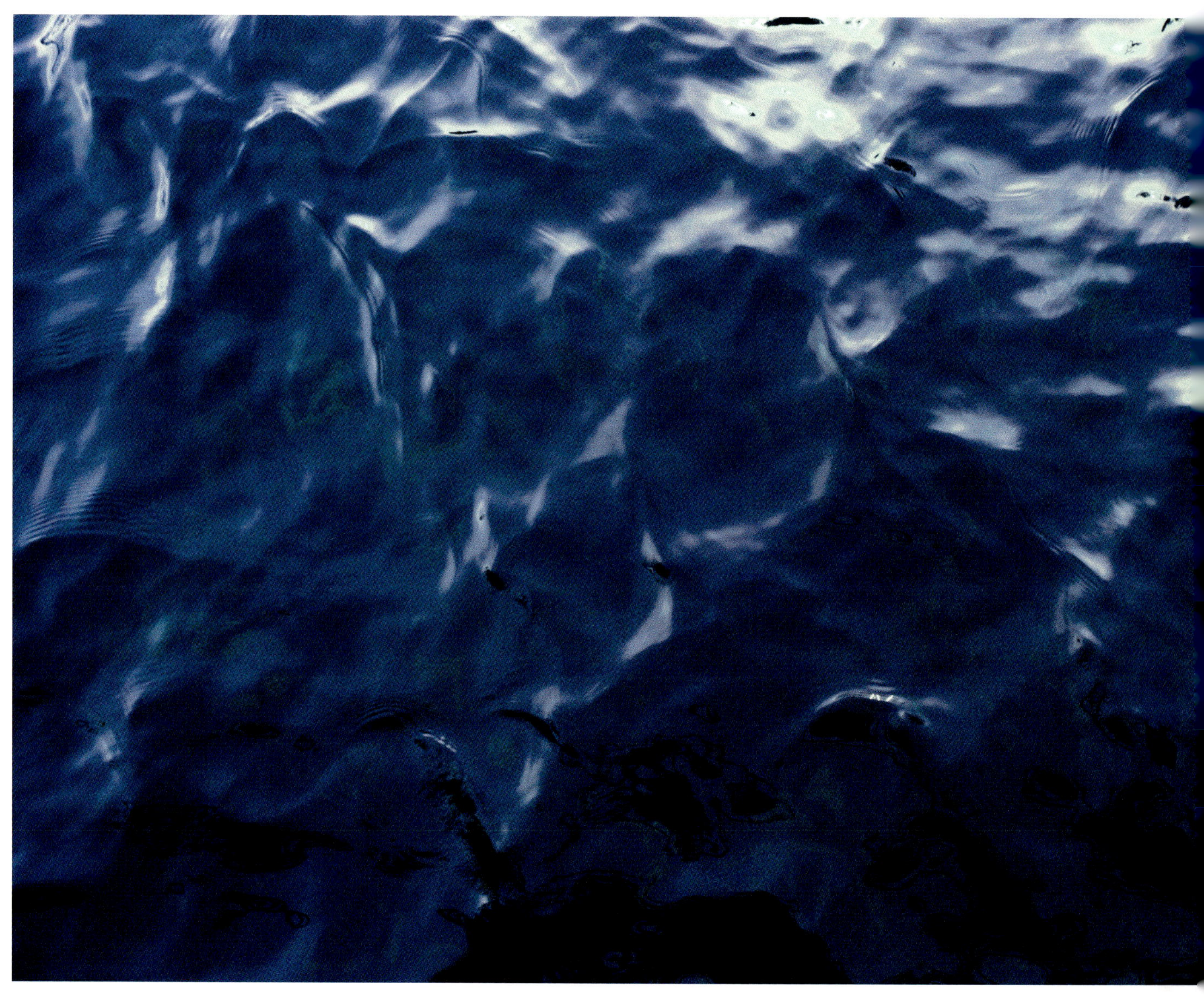

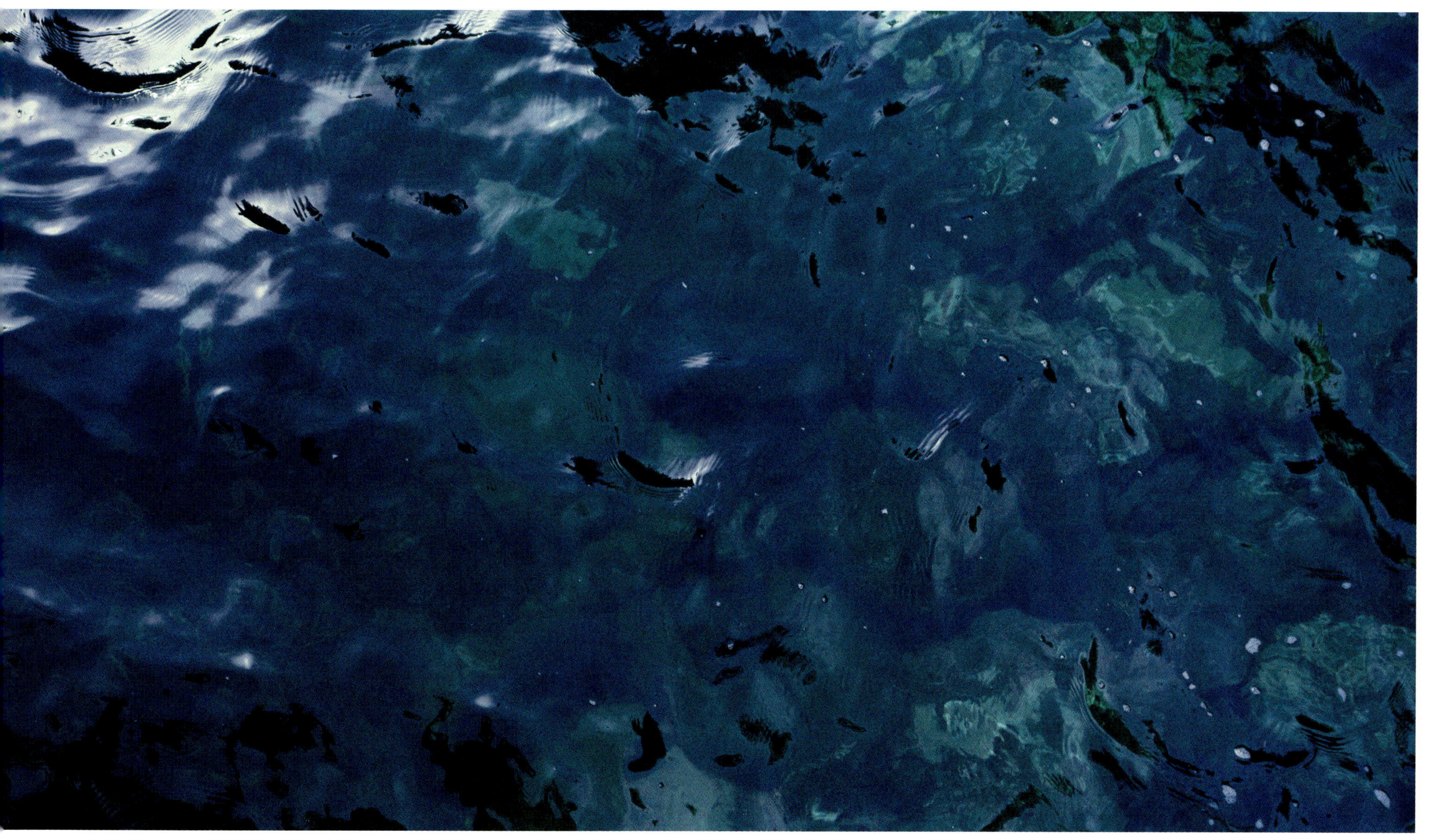

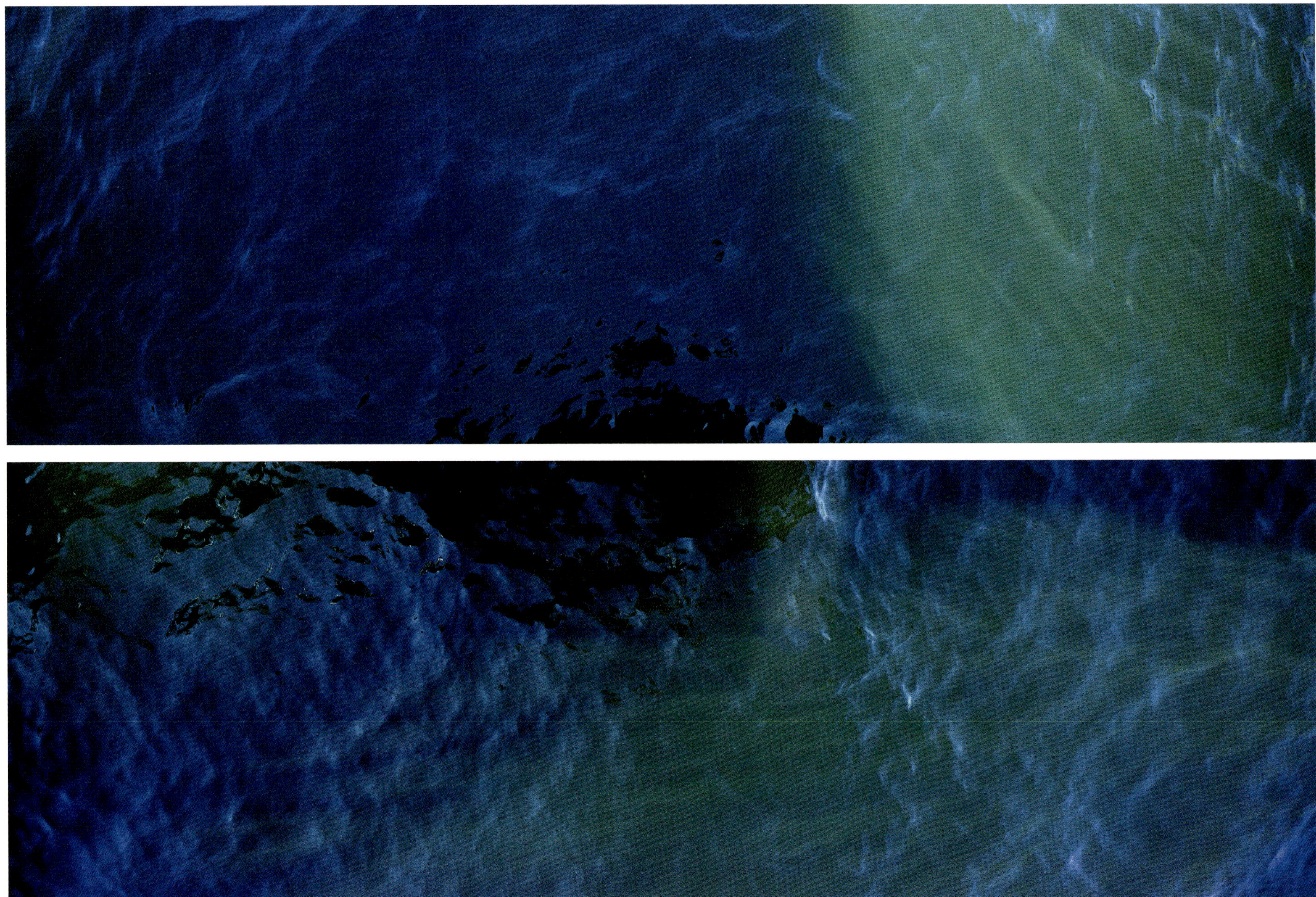

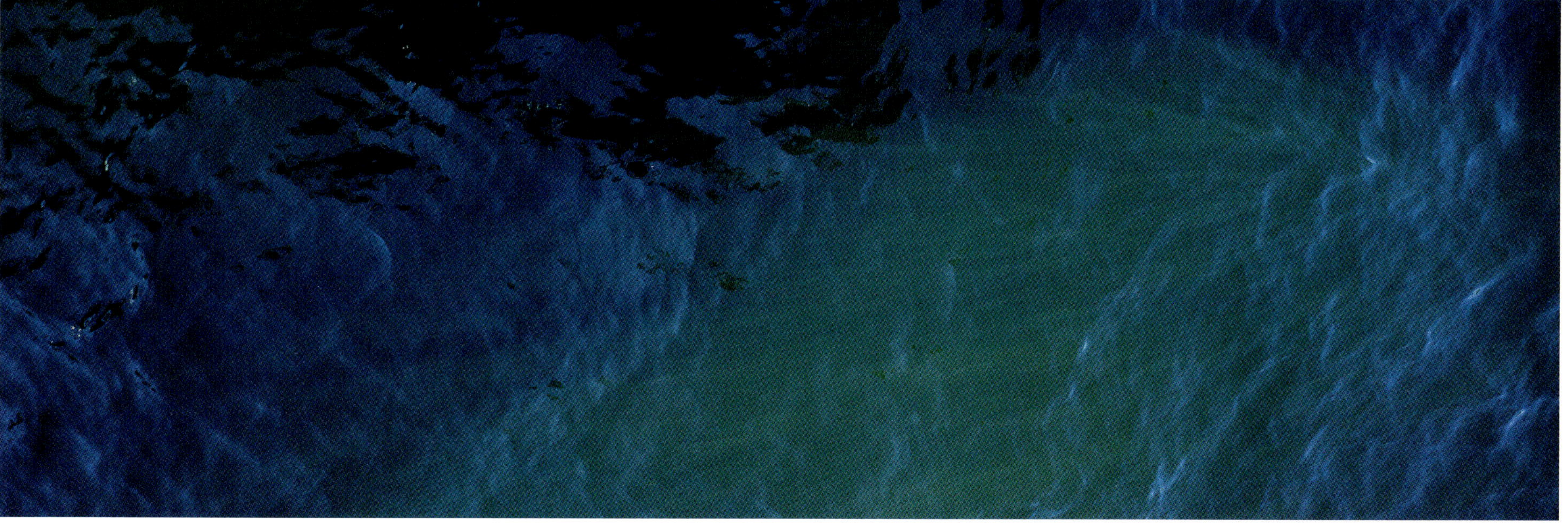

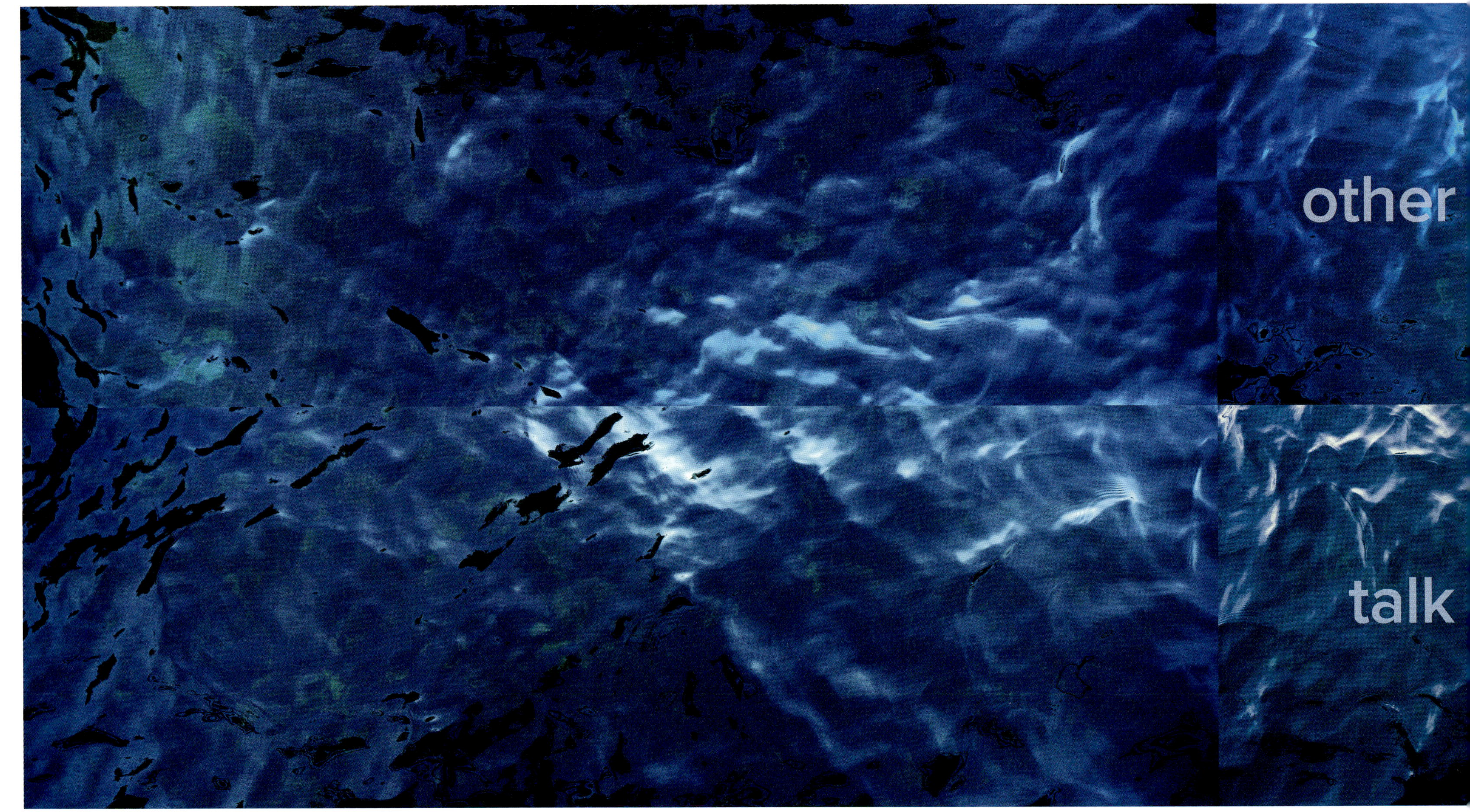
other
talk

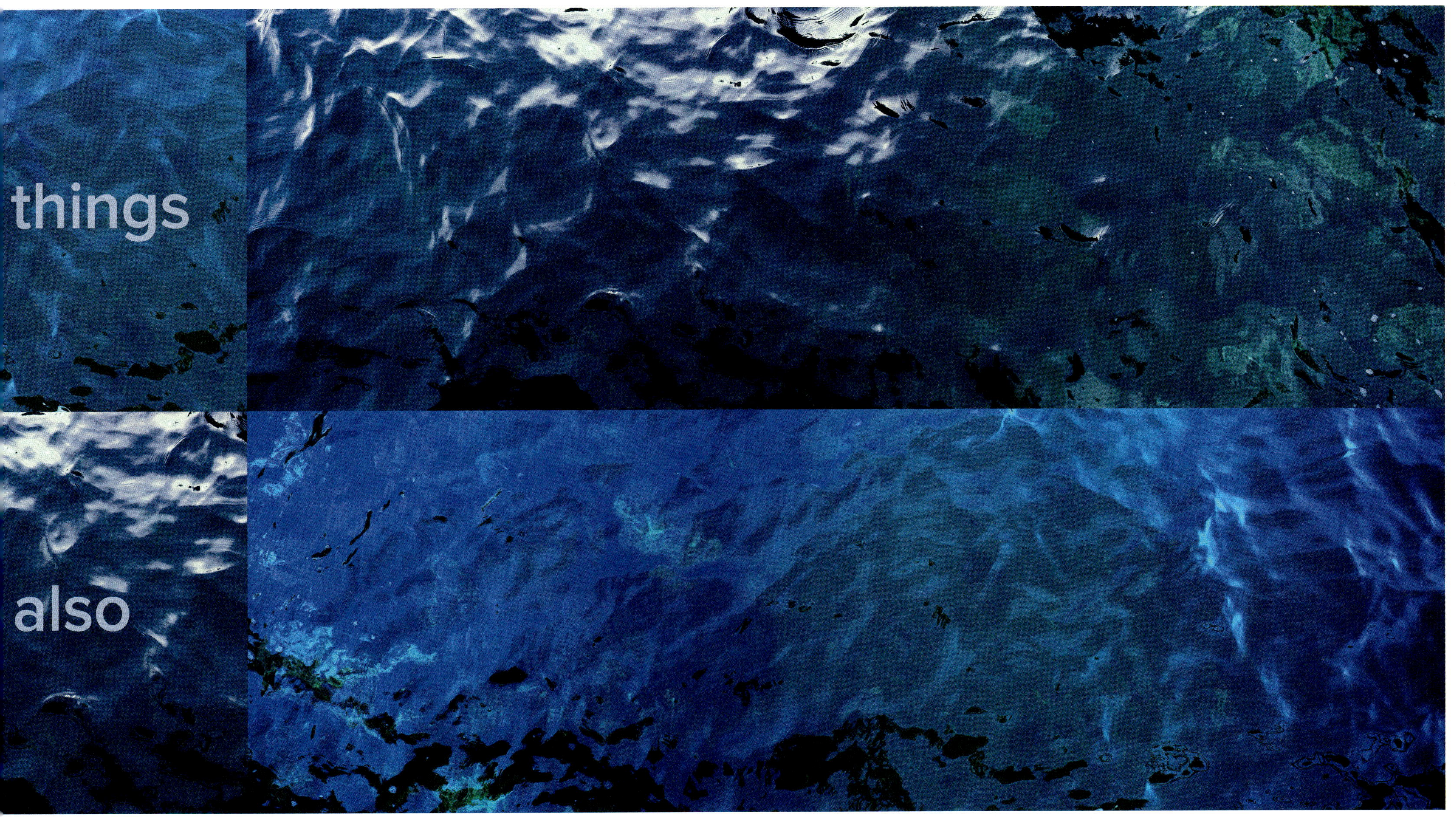
things
also

GLOSSARY

7imlamelwet (M law mel wit): Melanie Rivers (Medicine)
Chee Mamuk: Chinook language word meaning "new work," the name of the Aboriginal Program of the STI/HIV Division of the B.C. Centre for Disease Control
Chiy̓áxw (Chee-YAW-xw): protocol (unwritten laws)
Haykwílem (Hi-KWEE-lum): ancestral name of Eugene Harry
Huy chap a (Hoy chop a): thank you all
Huy chexw a (Hoy chook a): thank you
Kwa kwayx welh-aynexws (K-WHY k-why-ah-x wulh EYE-nooks): Wild Spirit Places
Kwelánexw (Kwel-AH-nook): William Nahanee
Nexw-áyantsut (Nook-EYE-en-tsote): place of transformation
Níchim/Nexwsustsáylh (NAY-cheem/nook OH-ts-eye-lh): Speaker/Teacher
ninám̓in (Naa min): a nickname that is given to someone, rather than an ancestral name
S7áplek̲ (S7-OP-u-luck): ancestral name of Bob Baker (Speaker)
Sk̲wx̲wú7mesh (Squ-HO-mish): the Squamish People
Sk̲wx̲wú7mesh Sníchim (Sk-HO-mish SNAY-cheem): the Squamish language
Slánay̓ Sp'ák̲w'us (Slh-ON-eye SPOCK-woes): Nancy Bleck (Eagle Woman)
Sts'íts'ap (sts-AY-ts-op): work
Tawx'sin Yexwulla/Púlxtn (Talk-shin Yook-Wulla/Poolxtn): Aaron Nelson-Moody (Splashing Young Eagle)
telálsemk̲in siy̓ám̓ (Ta-LALL-sum-cane, See-YAHM): Chief Bill Williams, one of sixteen hereditary Chiefs of the Squamish Nation, co-founder of Utsám̓ Witness
Temlh (tum-lh(th): a cedar pigment used to paint the body for spiritual protection, as part of regalia
Tk̲wáyani7m (t-k-WHY-a-nay7-um): Verification Ceremony, to listen
Tselk̲wílem (Tsull-KWAY-lum): ancestral name of Byron Joseph (Speaker)
Tsewátseltn (Tse-WATTS-ol-ten): Drew Leathem (Resourceful Person)
T'uy̓tanat (TOY-ten-ought): Cease Wyss (Medicine Woman)
Utsám̓ (OATS-ahm): to witness
X̲álek̲/Sek̲yú siy̓ám̓ (X-ALL-uck/Suck-YO See-YAHM): ancestral name of Chief Ian Campbell
X̲álek̲-t/Sek̲yú-t siy̓ám̓ (XALL-uck/Suck-YO See-YAHM): Chief Ian's grandfather, the late Chief Lawrence Baker
X̲ay Temíxw (X-eye Tum-AY-xw): (Sacred Land) Land Use Plan
Xwelák̲tn (Xwel-AHCK-ten): ancestral name of Rick Harry
X̲wex̲wsél̓k̲n (Xoh-xw-SULK-n): John Clarke (Mountain Goat)
Yemk̲s (Yum-ks): ancestral name of Rudy Reimer

ACKNOWLEDGEMENTS

A BOOK, especially this book, takes a community to produce. We apologize in advance for any names of people we may have missed. Many thanks are due.

Thank you to those who were interviewed for this book: Amir Ali Alibhai, Lisa Baile, Celia Brauer, Chief Ian Campbell, Joe Foy, Eugene Harry, Reena Lazar, Drew Leathem, Aaron Nelson-Moody, Devora Neumark, Melanie Rivers, Zool Suleman, Marc Williams and Cease Wyss.

Thank you to all those who read and commented on the manuscript: Lisa Baile, Betsy Carson, Marian Dodds, Sandy Haksi, Ivailo Ivanov, Susan Leech, Zahed Mardukhi, Allan MacDonald, Aaron Nelson-Moody, David Ng, Melanie Rivers, Stephanie Sersli, Gayle Stoodley and June Thomson.

Thanks also to those who gave feedback and support on the book project: Mark Achbar, Lisa Barrett, Heather Bohn, Lynn Booth, Phillip Djwa, Kim Elliot, Siobhan Flanagan, Marc Glassman, Colette Gunson, Lisa Jackson, Paul Lang, Norm Leech, Oonagh Maley, Samantha McGavin, Scott Nelson, Andrea Nemtin, Joanne Norris, Irwin Oostindie, John Sakamoto-Kramer, Carolyn Stock, Skylar Stock, Denise Thomas, Lauri Thompson and Denise Williams. Thank you to Becky Campbell for the Squamish language translation.

Thank you to Terry Sunderland, for graphic assistance; David Ng and Bella Sie, for video editing our book trailer; Atef Abdelkefi, for designing our website; and to Julius Booth, our marketing intern.

A special thank you to our talented editorial and design team: Figure 1 publisher Chris Labonté; director of sales and marketing Richard Nadeau; and creative director Peter Cocking; and our fabulous editor, Lucy Kenward.

Deep gratitude goes out to the ones who started this publishing journey with us: Scott McIntyre of D&M Publishers and Margaret Reynolds of the Association of Book Publishers of BC.

For their support before, during and after the entire Utsám̓ Witness project, Chief Bill Williams and Nancy Bleck wish to thank their families: Chief Bill Williams' grandparents Chief George Williams and Monica Williams; parents, Chief David Williams and Laura Williams; and his immediate family, Bertha Joseph, Christopher and Marc Williams; Nancy Bleck's parents, Hans Bleck and Renate Bleck; husband, Ivailo Ivanov; and son, Sasha Ivanov Bleck.

Special thanks to Sasha, for not only putting up with our busyness for more than one summer, but for prodding us by asking if we were on the last page yet!

Our sincerest thank you goes to the following people for generously donating their time, advice and valuable assistance to the Utsám̓ Witness project over the years it was active. Many of these people have helped in many of the ways listed below, though we mention them just once.

Early days of Witness: Doug Brown, Bryan Evans, Daniel Gautreau, Harald Gravelsins, Marian Halle, Dwayne Himmelsbach, Shayna Hornstein, Paul Hundal, Rick Hurney, Jared Irwin, Heather Kirk, sylvi macCormac, Scott Mason, Coral McFadden, Shel Neufeld, Peter Pare, Heather Ramsay, Susan Schuppli, Sandra Semchuk, Greg Stoltmann, Toby Toman, Hali Tsui, Geza Vamos, Lorna Williams, Jeremy Williams. Also the Carnegie Centre, Landsea Tours and Squamish Nation Peace Keepers.

The important role that the Roundhouse Community Centre brought to this project is immense and undeniable. Our gratitude goes to the people behind the scenes: Gregory Byrne, Skai Fowler, Elizabeth Kidd, Shirley Mae, Percy Nacario, Irwin Oostindie, Derek Simmons, Karen Stanley, Kim Stuart.

Sims Creek camping volunteers made the journey of bringing people to the land and waters possible. Deep thanks go to: Dennis Alvey, Anissa Au, Melinda Averball, Sabine Bartel, Michael Battles, Sarah Belanger, Beth Belcher, Rob Benany, Eden Bishop, Sabine Bitter, Gavin Blackstock, Sabrina Bonfonti, Rachel Bower, Margaret Bridgeman, Peter Burns, Janey Chang, Chanti, Hugh Chapman, Grace Darney, Justin Dawson, Jessica Duncan-Wersta, Stacy Ellwein, Caroline Farquhar, Natalie Ferrari-Morton, Daniel Ferrari-Morton, Evelyn Forrest, Kim Foster, Bernadette Fox, Kelli Gallagher, Lauren Goldman, Yael Greenfeld, Paul Grewal, James Griffiths, Miriam Grob, Ian Gunn, Kim Hagen, Jess Henry, Jennifer Hill, Dorothy Holt, Sarah Joy Hopkin, Meredith Hunt, Randa Jabaji, Kevin Kirkpatrick, Michelle Kotko, David Lane, Genny Lau, Meredith Laycock, Lorelei Lester, Stephanie Liebe-McGinnis, Megan Long, Andrew Luke, Rennard Lusterio, Corine Madill, Rick McCallion, Devon McClelland, Dan McDonald, Mitzi McFarlane, Gord McGee, Aaron McKean, Laila Meadus, Sandra Mott, Kiran Pal-Pross, Mary Ann Pare, Sanya Pleshakov, Miki Promislow, Alivira Quek, Nigel Reeves, Mark Robinson, Robert Safarik, Ken Salmon, Abir Saudi, Maggie Segger, Geoffrey Senchenko, Christy Steckler, Lindsay Stephenson, Suzanne, Eloginy Tharmendran, Owen Thomas, Woody Thompson, Anton van Walraven, Robin Walker, Fred Wilson, Danielle Wilson-Brown, Chiang Yuan.

Workshop presenters: Lisa Andrew, Alroy Baker, Bob Baker, Thais Baker, Michael Barkusky, Laurel Brewster, Constance Brissenden, Cheri Burta, Suzanne Diamond, Eric Donnelly, Fin Donnelly, Leonardo Frid, Terry Glavin, Brandon Goldsmith, Karen Goodfellow, Dr. Kurt Grimm, Marian Halle, Dr. Alton Harestad, Eugene Harry, Katy Holm, Terry Hunter, Chief Gibby Jacobs, Karen Jamieson, Valerie Langer, Annette Lehnacker, Larry Loyie, Trevor Lummy, Alan MacDonald, Bruce MacDonald, Ian Marcuse, Chief Joe Mathias, Robert Morris, Maurice Nahanee, William Nahanee, Christy Neufeld, Gerry Oleman, Sarah Orlowski, Devon Page, Marie Preissl, Gordon Prest, Rudy Reimer, Dr. Richard Ring, Cheryl Rivers, Heather Royal-Brant, Kira Schaffer, Allwyn Stewart, Terry Taylor, Andrea Thompson, Bob Turner, Vera Wabegijig, Savannah Walling, Guy Warrington, John Weighardt, Charlene and Linda Williams, Tracy Williams, Gary Yabsley.

Cultural Speakers: Ann Baker, Dale Harry, Rick Harry, Byron Joseph and the Cultural Youth Ambassadors.

Our supporters and friends who have assisted our work from Montreal, Quebec: Diane Conrad, Guy Lamaree, Scott MacLeod, Anita Sinner, Dana Velan, Tom Velan, Gaetane Verna. Special mention goes to the people of Kanesatake and to Jacob Cree, Marie David, Beverly Nelson and Susan Oke.

Academics, writers, artists and designers: Stella Archer, Dr. Rosi Braidotti, Beth Carruthers, Daniel Collins, Zach Embree, John Grande, Greg Mauer, Randy Stoltmann, Rachel Thompson, Petra Ukuru and Martyn Williams.

By participating in the camping weekends and events, many more people—more than can all be mentioned by name—contributed to the wider Utsám̓ Witness project and the work that came out of it. Sincerest gratitude, *Huy chewx a*, to all of you.

IMAGE CREDITS

photographs by Nancy Bleck unless indicated
all dimensions are given as height x width

LAND SPEAK

p 12 **Thimbleberries**, photo-canvas heat transfer, 4.5′ × 5.5′, 1995
p 13 **Foliage**, photo-canvas heat transfer, 4.5′ × 5.5′, 1995
p 14 **Moss and Rocks I**, photo-canvas heat transfer, 4.5′ × 5.5′, 1995
p 15 **Moss and Rocks II**, photo-canvas heat transfer, 4.5′ × 5.5′, 1995
p 16 **Upper Lil'wat Sandbar**, photo-canvas heat transfer, 4.5′ × 5.5′, 1995
p 17 **Rocks**, photo-canvas heat transfer, 4.5′ × 5.5′, 1995
p 18 **Vortex I, II, III**, photo-canvas heat transfer, 4.5′ × 5.5′, triptych, 1995
p 19 **Base Camp**, photo-canvas heat transfer, 4.5′ × 5.5′, 1995
p 21 **Night**, photo-canvas heat transfer, 4.5′ × 5.5′, 1995
p 22 **Crisscross**, photo-canvas heat transfer, 4.5′ × 5.5′, 1996
p 23 **Roots**, photo-canvas heat transfer, 4.5′ × 5.5′, 1996
p 24 **Have Fun!** photo-canvas heat transfer, 4.5′ × 5.5′, 1996
p 25 **Cedar Burn I**, photo-canvas heat transfer, 4.5′ × 5.5′, 1995
p 26 **Cedar Burn II**, photo-canvas heat transfer, 4.5′ × 5.5′, 1995
p 27 **Cedar Burn III**, photo-canvas heat transfer, 4.5′ × 5.5′, 1995
p 29 **Smoke**, photo-canvas heat transfer, 4.5′ × 5.5′, 1995
p 30 **Untitled**, photo-canvas heat transfer, 4.5′ × 5.5′, 1995
p 31 **Untitled**, photo-canvas heat transfer, 4.5′ × 5.5′, 1995
p 33 **Elaho Cedar**, photo-canvas heat transfer, 4.5′ × 5.5′, 1995

CALL TO WITNESS

p 46 detail from **Witness**, image & text banner, photo-canvas heat transfer, 3′ × 37′, 1997
p 47 detail from **Witness**
p 48 detail from **Witness**
p 49 detail from **Witness**
p 50 detail from **Witness**
p 51 detail from **Witness**

PANORAMA DOCUMENTS

p 54 **Gene Ceremony I**, c-print, 2′6″ × 7′3″, 1998
p 55 **Gene Ceremony II**, c-print, 2′6″ × 7′3″, 1998
p 56 **Elaho Logging I**, c-print, 2′6″ × 7′3″, 1998
p 57 **Elaho Logging II**, c-print, 2′6″ × 7′3″, 1998
p 58 **Hollow Tree I**, c-print, 2′6″ × 7′3″, 1999
p 59 **Hollow Tree II**, c-print, 2′6″ × 7′3″, 1999
p 60 **Untitled**, c-print, 2′6″ × 7′3″, 1999
p 61 **Untitled**, c-print, 2′6″ × 7′3″, 1999
p 62 **Untitled**, c-print, 2′6″ × 7′3″, 1999
p 63 **Cedar 98.8**, c-print, 2′6″ × 7′3″, 1998
p 64 **G Main, Mile 56.5**, c-print, 2′6″ × 7′3″, 1998
p 65 **Irwin's Truck**, c-print, 2′6″ × 7′3″, 1998
p 66 **Cedar Woman I**, c-print, 2′6″ × 7′3″, 1999
p 67 **Cedar Woman II**, c-print, 2′6″ × 7′3″, 1999
p 69 top: **Forest Silence I**, c-print, 2′6″ × 7′3″, 1999
bottom: **Forest Silence II**, c-print, 2′6″ × 7′3″, 1999
p 70 **Logger's Blockade**, triptych, c-print, each 2′6″ × 7′3″, 1997
p 71 **Log Sort**, triptych, c-print, each 2′6″ × 7′3″, 1997
p 72 **Untitled**, c-print, 2′6″ × 7′3″, 1997
p 73 **Untitled**, c-print, 2′6″ × 7′3″, 1997
p 74 **Chiỷaxw**, c-print, 2′6″ × 7′3″, 2005
p 77 **Shel and Christy's Wedding**, diptych, c-print, each 2′6″ × 7′3″, 2003
p 78 **Sims Ceremony I**, c-print, 2′6″ × 7′3″, 1998
p 79 **Sims Ceremony II**, c-print, 2′6″ × 7′3″, 1998

CEDAR PEOPLE

p 92 **Next Generation**, c-print, 2′6″ × 7′3″, 2006
p 94 **Breach of Protocol**, photo-canvas heat transfer, 2′6″ × 12′, 2000
p 96 **Kahkalhil, Wild Woman of the Woods Eating Her Children**, photo-canvas heat transfer, 2′6″ × 12′, 2000

THE WITNESS PROJECT received support and contributions from: Colorific Photo & Digital Imaging Ltd., Emerald City, Landsea Tours, Printing Ink, the Society Promoting Environmental Conservation (SPEC), Wolfe Chev Olds.

Financial assistance in the printing of this book from Aqualini Group, Hans Bleck, Velan Foundation, Vancity, The Squamish Nation, Western Canada Wilderness Committee, The Roundhouse, Mark Achbar and Siobhan Flanagan, and with in-kind assistance from Utsám̓ Witness Society and Hello Cool World.

NANCY BLECK acknowledges financial support for her photography:
Peter Pare and Lisa Baile, 1999
Landsea Tours, 2000
The Canada Council, 2003
The Velan Foundation, 2001 and 2012

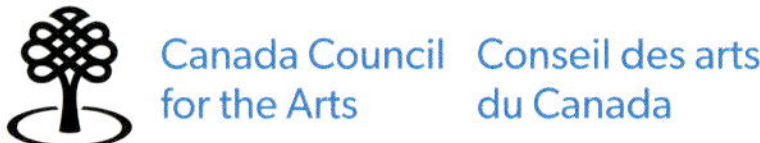

www.PicturingTransformation.com

THANK YOU to our community partners:

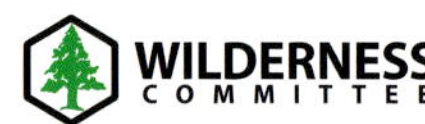

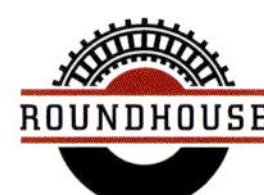

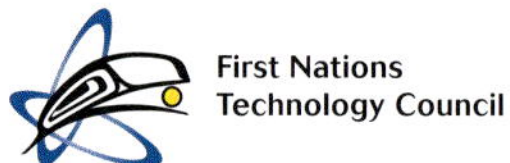

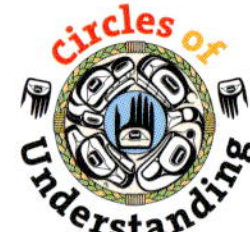

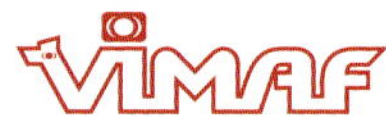

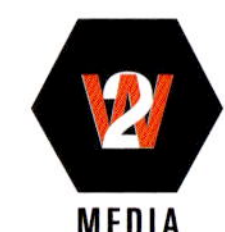

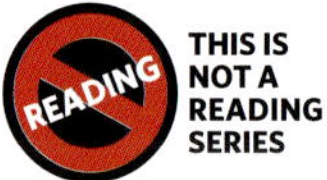

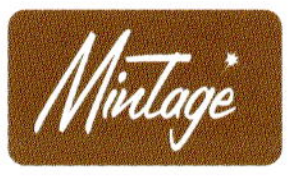

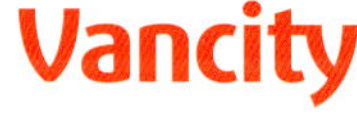

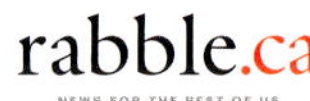

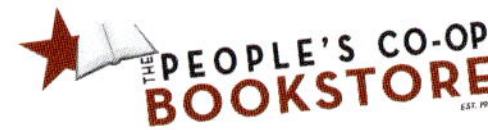

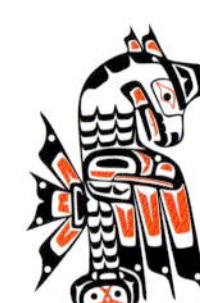

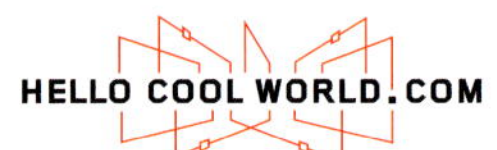

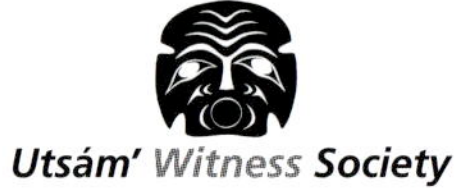